# Sams'
# Teach Yourself
# SQL
## in 24 Hours

D0130499

Active Leadership in Education
Enterprise and Engagement

# Using the *Sams' Teach Yourself in 24 Hours* Series

Welcome to the *Sams' Teach Yourself in 24 Hours* series!
You're probably thinking, "What, they want me to stay up
all night and learn this stuff?" Well, no, not exactly. This
series introduces a new way to teach you about exciting new
products: 24 one-hour lessons, designed to keep your interest and keep you learning. Because the learning process is
broken into small units, you will not be overwhelmed by
the complexity of some of the new technologies that are
emerging in today's market. Each hourly lesson has a number of special items, some old, some new, to help you along.

## Minutes

The first 10 minutes of each hour lists the topics and skills
that you will learn about by the time you finish the hour.
You will know exactly what the hour will bring with no sur-
prises.

## Minutes

Twenty minutes into the lesson, you will have been introduced to many of the newest features of the software application. In the constantly evolving computer arena, knowing
everything a program can do will aid you enormously now
and in the future.

## Minutes

Before 30 minutes have passed, you will have learned at
least one useful task. Many of these tasks take advantage of
the newest features of the application. These tasks use a
hands-on approach, telling you exactly which menus and
commands you need to use to accomplish the goal. This
approach is found in each lesson of the *24 Hours* series.

## 40 Minutes

You will see after 40 minutes that many of the tools you have come to expect from the *Sams' Teach Yourself* series are found in the *24 Hours* series as well. Notes and Tips offer special tricks of the trade to make your work faster and more productive. Warnings help you avoid those nasty time-consuming errors.

## 50 Minutes

By the time you're 50 minutes in, you'll probably run across terms you haven't seen before. Never before has technology thrown so many new words and acronyms into the language, and the New Terms elements in this series will carefully explain each and every one of them.

## 60 Minutes

At the end of the hour, you may still have questions that need to be answered. You know the kind—questions on skills or tasks that come up every day for you, but that weren't directly addressed during the lesson. That's where the Q&A section can help. By answering the most frequently asked questions about the topics discussed in the hour, Q&A not only answers your specific question, it provides a succinct review of all that you have learned in the hour.

Sams'
**Teach Yourself**
# SQL

**in 24 Hours**

Sams'
**Teach Yourself**

# SQL

## in 24 Hours

*Ryan K. Stephens*
*Ronald R. Plew*

**SAMS**
PUBLISHING

201 West 103rd Street
Indianapolis, Indiana  46290

**Publisher**   Joseph B. Wikert
**Executive Editor**   Rosemarie Graham
**Managing Editor**   Patrick Kanouse

**Development Editor**
Todd Bumbalough

**Technical Editors**
Todd Bumbalough
Daniel C. Marsh

**Project Editor**
Andrew Cupp

**Copy Editor**
Tonya Maddox

**Team Coordinator**
Lorraine Schaffer

**Cover Designer**
Tim Amrhein

**Book Designer**
Gary Adair

**Production Team**
Marcia Deboy
Michael Dietsch
Jenny Earhart
Cynthia Fields
Maureen West

**Indexers**
Greg Pearson
Kelly Talbot

# Overview

# Contents

# Acknowledgments

I have to thank God for all of the excellent opportunities that I have had and for my ability to complete all of these projects. I would like to thank my partner in life, Tina, for her patience and support throughout the length of this project and many others. This book is dedicated to my wonderful nephews and nieces, Brandon, Jacob, Mariah, and Tiffany.

—*Ryan*

This book is dedicated to my family: my wife, Linda; my mother, Betty; my children, Leslie, Nancy, Angela, and Wendy; my grandchildren, Andy, Ryan, Holly, Morgan, Schyler, Heather, Gavin, and Regan; and my sons-in law, Jason, Dallas, and Andy. Thanks for being patient with me during this busy time. Love all of you.

—*Poppy*

# About the Authors

**Ryan Stephens** is President and CEO for Perpetual Technologies, Inc., a growing database consulting firm out of Indianapolis, Indiana. He is an Oracle database administrator and is currently managing numerous development and production databases. He has specialized in Oracle databases and SQL for more than seven years. Ryan is also an adjunct professor at Indiana University-Purdue University in Indianapolis, where he teaches SQL, PL/SQL, and Oracle database administration. Ryan has also done Oracle database and SQL work for organizations such as the Military Department of Indiana, Unisys Corporation, EDS, and the State of Indiana. Ryan resides in Indianapolis with his wife Tina.

**Ronald R. Plew** is vice-president and CIO for Perpetual Technologies, Inc. in Indianapolis, IN. His duties also include Oracle database consulting. Ron is an adjunct professor at Indiana University-Purdue University in Indianapolis, where he teaches SQL and various database courses. He holds a Bachelor of Science degree in Business/Management from Indiana Institute of Technology. Ron also serves in the Indiana Army National Guard, where he is the Detachment Sergeant and programmer for the 826th Personnel Detachment. Ron's hobbies include golf, chess, and collecting Indy 500 racing memorabilia. He shares ownership of Plew's Indy 500 Museum with his brothers, Mark and Dennis; his sister, Arleen; and Mother, Betty. Ron lives in Indianapolis with his wife Linda.

# Introduction

## Who Should Read This Book?

Welcome to the world of relational databases and SQL! This book is written for those self-motivated individuals out there that would like to get an edge on relational database technology by learning the Structured Query Language, SQL. This book was written primarily for those with very little or no relative experience with relational database management systems using SQL. This book may also apply to those who have some experience with relational databases, but need to learn how to navigate within the database, issue queries against the database, build database structures, manipulate data in the database, and more. This book was not geared towards individuals with significant relational database experience who have been using SQL on a regular basis.

## What This Book Intends to Accomplish

This book was written for individuals with little or no experience using SQL, or those who have used a relational database, but their tasks have been very limited within the realm of SQL. Keeping this thought in mind, it should be noted up front that this book is strictly a learning mechanism, and one in which we have presented the material from ground zero and have provided examples and exercises with which to begin to apply the material covered. This book is not a reference and should not be relied upon as a reference.

## What You Need

You may be wondering, what do I need in order to make this book work for me? Theoretically, you should be able to pick up this book, study the material for the current hour, study the examples, and either write out the exercises or run them on a relational database server. However, it would be to your benefit to have access to a relational database system to apply the material in each lesson. The relational database to which you have access is not a major factor, because SQL is the standard language for all relational databases. Some database systems that you may use include Oracle, Sybase, Informix, Microsoft SQL Server, Microsoft Access, and dBase.

## Conventions Used in This Book

For the most part, we have tried to keep conventions in this book as simple as possible.

Many new terms are identified and are printed in italics.

In the listings, all code that you type in (input) appears in **boldface monospace**. Output appears in standard monospace.

SQL code and keywords have been placed in uppercase for your convenience and general consistency.

```
SELECT * FROM PRODUCTS_TBL;

PROD_ID    PROD_DESC                      COST
---------- ------------------------------ ----------
11235      WITCHES COSTUME                29.99
222        PLASTIC PUMPKIN 18 INCH        7.75
13         FALSE PARAFFIN TEETH           1.1
90         LIGHTED LANTERNS               14.5
15         ASSORTED COSTUMES              10
9          CANDY CORN                     1.35
6          PUMPKIN CANDY                  1.45
87         PLASTIC SPIDERS                1.05
119        ASSORTED MASKS                 4.95

9 rows selected.
```

The following special design features enhance the text:

There are syntax boxes to draw your attention to the syntax of the commands discussed during each hour.

```
select [ all ¦ * ¦ distinct column1, column2 ]
from table1 [ , table2 ];
```

**NOTE**

Notes are provided to expand on the material covered in each hour of the book.

**WARNING**

Warnings are provided to warn the reader about "disasters" that could occur and certain precautions that should be taken.

**TIP**

Tips are also given to supplement the material covered during appropriate hours of study.

# ANSI SQL and Vendor Implementations

One thing that is difficult about writing a book like this on standard SQL is that although there is an ANSI standard for SQL, each database vendor has its own implementation of SQL.

With each implementation comes variations from the actual standard, enhancements to the standard, and even missing elements from the standard.

The expected question is, "Because there is an ANSI standard for SQL, what is so difficult about teaching standard SQL?" The answer to this question begins with the statement that ANSI SQL is just that, a standard. ANSI SQL is not an actual language. In order to teach you SQL, we had to come up with examples and exercises, which involves using one or more implementations of SQL. And because each vendor has its own implementation with its own specifications for the language of SQL, these variations, if not handled properly in this book, could actually cause confusion concerning the syntax of various SQL commands. Therefore, we have tried to stay as close to the ANSI standard as possible, foremost discussing the ANSI standard and then showing examples from different implementations that are very close, if not the same as the exact syntax that ANSI prescribes.

We have, however, accompanied examples of variations among implementations with notes for reminders and tips on what to watch out for. Just remember this—each implementation differs slightly from other implementations. The most important thing is that you understand the underlying concepts of SQL and its commands. Although slight variations do exist, SQL is basically the same across the board and is very portable from database to database, regardless of the particular implementation.

# Understanding the Examples and Exercises

We have chosen to use Oracle for most of the examples in this book; however, we have also shown examples from Sybase, Microsoft SQL Server, and dBase. Oracle was used the most for various reasons, including Oracle's compliance with ANSI SQL, and the fact that Oracle is one of the most popular relational database products today. As stated, there are some differences in the exact syntax among implementations of SQL. For example, if you attempt to execute some examples in this book, you may have to make minor modifications to fit the exact syntax of the implementation that you are using. We have tried to keep all of the examples compliant with the standard; however, we have intentionally shown you some examples that are not exactly compliant. The basic structure for all of the commands is the same. In order to learn SQL, you have to start with an implementation using practical examples. You should be able to emulate the database and examples used in this book without very much difficulty. Any adjustments that you may have to make to the examples in this book to fit your implementation exactly will only help you to better understand the syntax and features of your implementation.

Good luck!

# PART
# I

## A SQL Concepts Overview

## Hour

# Hour 1

# Welcome to the World of SQL

Welcome to the world of SQL and the vast, growing database technologies of today's businesses all over the world. By reading this book, you have begun accepting the knowledge that will soon be required for survival in today's world of relational databases and data management. Unfortunately, because it is first necessary to provide a background of SQL and cover some preliminary concepts that you need to know, the majority of this chapter is text in paragraph format. Bear with the book; this will be exciting, and the "boring stuff" in this hour definitely pays off.

The highlights of this hour include

- ☐ An introduction to and brief history of SQL
- ☐ An introduction to database management systems
- ☐ An overview of some basic terms and concepts
- ☐ An introduction to the database used in this book

# SQL Definition and History

Every business has data, which requires some organized method, or mechanism, for maintaining the data. This mechanism is referred to as a *database management system* (DBMS). Database management systems have been around for years, many of which started out as flat-file systems on a mainframe. With today's technologies, the accepted use of database management systems has begun to flow in other directions, driven by the demands of growing businesses, increased volumes of corporate data, and of course, Internet technologies.

The modern wave of information management is primarily carried out through the use of a *relational database management system* (RDBMS), derived from the traditional DBMS. Relational databases and client/server technologies are typical combinations used by current businesses to successfully manage their data and stay competitive in their appropriate markets. The next few sections discuss the relational database and client/server technology in order to provide you with a stronger foundation of knowledge for the standard relational database language—SQL.

## What Is SQL?

SQL, Structured Query Language, is the standard language used to communicate with a relational database. The prototype was originally developed by IBM using Dr. E.F. Codd's paper ("A Relational Model of Data for Large Shared Data Banks") as a model. In 1979, not long after IBM's prototype, the first SQL product, ORACLE, was released by Relational Software, Inc. (it was later renamed Oracle Corporation). It is, today, one of the distinguished leaders in relational database technologies. SQL is pronounced either of two ways: as the letters S–Q–L, or as "sequel"; both pronunciations are acceptable.

If you travel to a foreign country, you may be required to know that country's language in order to get around. For example, you may have trouble ordering from a menu via your native tongue if the waiter speaks only his country's language. Look at a database as a foreign land, in which you seek information. SQL is the language that you use to express your needs to the database. Just as you would order a meal from a menu in another country, you may request specific information from within a database in the form of a query, using SQL.

## What Is ANSI SQL?

The American National Standards Institute (ANSI) is an organization that approves certain standards in many different industries. SQL has been deemed the standard language in relational database communication, originally approved in 1986 based on IBM's implementation. In 1987, the ANSI SQL standard was accepted as the international standard by the International Organization for Standardization (ISO). The current standard is referred to as SQL/92, much revised since 1986.

1

**NEW TERM** *ANSI* stands for American National Standards Institute, an organization responsible for devising standards for various products and concepts.

With any standard come numerous, obvious advantages, as well as some disadvantages. Foremost, a standard steers vendors in the appropriate industry direction for development; in the case of SQL, providing a basic skeleton of necessary fundamentals which, as an end result, allows consistency between various implementations and better serves increased portability (and not only database programs, but databases in general and individuals who manage databases).

Some may argue that a standard is not so good, limiting the flexibility and possible capabilities of a particular implementation. However, most vendors who comply with the standard have added product-specific enhancements to standard SQL to fill in these gaps.

A standard is good, considering the advantages and disadvantages. The expected standard demands features that should be available in any complete SQL implementation and outlines basic concepts that not only force consistency between all competitive SQL implementations, but increases the value of a SQL programmer or relational database user in today's database market.

**NEW TERM** A *SQL implementation* is a particular vendor's SQL product.

## What Is a Database?

In very simple terms, a *database* is a collection of data. Some like to think of a database as an organized mechanism that has the capability of storing information, through which a user can retrieve the stored information in an effective and efficient manner.

People use databases every day without realizing it. A phone book is a database. The data contained consists of individuals' names, addresses, and telephone numbers. The listings are alphabetized, or indexed, which allows the user to reference a particular local resident with ease. Ultimately, this data is stored in a database somewhere on a computer. After all, each page of a phone book is not manually typed each year a new edition is released.

The database has to be maintained. As people move to different cities or states, entries may have to be added or removed from the phone book. Likewise, entries will have to be modified for people changing names, addresses, or telephone numbers, and so on. Figure 1.1 illustrates a simple database.

**Figure 1.1.**
*The database.*

## An Introduction to the Relational Database

A *relational database* is a database divided into logical units called *tables*, where tables are related to one another within the database. A relational database allows data to be broken down into logical, smaller, more manageable units, allowing for easier maintenance and providing more optimal database performance according to the level of organization. In Figure 1.2, you can see that tables are related to one another through a common key in a relational database.

**Figure 1.2.**
*The relational database.*

Again, tables are related in a relational database, allowing adequate data to be retrieved in a single query (although the desired data may exist in more than one table). By having common *keys*, or *fields*, among relational database tables, data from multiple tables can be joined to form one large result set. As you venture deeper into this book, you see more of the relational database's advantages, including overall performance and easy data access.

NEW TERM   *Relational database* is a database composed of related objects, primarily tables.

NEW TERM   A *table* is the most basic means of storage for data in a database.

## An Introduction to Client/Server Technology

In the past, the computer industry was predominately ruled by the mainframe computers; large, powerful systems capable of high storage capacity and high data processing capabilities. Users communicated with the mainframe through dumb terminals—terminals that did not think on their own, but solely relied upon the mainframe's CPU, storage, and memory. Each terminal had a data line attached to the mainframe. The mainframe environment definitely

1

served its purpose, and does today in many businesses, but a greater technology was soon to be introduced: the client/server model.

In the *client/server system*, the main computer, called the *server*, is accessible from a network, typically a local area network (LAN) or a wide area network (WAN). The server is normally accessed by personal computers (PCs), or by other servers, instead of dumb terminals. Each PC, called a *client*, is provided access to the network, allowing communication between the client and the server, thus explaining the name client/server. The main difference between client/server and mainframe environments is that the user's PC in a client/server environment is capable of thinking on its own, capable of running its own processes using its own CPU and memory, but readily accessible to a server computer through a network. A client/server system is much more flexible for today's overall business needs in most cases, and is much preferred.

Relational database systems reside on both mainframes and on client/server platforms. Although a client/server system is preferred, the continued use of mainframes can certainly be justified according to a company's needs. A high percentage of companies have recently been leaving their mainframe systems behind and moving their data to a client/server system, motivated by the urge to stay current with new technologies, provide more flexibility to better suit their business needs, and make old systems Year 2000-compliant.

The switch to a client/server system has proven beneficial for some companies, while others have failed in the client/server implementation and have, as a result, wasted millions of dollars, causing some to return to their mainframes; others still hesitate to make a change. The lack of appropriate expertise—a result of new technology combined with a lack of training—is the main reason for failed implementations. Nevertheless, an understanding of the client/server model is imperative with the rising (and sometimes unreasonable) demands placed on today's businesses, as well as the development of Internet technologies and network computing. Figure 1.3 illustrates the concept of client/server technology.

**Figure 1.3.**

*The client/server model.*

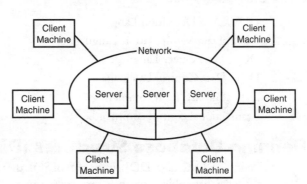

## Some Popular Relational Database Vendors

Some of the most predominant database vendors include Oracle, Microsoft, Informix, Sybase, and IBM. Although there are many more, this list includes names that you may have recognized on the bookshelf, in the newspaper, magazines, the stock market, or on the World Wide Web.

### Differences Between Implementations

As each individual in this world is unique in both features and nature, so is each vendor-specific implementation of SQL. A database server is a product, like any other product on the market, manufactured by a widespread number of vendors. It is to the benefit of the vendor to ensure that their implementation is compliant with the current ANSI standard for portability and user convenience. For instance, if a company is migrating from one database server to another, it would be rather discouraging for the database users to have to learn another language in order to maintain functionality with the new system.

With each vendor's SQL implementation, however, you find that there are enhancements that serve the purpose for each database server. These enhancements, or *extensions*, are additional commands and options that are simply a bonus to the standard SQL package and available with a specific implementation.

# Types of SQL Commands

The following sections discuss the basic categories of commands used in SQL to perform various functions. These functions include building database objects, manipulating objects, populating database tables with data, updating existing data in tables, deleting data, performing database queries, controlling database access, and overall database administration.

The main categories are

☐ DDL, Data Definition Language
☐ DML, Data Manipulation Language
☐ DQL, Data Query Language
☐ DCL, Data Control Language
☐ Data administration commands
☐ Transactional control commands

# Defining Database Structures (DDL)

Data Definition Language, DDL, is the part of SQL that allows a database user to create and restructure database objects, such as the creation or the deletion of a table.

1

The main DDL commands discussed during following hours include:

```
CREATE TABLE
ALTER TABLE
DROP TABLE
CREATE INDEX
ALTER INDEX
DROP INDEX
```

These commands are discussed in detail during Hour 3, "Managing Database Objects," and Hour 17, "Improving Database Performance."

## Manipulating Data (DML)

Data Manipulation Language, DML, is the part of SQL used to manipulate data within objects of a relational database.

There are three basic DML commands:

```
INSERT
UPDATE
DELETE
```

These commands are discussed in detail during Hour 5, "Manipulating Data."

## Selecting Data (DQL)

Though comprised of only one command, Data Query Language, DQL, is the most concentrated focus of SQL for a relational database user. The command is as follows:

```
SELECT
```

This command, accompanied by many options and clauses, is used to compose queries against a relational database. Queries from simple to complex, from vague to specific can be easily created. The SELECT command is discussed in exhilarating detail during Hours 7 through 16.

**NEW TERM**   A *query* is an inquiry to the database for information.

## Data Control Language (DCL)

Data control commands in SQL allow you to control access to data within the database. These DCL commands are normally used to create objects related to user access and also control the distribution of privileges among users. Some data control commands are as follows:

```
ALTER PASSWORD
GRANT
REVOKE
CREATE SYNONYM
```

You find that these commands are often grouped with other commands, and may appear in a number of different chapters.

## Data Administration Commands

Data administration commands allow the user to perform audits and perform analyses on operations within the database; they can also be used to help analyze system performance. Two general data administration commands are as follows:

```
START AUDIT
STOP AUDIT
```

Do not get data administration confused with database administration. *Database administration* is the overall administration of a database, which envelops the use of all levels of commands.

## Transactional Control Commands

In addition to the three previously introduced categories of commands, there are commands that allow the user to manage database transactions.

- ☐ COMMIT    Used to save database transactions
- ☐ ROLLBACK    Used to undo database transactions
- ☐ SAVEPOINT    Creates points within groups of transactions in which to ROLLBACK
- ☐ SET TRANSACTION    Places a name on a transaction

Transactional commands are discussed extensively during Hour 6, "Managing Database Transactions."

# An Introduction to the Database Used in This Book

Before continuing with your journey through SQL fundamentals, the next step is introducing the tables and data that you use throughout the course of instruction for the next 23 one-hour lessons. The next two sections provide an overview of the specific tables (the database) being used, their relationship to one another, their structure, and examples of the data contained.

1

## Diagram of the Tables in This Book

Figure 1.4 reveals the relationship between the tables that you use for examples, quiz questions, and exercises in this book. Each table is identified by the table name as well as each residing field in the table. Follow the mapping lines to compare the specific tables' relationship through a common field, in most cases referred to as the *primary key* (which is discussed soon).

**Figure 1.4.**

*Table relationships for this book.*

## Table-Naming Standards

Table-naming standards, as well as any standard within a business, is critical to maintain control. After studying the tables and data in the previous sections, you probably noticed that each table's suffix is _TBL. This is a naming standard selected for use, such as what's been used at various client sites. The _TBL simply tells you that the object is a table; there are many different types of objects in a relational database. For instance, in later chapters you see that the suffix _INX used to identify indexes on tables. Naming standards exist almost exclusively for overall organization and assist immensely in the administration of any relational database.

**NOTE**

You should not only adhere to the object naming syntax of any SQL implementation, but also follow local business rules and make names descriptive and related to the data groupings for the company.

## A Look at the Data

This section offers a picture of the data contained in each one of the tables used in this book. Take a few minutes and study the data, the variations, and the relationships between the tables and the data itself. Notice that some fields may not require data, which is specified when each table is created in the database.

EMPLOYEE_TBL

| EMP_ID | LAST_NAM | FIRST_NA | M | ADDRESS | CITY | ST | ZIP | PHONE |
|--------|----------|----------|---|---------|------|----|----|-------|
| 311549902 | STEPHENS | TINA | D | RR 3 BOX 17A | GREENWOOD | IN | 47890 | 3178784465 |
| 442346889 | PLEW | LINDA | C | 3301 BEACON | INDIANAPOLIS | IN | 46224 | 3172978990 |
| 213764555 | GLASS | BRANDON | S | 1710 MAIN ST | WHITELAND | IN | 47885 | 3178984321 |
| 313782439 | GLASS | JACOB | | 3789 RIVER BLVD | INDIANAPOLIS | IN | 45734 | 3175457676 |
| 220984332 | WALLACE | MARIAH | | 7889 KEYSTONE | INDIANAPOLIS | IN | 46741 | 3173325986 |
| 443679012 | SPURGEON | TIFFANY | | 5 GEORGE COURT | INDIANAPOLIS | IN | 46234 | 3175679007 |

EMPLOYEE_PAY_TBL

| EMP_ID | POSITION | DATE_HIRE | PAY_RATE | DATE_LAST | SALARY | BONUS |
|--------|----------|-----------|----------|-----------|--------|-------|
| 311549902 | MARKETING | 23-MAY-89 | | 01-MAY-97 | 4000 | |
| 442346889 | TEAM LEADER | 17-JUN-90 | 14.75 | 01-JUN-97 | | |
| 213764555 | SALES MANAGER | 14-AUG-94 | | 01-AUG-97 | 3000 | 2000 |
| 313782439 | SALESMAN | 28-JUN-97 | | | 2000 | 1000 |
| 220984332 | SHIPPER | 22-JUL-96 | 11 | 01-JUL-97 | | |
| 443679012 | SHIPPER | 14-JAN-91 | 15 | 01-JAN-97 | | |

CUSTOMER_TBL

| CUST_ID | CUST_NAME | ADDRESS | CUST_CITY | ST | ZIP | CUST_PHONE | CUST_FAX |
|---------|-----------|---------|-----------|----|----|-----------|----------|
| 232 | LESLIE GLEASON | 798 HARDAW AY DR | INDIANAPOLIS | IN | 47856 | 3175457690 | |
| 109 | NANCY BUNKER | APT A 4556 WATERWAY | BROAD RIPPLE | IN | 47950 | 3174262323 | |
| 345 | ANGELA DOBKO | RR3 BOX 76 | LEBANON | IN | 49967 | 7658970090 | |
| 090 | WENDY WOLF | 3345 GATEW AY DR | INDIANAPOLIS | IN | 46224 | 3172913421 | |
| 12 | MARYS GIFT SHOP | 435 MAIN S T | DANVILLE | IL | 47978 | 3178567221 | 3178523434 |
| 432 | SCOTTYS MARKET | RR2 BOX 17 3 | BROWNSBURG | IN | 45687 | 3178529835 | 3178529836 |
| 333 | JASONS AND DALL AS GOODIES | LAFAYETTE SQ MALL | INDIANAPOLIS | IN | 46222 | 3172978886 | 3172978887 |

```
21        MORGANS CANDIES 5657 W    INDIANAPOLIS IN 46234 3172714398
          AND TREATS      TENTH ST

43        SCHYLERS NOVELT 17 MAPLE  LEBANON      IN 48990 3174346758
          IES             ST

287       GAVINS PLACE    9880 ROCKV INDIANAPOLIS IN 46244 3172719991 3172719992
                          ILLE RD

288       HOLLYS GAMEARAM 567 US 31  WHITELAND    IN 49980 3178879023

590       HEATHERS FEATHE 4090 N SHA INDIANAPOLIS IN 43278 3175456768
          RS AND THINGS   DELAND AVE

610       RAGANS HOBBIES  451 GREEN  PLAINFIELD   IN 46818 3178393441 3178399090

560       ANDYS CANDIES   RR 1       NASHVILLE    IN 48756 8123239871
                          BOX 34

221       RYANS STUFF     2337 S     INDIANAPOLIS IN 47834 3175634402
                          SHELBY ST
```

```
ORDERS_TBL

ORD_NUM   CUST_ID PROD_ID        QTY ORD_DATE
--------- ------- ----------- ------- --------
56A901    232     11235            1 22-OCT-97
56A917    12      907            100 30-SEP-97
32A132    43      222             25 10-OCT-97
16C17     090     222              2 17-OCT-97
18D778    287     90              10 17-OCT-97
23E934    432     13              20 15-OCT-97
```

```
PRODUCTS_TBL

PROD_ID   PROD_DESC                      COST
--------- ------------------------- ----------
11235     WITCHES COSTUME               29.99
222       PLASTIC PUMPKIN 18 INCH        7.75
13        FALSE PARAFFIN TEETH           1.10
90        LIGHTED LANTERNS              14.50
15        ASSORTED COSTUMES             10.00
9         CANDY CORN                     1.35
6         PUMPKIN CANDY                  1.45
87        PLASTIC SPIDERS                1.05
119       ASSORTED MASKS                 4.95
```

# A Closer Look at What Composes a Table

The storage and maintenance of valuable data is the reason for any database's existence. You have just viewed the data that is used to explain SQL concepts in this book. The following sections take a closer look at the elements within a table. Remember, a table is the most common and simplest form of data storage in a relational database.

## A Field

Every table is broken up into smaller entities called *fields*. The fields in the PRODUCTS_TBL table consist of PROD_ID, PROD_DESC, and COST. These fields categorize the specific information that is maintained in a given table.

> **NEW TERM**    A *field* is a column in a table that is designed to maintain specific information about every record in the table.

## A Record, or Row, of Data

A *record*, also called a *row* of data, is each individual entry that exists in a table. Looking at the last table, PRODUCTS_TBL, consider the following first record in that table:

```
11235      WITCHES COSTUME                 29.99
```

The record is obviously composed of a product identification, product description, and unit cost. For every distinct product, there should be a corresponding record in the PRODUCTS_TBL table. A record is a horizontal entity in a table.

> **NEW TERM**    A *row of data* is an entire record in a relational database table.

## A Column

A *column* is a vertical entity in a table, containing all data in a table based on a specific field. For example, a column in the PRODUCTS_TBL having to do with the product description would consist of the following:

```
WITCHES COSTUME
PLASTIC PUMPKIN 18 INCH
FALSE PARAFFIN TEETH
LIGHTED LANTERNS
ASSORTED COSTUMES
CANDY CORN
PUMPKIN CANDY
PLASTIC SPIDERS
ASSORTED MASKS
```

This column is based on the field PROD_DESC, the product description. A column pulls information about a certain field from every record within a table.

> **NEW TERM**    A *column* contains all information associated with a specific field in a table.

## The Primary Key

A *primary key* distinguishes unique records for a table in a relational database. The primary key in the PRODUCTS_TBL table is PROD_ID, which is typically initialized during the table creation process. The nature of the primary key is to ensure that all product identifications are unique, so that each record in the PRODUCTS_TBL table has its own PROD_ID. Primary keys alleviate the possibility of a duplicate record in a table and are used in other ways, which you read about later.

1

**New Term** A *primary key* is a column that makes each row of data in the table unique.

### A NULL **Value**

A NULL value in a table is a value in a field that appears to be blank. A field with a NULL value is a field with no value. It is very important to understand that a NULL value is different than a zero value or a field that contains spaces. A field with a NULL value is one that has been left blank during record creation. Notice that in the EMPLOYEE_TBL table, not every employee has a middle initial. Those records for employees who do not have an entry for middle initial signify a NULL value.

**New Term** NULL is the term used to represent a missing value.

Additional table elements are discussed in detail during the next two hours.

# Summary

You have been introduced to the standard language of SQL and have been given a brief history and thumbnail of how the standard has evolved over the last several years. Database systems and current technologies were also discussed, including the relational database and client/server systems, both of which are vital to your understanding of SQL. The main SQL language components and the fact that there are numerous players in the relational database market, and likewise, many different flavors of SQL, were discussed. Despite ANSI SQL variations, most vendors do comply, to some extent, with the current standard, rendering consistency across the board and forcing the development of SQL applications that are portable.

The database that will be used during your course of study was also introduced. The database, as you have seen it so far, has consisted of a few tables, which are related to one another, and the data that each table contains at this point (at the end of Hour 1). You should have acquired some overall background knowledge of the fundamentals of SQL and should understand the concept of a relational database. After a few refreshers in the Workshop for this hour, you should feel very confident about continuing to the next hour.

# Q&A

**Q** **If I learn SQL, will I be able to use any of the implementations that use SQL?**

**A** Yes, you will be able to communicate with a database whose implementation is ANSI SQL-compliant. If an implementation is not completely compliant, you should be able to pick it up quickly with some adjustments.

**Q** **In a client/server environment, is the PC the client or the server?**

**A** The PC is known as the client.

**Q  Do I have to use _tbl for each table I create?**

**A  Certainly not.** The use of _tbl is a standard chosen for use in order to name and easily identify the tables in your database. You could spell out _tbl as _table, or may want to avoid using a suffix. For example, employee_tbl could simply be employee.

**Q  What happens when I am inserting a new record into a table and am missing, for example, a new employee's phone number—and the column for the phone number entry is not null?**

**A  One of two things,** because the column was specified as not null (something has to be entered), and because you do not have the necessary information, you could delay inserting the record until you have the phone number. Another option is to change the column from NOT NULL to NULL, thereby allowing you to update the phone number later when the information is received.  Changing the column definitions is discussed in Hour 3.

# Workshop

The following workshop is composed of a series of quiz questions and practical exercises. The quiz questions are designed to test your overall understanding of the current material. The practical exercises are intended to afford you the opportunity to apply the concepts discussed during the current hour, as well as build upon the knowledge acquired in previous hours of study. Please take time to complete the quiz questions and exercises before continuing. You may refer to the answers in Appendix C.

## Quiz

1.  What does the acronym SQL stand for?
2.  What are the six main categories of SQL commands?
3.  What are the four transactional control commands?
4.  What is the main difference between client/server technologies and the mainframe?
5.  If a field is defined as null, does that mean that something has to be entered into that field?

## Exercises

1.  Identify the categories in which the following SQL commands fall:

```
create table
delete
select
insert
alter table
update
```

# PART II

## Building Your Database

## Hour

# Hour 2

# Defining Data Structures

In this second hour you learn more about the data you viewed at the end of Hour 1. You learn the characteristics of the data itself and how such data is stored in a relational database. There are several datatypes, as you soon discover.

The highlights of this hour include

- ☐ A look at the underlying data of a table
- ☐ An introduction to the basic datatypes
- ☐ Instruction on the use of various datatypes
- ☐ Examples depicting differences between datatypes

## What Is Data?

*Data* is a collection of information stored in a database as one of several different datatypes. Data includes names, numbers, dollar amounts, text, graphics, decimals, figures, calculations, summarization, and just about anything else you can possibly imagine. Data can be stored in uppercase, lowercase, or mixed case. Data can be manipulated or changed; most data does not remain static for its lifetime.

*Datatypes* are used to provide rules for data for particular columns. A datatype deals with the way values are stored in a column as far as the length allocated for a column and whether values such as alphanumeric, numeric, and date and time data are allowed.

The data is the purpose of any database and must be protected. The protector of the data is normally the DBA, although it is every database user's responsibility to ensure that measures are taken to protect data. Data security is discussed in-depth in Hour 18, "Managing Database Users," and Hour 19, "Managing Database Security."

# Basic Datatypes

The following sections discuss the basic datatypes supported by ANSI SQL. Datatypes are characteristics of the data itself, whose attributes are placed on fields within a table. For example, you can specify that a field must contain numeric values, disallowing the entering of alphanumeric strings. After all, you would not want to enter alphabetic characters in a field for a dollar amount.

> **Note**
>
> Every implementation of SQL seems to have its own specific datatypes. The use of implementation-specific datatypes is necessary in order to support the philosophy of each implementation on how to handle the storage of data. However, the basics are the same among all implementations.

The very basic datatypes, as with most other languages, are:

- ☐ Character strings
- ☐ Numeric strings
- ☐ Date and time values

## Fixed-Length Characters

*Constant characters*, those strings that always have the same length, are stored using a fixed-length datatype. The standard for an SQL fixed-length character is:

```
CHARACTER(n)
```

*n* represents a number identifying the *allocated*, or maximum length, of the particular field with this definition.

Some implementations of SQL use the CHAR datatype to store fixed-length data. Alphanumeric data can be stored in this datatype. An example of a constant length datatype would be for a state abbreviation, as all state abbreviations are two characters.

Spaces are normally used to fill extra spots when using a fixed-length datatype; if a field's length was set to 10 and data entered filled only five places, then the remaining five spaces are recorded as spaces. The padding of spaces ensures that each value in a field is a fixed length.

**WARNING**

Be careful not to use a fixed-length datatype for fields that may contain varying-length values, such as an individual's name. If you use the fixed-length datatype inappropriately, problems such as the waste of available space and the inability to make accurate comparisons between data will eventually be encountered.

2

## Variable Characters

SQL supports the use of *varying-length strings*, strings whose length is not constant for all data. The standard for an SQL varying-length character is:

```
CHARACTER VARYING(n)
```

*n* represents a number identifying the allocated, or maximum length, of the particular field with this definition.

A common datatype for variable-length character values are the VARCHAR and VARCHAR2 datatypes. VARCHAR is the ANSI standard, which Microsoft SQL Server uses; VARCHAR2 is used by Oracle and should be used in Oracle, because VARCHAR's usage in the future may change. The data stored can be alphanumeric.

Remember that fixed-length datatypes typically pad spaces to fill in allocated places not used by the field. The varying-length datatype does not work this way. For instance, if the allocated length of a varying-length field is 10, and a string of five characters is entered, then the total length of that particular value is only 5. Spaces are not used to fill unused places in a column.

**TIP**

Always use the varying-length datatype for non-constant character strings to save database space.

## Numeric Values

Numeric values are stored in fields that are defined as some type of number, typically referred to as NUMBER, INTEGER, REAL, DECIMAL, and so on.

The standards for SQL numeric values are

```
BIT(n)

BIT VARYING(n)

DECIMAL(n,n)
```

```
INTEGER
SMALLINT
FLOAT(p)
REAL(s)
DOUBLE PRECISION(P)
```

*n* represents a number identifying the allocated, or maximum length, of the particular field for each appropriate definition.

A common numeric datatype in SQL implementations is NUMBER, which accommodates the direction for numeric values provided by ANSI. Numeric values can be stored as zero, positive, negative, fixed, and floating-point numbers. An example using NUMBER:

```
NUMBER(5)
```

This example restricts the maximum value entered in a particular field to 99999.

## Decimal Values

Decimal values are numeric values that include the use of a decimal point. The standard for a decimal in SQL follows, where the first *n* is the precision and the second *n* is the decimal's scale:

```
DECIMAL(n,n)
```

 The *precision* is the total length of the numeric value. In a numeric defined DECIMAL(4,2), the precision is 4, which is the total length allocated for a numeric value.

 The *scale* is the number of digits to the right of the decimal point. The scale is 2 in the previous DECIMAL(4,2) example.

34.33 inserted into a DECIMAL(3,1) is typically rounded to 34.3.

If a numeric value was defined as the following datatype, then the maximum value allowed would be 99.99:

```
DECIMAL(4,2)
```

The precision is 4, which represents the total length allocated for an associated value. The scale is 2, which represents the number of *places*, or *bytes*, reserved to the right side of the decimal point. The decimal point itself does not count as a character.

Allowed values for a column defined as DECIMAL(4,2) include:

```
12
12.4
12.44
12.449
```

**2**   The last numeric value, 12.449, is rounded off to 12.45 upon input into the column.

## Integers

An *integer* is a numeric value that does not contain a decimal, only whole numbers (both positive and negative).

Valid integers include

```
1
0
-1
99
-99
199
```

## Floating-Point Decimals

*Floating-point decimals* are decimal values whose precision and scale are variable lengths and virtually without limit. Any precision and scale is acceptable. The REAL datatype designates a column with single-precision, floating-point numbers. The DOUBLE PRECISION datatype designates a column that contains double-precision, floating-point numbers. To be considered a single-precision floating point, the precision must be between 1 and 21 inclusive. To be considered a double-precision floating point, the precision must be between 22 and 53 inclusive.

```
FLOAT
FLOAT(15)
FLOAT(50)
```

## Dates and Time

Date and time datatypes are quite obviously used to keep track of information concerning dates and time. Standard SQL supports what are called DATETIME datatypes, which include the following specific datatypes:

```
DATE
TIME
INTERVAL
TIMESTAMP
```

The elements of a DATETIME datatype consist of

```
YEAR
MONTH
DAY
HOUR
MINUTE
SECOND
```

**NOTE** The SECOND element can also be broken down to fractions of a second. The range is from `00.000` to `61.999`.

Be aware that each implementation of SQL may have its own customized datatype for dates and times. The previous datatypes and elements are standards to which each SQL vendor should adhere, but be advised that most implementations have their own datatype for date values, varying in both appearance and the way date information is actually stored internally.

A length is not normally specified for a date datatype. Later, you learn more about dates, how date information is stored in some implementations, how to manipulate dates and times using conversion functions, and study practical examples of how dates and time are used in the real world.

## Literal Strings

A *literal string* is a series of characters, such as a name or a phone number, that is explicitly specified by a user or program. Literal strings consist of data with the same attributes as the previously discussed datatypes, but the value of the string is known; the value of a column itself is usually unknown, because there is typically a different value for a column associated with each row of data in a table.

You do not actually specify datatypes with literal strings—you simply specify the string. Some examples of literal strings follow:

```
'Hello'
45000
'45000'
3.14
'November 1, 1997'
```

The alphanumeric strings are enclosed by single quotation marks, whereas the number value `45000` is not. Also notice that the second numeric value of `45000` is enclosed by quotation marks. Generally speaking, character strings require quotation marks, whereas numeric strings don't. You see later how literal strings are used with database queries.

## NULL **Datatypes**

This chapter has already touched on the concept of a NULL value. As you should know, a NULL value is a missing value, or a column in a row of data that has not been assigned a value. NULL values are used in nearly all parts of SQL, including the creation of tables, search conditions for queries, and even in literal strings.

The following are two methods for referencing a NULL value:

- [ ] NULL (the keyword NULL itself)
- [ ] ' ' (single quotation marks with nothing in between)

The following does not represent a NULL value, but a literal string containing the characters N-U-L-L:

'NULL'

# Summary

There are several datatypes available with SQL. If you have programmed in other languages, you probably recognize many of the datatypes mentioned. Datatypes allow different types of data to be stored in the database, ranging from simple characters to decimal points, to date and time. The concept of datatypes is the same in all languages, whether programming in a third-generation language such as C and passing variable, or using a relational database implementation and coding in SQL. Of course, each implementation has its own names for standard datatypes, but they basically work the same.

Care must be taken in planning for both the near and distant futures when deciding on datatypes, lengths, scales, and precisions in which to store your data. Business rules and how you want the end user to access the data are other factors in deciding upon specific datatypes. You should know the nature of the data itself and how data in the database is related in order to assign proper datatypes.

## Q&A

**Q  How is it that I can enter numbers such as a person's social security number in fields defined as character fields?**

**A**  Numeric values are still alphanumeric, which are allowed in character datatypes. Typically, the only data stored as numeric values are values used in computations. However, it may be helpful for some to define all numeric fields with a numeric datatype to help control the data entered in that field.

**Q  I still do not understand the difference between constant-length and varying-length datatypes. Can you explain?**

**A**  Say you have an individual's last name defined as a constant datatype with a length of 20 bytes. Suppose the individual's name is Smith. When the data is inserted into the table, 20 bytes are taken, 5 for the name and 15 for the extra spaces (Remember that this is a constant-length datatype). If you use a varying-length datatype with a length of 20 and inserted Smith, only 5 bytes of space are taken.

# Workshop

The following workshop is composed of a series of quiz questions and practical exercises. The quiz questions are designed to test your overall understanding of the current material. The practical exercises are intended to afford you the opportunity to apply the concepts discussed during the current hour, as well as build upon the knowledge acquired in previous hours of study. Please take time to complete the quiz questions and exercises before continuing. You may refer to the answers in Appendix C.

## Quiz

1. True or false: An individual's social security number can be any of the following datatypes: constant-length character, varying-length character, numeric.

2. True or false: The scale of a numeric value is the total length allowed for values.

3. Do all implementations use the same datatypes?

4. What is the precision and scale of the following?
   ```
   DECIMAL(4,2)
   DECIMAL(10,2)
   DECIMAL(14,1)
   ```

5. Which numbers could be inserted into a column whose datatype is DECIMAL(4,1)?

   a. 16.2

   b. 116.2

   c. 16.21

   d. 1116.2

   e. 1116.21

## Exercises

1. Take the following column titles, assign them to a datatype, and decide on the proper length.

   a. ssn

   b. state

   c. city

   d. phone_number

   e. zip

   f. last_name

   g. first_name

   h. middle_name

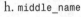

**2**

      i. salary

      j. hourly_pay_rate

      k. date_hired

2. Take the same column titles and decide whether they should be null or NOT NULL, realizing that in some cases where a column would normally be NOT NULL, the column could be NULL or vice-versa, depending on the application.

      a. ssn

      b. state

      c. city

      d. phone_number

      e. zip

      f. last_name

      g. first_name

      h. middle_name

      i. salary

      j. hourly_pay_rate

      k. date_hired

2

# Hour 3

# Managing Database Objects

In this hour you learn about database objects: what they are, how they act, how they are stored, and how they relate to one another. Database objects are the underlying backbone of the relational database. These *objects* are logical units within the database that are used to store information, and are referred to as the *back-end database*. The majority of the instruction during this hour revolves around the table, but keep in mind that there are other database objects, many of which are discussed in later hours of study.

The highlights of this hour include

- ☐ An introduction to database objects
- ☐ An introduction to the schema
- ☐ An introduction to the table
- ☐ A discussion of the nature and attributes of tables
- ☐ Examples for the creation and manipulation of tables
- ☐ A discussion of table storage options
- ☐ Concepts on referential integrity and data consistency

# What Are Database Objects?

A *database object* is any defined object in a database that is used to store or reference data. Some examples of database objects include tables, views, clusters, sequences, indexes, and synonyms. The table is Hour 3's focus, because it is the simplest form of data storage in a relational database.

# What Is a Schema?

A *schema* is a collection of database objects (as far as this hour is concerned, tables) associated with one particular database username. This username is called the *schema owner*, or the owner of the related group of objects. You may have one or multiple schemas in a database. Basically, any user who creates an object has just created his or her own schema. A schema can consist of a single table and has no limits to the number of objects that it may contain, unless restricted by a specific database implementation.

**NEW TERM**   A *schema* is a collection of related objects in a database that are owned by a common database user account.

Say you have been issued a database username and password by the database administrator. Your username is USER1. Suppose you log on to the database, then create a table called EMPLOYEE_TBL. Your table's actual name is USER1.EMPLOYEE_TBL. The schema name for that table is USER1, which is also the owner of that table. You have just created the first table of a schema.

The good thing about schemas is that when you access a table that you own (in your own schema), you do not have to refer to the schema name. For instance, you could refer to your table as either one of the following:

```
EMPLOYEE_TBL
USER1.EMPLOYEE_TBL
```

The first option is preferred because it requires fewer keystrokes. If another user were to query one of your tables, the user would have to specify the schema, as follows:

```
USER1.EMPLOYEE_TBL
```

In Hour 20, "Creating and Using Views and Synonyms," you learn about the distribution of permissions so that other users can access your tables. You also learn about synonyms, which allow you to give a table another name so that you do not have to specify the schema name when accessing a table. Figure 3.1 illustrates two schemas in a relational database.

**Figure 3.1.**

*Schemas in a database.*

There are, in Figure 3.1, two user accounts in the database that own tables: USER1 and USER2. Each user account has its own schema. Some examples for how the two users may access their own tables and tables owned by the other user follow:

USER1 accesses own `table1`:          `TABLE1`

USER1 accesses own test:             `TEST`

USER1 accesses USER2's `table10`:     `USER2.TABLE10`

USER1 accesses USER2's test:         `USER2.TEST`

Both users have a table called `TEST`. Tables can have the same names in a database as long as they belong to different schemas. If you look at it this way, table names are always unique in a database, because the schema owner is actually part of the table name. For instance, `USER1.TEST` is different than `USER2.TEST`. If you do not specify a schema with the table name when accessing tables in a database, the database server looks for a table that you own by default. That is, if USER1 tries to access `TEST`, the database server looks for a USER1-owned table named `TEST` before it looks for other objects owned by USER1, such as synonyms to tables in another schema. Hour 21, "Working with the System Catalog," helps you fully understand how synonyms work.

**NOTE**

Every database server has rules concerning how you may name objects and elements of objects, such as field names. You must check your particular implementation for the exact naming conventions or rules.

# A Table: The Primary Storage for Data

The *table* is the primary storage object for data in a relational database. A table consists of row(s) and column(s), both of which hold the data. A table does take up physical space in a database and can be permanent or temporary.

## Fields and Columns

A *field*, also called a *column* in a relational database, is part of a table that is assigned a specific datatype; a field should be named to correspond with the type of data that will be entered into that column. Columns can be specified as NULL or NOT NULL, meaning that if a column is NOT NULL, something must be entered. If a column is specified as NULL, nothing has to be entered.

Every database table must consist of at least one column. *Columns* are those elements within a table that hold specific types of data, such as a person's name or address. For example, a valid column in a customer table may be the customer's name.

Generally, a name must be one continuous string. An object name must typically be one continuous string and may be limited to the number of characters used according to each implementation of SQL. It is typical to use underscores with names to provide separations between characters. For example, a column for the customer's name can be named CUSTOMER_NAME instead of CUSTOMERNAME.

**NOTE**

> Be sure to check your implementation for rules when naming objects and other database elements.

## Rows

A *row* is a record of data in a database table. For example, a row of data in a customer table might consist of a particular customer's identification number, name, address, phone number, fax number, and so on. A row comprises fields that contain data from one record in a table. A table can contain as little as one row of data and up to as many as millions of rows of data, or records.

## The CREATE TABLE Statement

The CREATE TABLE statement is obviously used to create a table. Although the very act of creating a table is quite simple, much time and effort should be put into planning table structures before the actual execution of the create table statement.

Some elementary questions need to be answered when creating a table:

- ☐ What type of data will compose the table?
- ☐ What will be the table's name?
- ☐ What column(s) will compose the primary key?
- ☐ What names shall be given to the columns (fields)?
- ☐ What datatype will be assigned to each column?
- ☐ What will be the allocated length for each column?
- ☐ Which columns in a table require data?

After these questions are answered, the actual CREATE TABLE statement is simple.

The basic syntax to create a table is as follows:

```
CREATE TABLE table_name
( field1  datatype  [ not null ],
  field2  datatype  [ not null ],
  field3  datatype  [ not null ],
  field4  datatype  [ not null ],
  field5  datatype  [ not null ] )
```

**NOTE**

In this chapter's examples, you use the popular datatypes CHAR (constant-length character), VARCHAR (variable-length character), NUMBER (numeric values, decimal and non-decimal), and DATE (date and time values).

You create a table called EMPLOYEE_TBL in the following example:

**TYPE**

```
CREATE TABLE EMPLOYEE_TBL
(EMP_ID          CHAR(9)        NOT NULL,
 EMP_NAME        VARCHAR(40)    NOT NULL,
 EMP_ST_ADDR     VARCHAR(20)    NOT NULL,
 EMP_CITY        VARCHAR(15)    NOT NULL,
 EMP_ST          CHAR(2)        NOT NULL,
 EMP_ZIP         NUMBER(5)      NOT NULL,
 EMP_PHONE       NUMBER(10)     NULL,
 EMP_PAGER       NUMBER(10)     NULL);
```

Eight different columns make up this table. Notice the use of the underscore character to break the column names up into what appears to be separate words (EMPLOYEE ID is stored as EMP_ID). Each column has been assigned a specific datatype and length, and by using the NULL/NOT NULL constraint, you have specified which columns require values for every row of data in the table. The EMP_PHONE is defined as NULL, meaning that NULL values are allowed in this column, because there may be individuals without a telephone number. The information concerning each column is separated by a comma, with parentheses surrounding all columns (a left parenthesis before the first column and a right parenthesis following the information on the last column).

A semicolon is the last character in the previous statement. Most SQL implementations have some character that terminates a statement or submits a statement to the database server. Oracle uses the semicolon. Transact-SQL uses the GO statement. This book uses the semicolon.

Each *record*, or row of data, in this table would consist of the following:

EMP_ID, EMP_NAME, EMP_ST_ADDR, EMP_CITY, EMP_ST, EMP_ZIP, EMP_PHONE, EMP_PAGER

In this table, each field is a column. The column EMP_ID could consist of one employee's identification number or many employees' identification numbers, depending upon the requirements of a database query or transactions. The column is a vertical entity in a table, whereas a row of data is a horizontal entity.

**NOTE**

NULL is the default value for a column; therefore, it does not have to be entered in the CREATE TABLE statement.

### storage **Clause**

Some form of a storage clause is available in many relational database implementations of SQL. The storage clause in a CREATE TABLE statement is used for initial table sizing and is usually done upon table creation. The syntax of a storage clause as used in one implementation is shown in the following example:

```
CREATE TABLE EMPLOYEE_TBL
(EMP_ID          CHAR(9)         NOT NULL,
 EMP_NAME        VARCHAR(40)     NOT NULL,
 EMP_ST_ADDR     VARCHAR(20)     NOT NULL,
 EMP_CITY        VARCHAR(15)     NOT NULL,
 EMP_ST          CHAR(2)         NOT NULL,
 EMP_ZIP         NUMBER(5)       NOT NULL,
 EMP_PHONE       NUMBER(10)      NULL,
 EMP_PAGER       NUMBER(10)      NULL)
STORAGE
    (INITIAL     3K
     NEXT        2K );
```

In some implementations, there are several options available in the storage clause. INITIAL allocates a set amount of space in bytes, kilobytes, and so on, for the initial amount of space to be used by a table. The NEXT part of the storage identifies the amount of additional space that should be allocated to the table if it should grow beyond the space allocated for the initial allocation. You find that there are other options available with the storage clause, and remember that these options vary from implementation to implementation. If the storage clause is omitted from most major implementations, there are default storage parameters invoked, which may not be the best for the application.

Notice the neatness of the create table statement. This is for ease of reading and error resolution. Indentation has been used to help.

**NOTE**

The storage clause differs between relational database implementations of SQL. The previous example used Oracle's storage clause, which was added to the CREATE TABLE statement. Remember that the ANSI standard for SQL is just that, a standard. The standard is not a language itself, but guidelines on how vendors should develop their SQL implementation. You also find that datatypes differ between implementations. Most issues concerning the actual storage and processing of data are implementation-specific.

## Naming Conventions

When selecting names for objects, specifically tables and columns, the name should reflect the data that is to be stored. For example, the name for a table pertaining to employee information could be named EMPLOYEE_TBL. Names for columns follow the same logic. When storing an employee's phone number, an obvious name for that column would be PHONE_NUMBER.

**NOTE** Check your particular implementation for name length limits and characters that are allowed; they could differ from other implementations.

## The ALTER TABLE Command

A table can be modified through the use of the ALTER TABLE command after that table's creation. You can add column(s), drop column(s), change column definitions, add and drop constraints, and in some implementations, modify table storage values. The standard syntax for the ALTER TABLE command follows:

```
alter table table_name [modify] [column column_name][datatype¦null not null]
[restrict¦cascade]
                      [drop]    [constraint constraint_name]
                      [add]     [column] column definition
```

### Modifying Elements of a Table

You can modify the attributes of a column with the ALTER TABLE command. The word attributes here refers to the following:

- ☐ The datatype of a column
- ☐ The length, precision, or scale of a column
- ☐ Whether the column can contain NULL values

**NEW TERM** The *attributes* of a column refer to the rules and behavior of data in a column.

The following example uses the ALTER TABLE command on EMPLOYEE_TBL to modify the attributes of the column EMP_ID:

**ALTER TABLE EMPLOYEE_TBL MODIFY (EMP_ID VARCHAR2(10));**

```
Table altered.
```

The column was already defined as datatype VARCHAR2 (a varying-length character), but you increased the maximum length from 9 to 10.

### Adding Mandatory Columns to a Table

One of the basic rules for adding columns to an existing table is that the column you are adding cannot be defined as NOT NULL if data currently exists in the table. NOT NULL means that a column must contain some value for every row of data in the table, so if you are adding a column defined as NOT NULL, then you are contradicting the NOT NULL constraint; the preexisting rows of data in the table do not have values for the new column.

There is, however, a way to add a mandatory column to a table:

1. Add the column and define it as NULL (the column does not have to contain a value).

2. Insert a value into the new column for every row of data in the table.

3. After ensuring that the column contains a value for every row of data in the table, you can alter the table to change the column's attribute to NOT NULL.

### Modifying Columns

There are many thoughts to take into consideration when modifying existing columns of a table.

Common rules for modifying columns:

☐ The length of a column can be increased to the maximum length of the given datatype.

☐ The length of a column can be decreased only if the largest value for that column in the table is less than or equal to the new length of the column.

☐ The number of digits for a number datatype can always be increased.

☐ The number of digits for a number datatype can be decreased only if the value with the most number of digits for that column is less than or equal to the new number of digits specified for the column.

☐ The number of decimal places for a number datatype can either be increased or decreased.

☐ The datatype of a column can normally be changed.

Some implementations may actually restrict you from using certain ALTER TABLE options. For example, you may not be allowed to drop columns from a table. In order to do this, you would have to drop the table itself, then rebuild the table with the desired columns. You could run into problems by dropping a column in one table that is dependent upon a column in another table, or a column that is referenced by a column in another table. Be sure to refer to your specific implementation documentation.

## Creating a Table from an Existing Table

A copy of an existing table can be created using a combination of the CREATE TABLE statement and the SELECT statement. The new table has the same column definitions. All columns or specific columns can be selected. New columns that are created via functions or a combination of columns automatically assume the size necessary to hold the data. The basic syntax for creating a table from another table is as follows:

SYNTAX

```
create table new_table_name as
select [ *|column1, column2 ]
from table_name
[ where ]
```

Notice some new keywords in the syntax, particularly the SELECT keyword. SELECT is a database query, and is discussed in more detail later. However, it is important to know that you can create a table based on the results from a query.

First, do a simple query to view the data in the PRODUCTS_TBL table.

**TYPE**

```
select * from products_tbl;
```

**OUTPUT**

```
PROD_ID     PROD_DESC                    COST
--------    ----------------------       --------
11235       WITCHES COSTUME              29.99
222         PLASTIC PUMPKIN 18 INCH       7.75
13          FALSE PARAFFIN TEETH          1.1
90          LIGHTED LANTERNS             14.5
15          ASSORTED COSTUMES            10
9           CANDY CORN                    1.35
6           PUMPKIN CANDY                 1.45
87          PLASTIC SPIDERS               1.05
119         ASSORTED MASKS                4.95
```

**NOTE**

SELECT * selects data from all fields in the given table.

Next, create a table called PRODUCTS_TMP based on the previous query:

```
create table products_tmp as
select * from products_tbl;
```

Table created.

Now, if you run a query on the PRODUCTS_TMP table, your results appear the same as if you had selected data from the original table.

**TYPE**

```
select *
from products_tmp;
```

**OUTPUT**

```
PROD_ID     PROD_DESC                    COST
--------    ----------------------       --------
11235       WITCHES COSTUME              29.99
222         PLASTIC PUMPKIN 18 INCH       7.75
13          FALSE PARAFFIN TEETH          1.1
90          LIGHTED LANTERNS             14.5
15          ASSORTED COSTUMES            10
9           CANDY CORN                    1.35
6           PUMPKIN CANDY                 1.45
87          PLASTIC SPIDERS               1.05
119         ASSORTED MASKS                4.95
```

**NOTE**

When creating a table from an existing table, the new table takes on the same storage attributes as the original table.

## Dropping Tables

**SYNTAX**

Dropping a table is actually one of the easiest things to do. When the restrict option is used and the table is referenced by a view or constraint, the drop statement returns an error. When the cascade option is used, the drop succeeds and all referencing views and constraints are dropped. The syntax to drop a table follows:

```
drop table table_name [ restrict|cascade ]
```

In the following example, you drop the table that you just created:

```
drop table products_tmp;
```

Table dropped.

**WARNING**

Whenever dropping a table, be sure to specify the schema name, or owner of the table, before submitting your command. You could drop the incorrect table. If you have access to multiple user accounts, ensure that you are connected to the database through the correct user account before dropping tables.

# Integrity Constraints

Integrity constraints are used to ensure accuracy and consistency of data in a relational database. Data integrity is handled in a relational database through the concept of referential integrity. There are many types of integrity constraints that play a role in referential integrity (RI).

## Primary Key Constraints

*Primary key* is the term used to identify one or more columns in a table that make a row of data unique. Although the primary key typically consists of one column in a table, more than one column can comprise the primary key. For example, either the employee's social security number or an assigned employee identification number is the logical primary key for an employee table. The objective is for every record to have a unique primary key, or value, for the employee's identification number. Because there is probably no need to have more than one record for each employee in an employee table, the employee identification number makes a logical primary key. The primary key is assigned upon table creation.

**3**

The following example identifies the EMP_ID column as the PRIMARY KEY for the EMPLOYEES table.

**TYPE**
```
CREATE TABLE EMPLOYEE_TBL
(EMP_ID          CHAR(9)          NOT NULL PRIMARY KEY,
 EMP_NAME        VARCHAR2(40)     NOT NULL,
 EMP_ST_ADDR     VARCHAR2(20)     NOT NULL,
 EMP_CITY        VARCHAR2(15)     NOT NULL,
 EMP_ST          CHAR(2)          NOT NULL,
 EMP_ZIP         NUMBER(5)        NOT NULL,
 EMP_PHONE       NUMBER(10)       NULL,
 EMP_PAGER       NUMBER(10)       NULL);
```

This method of defining a primary key is accomplished during table creation. The primary key in this case is an implied constraint. You can also specify a primary key explicitly as a constraint when setting up a table, as follows:

**TYPE**
```
CREATE TABLE EMPLOYEE_TBL
(EMP_ID          CHAR(9)          NOT NULL,
 EMP_NAME        VARCHAR2(40)     NOT NULL,
 EMP_ST_ADDR     VARCHAR2(20)     NOT NULL,
 EMP_CITY        VARCHAR2(15)     NOT NULL,
 EMP_ST          CHAR(2)          NOT NULL,
 EMP_ZIP         NUMBER(5)        NOT NULL,
 EMP_PHONE       NUMBER(10)       NULL,
 EMP_PAGER       NUMBER(10)       NULL),
 PRIMARY KEY (EMP_ID);
```

The primary key constraint in this example is defined after the column comma list in the CREATE TABLE statement.

## Unique Constraints

A unique column constraint in a table is similar to a primary key in that the value in that column for every row of data in the table must have a unique value. While a primary key constraint is placed on one column, you can place a unique constraint on another column even though it is not actually for use as the primary key.

Study the following example:

```
CREATE TABLE EMPLOYEE_TBL
(EMP_ID          CHAR(9)          NOT NULL      PRIMARY KEY,
 EMP_NAME        VARCHAR2(40)     NOT NULL,
 EMP_ST_ADDR     VARCHAR2(20)     NOT NULL,
 EMP_CITY        VARCHAR2(15)     NOT NULL,
 EMP_ST          CHAR(2)          NOT NULL,
 EMP_ZIP         NUMBER(5)        NOT NULL,
 EMP_PHONE       NUMBER(10)       NULL          UNIQUE,
 EMP_PAGER       NUMBER(10)       NULL);
```

The primary key in this example is EMP_ID, meaning that the employee identification number is the column that is used to ensure that every record in the table is unique. The primary key is a column that is normally referenced in queries, particularly to join tables. The column

EMP_PHONE has been designated as a UNIQUE value, meaning that no two employees may have the same telephone number. There is not a lot of difference between the two, except that the primary key is used to provide an order to data in a table, and in the same respect, join related tables.

## Foreign Key Constraints

A *foreign key constraint* is the main mechanism used to enforce referential integrity between tables in a relational database. A column defined as a foreign key is used to reference a column defined as a primary key in another table.

**NEW TERM**   A *foreign key* is a column in a child table that references a column in the parent table.

Study the creation of the foreign key in the next example:

```
CREATE TABLE EMPLOYEE_PAY_TBL
(EMP_ID              CHAR(9)        NOT NULL,
POSITION             VARCHAR2(15)   NOT NULL,
DATE_HIRE            DATE           NULL,
PAY_RATE             NUMBER(4,2)    NOT NULL,
DATE_LAST_RAISE      DATE           NULL,
FOREIGN KEY EMP_ID_FK (EMP_ID) REFERENCES EMPLOYEE_TBL (EMP_ID);
```

The EMP_ID column in this example has been designated as the foreign key for the EMPLOYEE_PAY_TBL table. This foreign key, as you can see, references the EMP_ID column in the EMPLOYEE_TBL table. This foreign key ensures that for every EMP_ID in the EMPLOYEE_PAY_TBL, there is a corresponding EMP_ID in the EMPLOYEE_TBL. This is called a *parent/child relationship*. The parent table is the EMPLOYEE_TBL table, and the child table is the EMPLOYEE_PAY_TBL table. Study Figure 3.2 for a better understanding of the parent table/child table relationship.

**Figure 3.2.**
*The parent/child table relationship.*

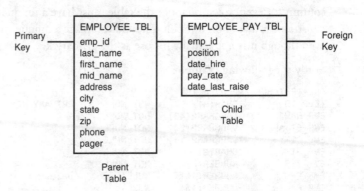

In this figure, the EMP_ID column in the child table references the EMP_ID column in the parent table. In order for a value to be inserted for EMP_ID in the child table, there must first exist a value for EMP_ID in the parent table. Likewise, in order for a value to be removed for EMP_ID in the parent table, all corresponding values for EMP_ID must first be removed from the child table. This is how referential integrity works.

**3**

A foreign key can be added to a table using the ALTER TABLE command, as shown in the next example:

```
alter table employee_pay_tbl
add constraint id_fk foreign key (emp_id)
references employee_tbl (emp_id);
```

**NOTE**  The options available with the ALTER TABLE command differ among different implementations of SQL, particularly when dealing with constraints. In addition, the actual use and definitions of constraints also vary, but the concept of referential integrity should be the same with all relational databases.

## NOT NULL **Constraints**

Previous examples use the keywords NULL and NOT NULL listed on the same line as each column and after the datatype. NOT NULL is a constraint that you can place on a table's column. This constraint disallows the entrance of NULL values into a column; in other words, data is required in a NOT NULL column for each row of data in the table. NULL is generally the default for a column, allowing NULL values in a column.

## Using Check Constraints

Check constraints can be utilized to check the validity of data entered into particular table columns. Check constraints are used to provide back-end database edits, although edits are commonly found in the front-end application as well. General edits restrict values that can be entered into columns or objects, whether within the database itself or on a window application. The check constraint is a way of providing another protective layer for the data.

The following example illustrates the use of a check constraint:

```
CREATE TABLE EMPLOYEE_TBL
(EMP_ID          CHAR(9)          NOT NULL,
 EMP_NAME        VARCHAR2(40)     NOT NULL,
 EMP_ST_ADDR     VARCHAR2(20)     NOT NULL,
 EMP_CITY        VARCHAR2(15)     NOT NULL,
 EMP_ST          CHAR(2)          NOT NULL,
 EMP_ZIP         NUMBER(5)        NOT NULL,
 EMP_PHONE       NUMBER(10)       NULL,
 EMP_PAGER       NUMBER(10)       NULL),
 PRIMARY KEY (EMP_ID),
 CONSTRAINT CHK_EMP_ZIP CHECK ( EMP_ZIP = '46234');
```

The check constraint in this table has been placed on the EMP_ZIP column, ensuring that all employees entered into this table have a zip code of '46234'. Perhaps that is a little restricting. Nevertheless, you can see how it works.

If you wanted to use a check constraint to verify that the zip code is within a list of values, your constraint definition could look like this:

```
CONSTRAINT CHK_EMP_ZIP CHECK ( EMP_ZIP in ('46234','46227','46745') );
```

If there is a minimum pay rate that can be designated for an employee, you could have a constraint that looks like this:

```
CREATE TABLE EMPLOYEE_PAY_TBL
(EMP_ID            CHAR(9)        NOT NULL,
POSITION          VARCHAR2(15)   NOT NULL,
DATE_HIRE         DATE           NULL,
PAY_RATE          NUMBER(4,2)    NOT NULL,
DATE_LAST_RAISE   DATE           NULL,
FOREIGN KEY EMP_ID_FK (EMP_ID) REFERENCES EMPLOYEE_TBL (EMP_ID),
CONSTRAINT CHK_PAY CHECK ( PAY_RATE > 12.50 ) );
```

In this example, any employee entered in this table must be paid more than $12.50 an hour. You can use just about any condition in a check constraint, as you can with an SQL query. You learn more about these conditions in later hours.

# Summary

You have learned a little about database objects in general, but have specifically learned about the table. The table is the simplest form of data storage in a relational database. Tables contain groups of logical information, such as employee, customer, or product information. A table is composed of various columns, with each column having attributes; those attributes mainly consist of datatypes and constraints such as NOT NULL values, primary keys, foreign keys, and unique values. You learned the CREATE TABLE command and options, such as storage parameters, that may be available with this command. You have also learned how to modify the structure of existing tables using the ALTER TABLE command. Although the process of managing database tables may not be the most basic process in SQL, it is our philosophy that if you first learn the structure and nature of tables, then you more easily grasp the concept of accessing the tables, whether through data manipulation operations or database queries. In later hours you learn about the management of other objects in SQL, such as indexes on tables and views.

## Q&A

**Q When I name a table that I am creating, is it necessary to use a suffix such as _tbl?**

**A** Absolutely not. You do not have to use anything. For example, a table to hold employee information could be named similar to the following, or anything else that would refer to what type of data is to be stored in that particular table:

```
employee
```

```
emp_tbl
```

```
employee_tbl

employee_table

worker
```

**Q Why is it so important to use the schema name when dropping a table?**

**A** Here's a true story about a new DBA that dropped a table: A programmer had created a table under his schema with the same name as a production table. That particular programmer left the company. The programmer's database account was being deleted from the database, but the DROP USER statement returned an error due to the fact that outstanding objects were owned by the programmer. After some investigation it was determined that the programmer's table was not needed, so a DROP TABLE statement was issued.

It worked like a charm—but the problem was that the DBA was logged in as the production schema when the DROP TABLE statement was issued. The DBA should have specified a schema name, or owner, for the table to be dropped. Yes, the wrong table in the wrong schema was dropped. It took approximately eight hours to restore the production database.

# Workshop

The following workshop is composed of a series of quiz questions and practical exercises. The quiz questions are designed to test your overall understanding of the current material. The practical exercises are intended to afford you the opportunity to apply the concepts discussed during the current hour, as well as build upon the knowledge acquired in previous hours of study. Please take time to complete the quiz questions and exercises before continuing. You may refer to the answers in Appendix C.

## Quiz

1. Will the following CREATE TABLE statement work? If not, what needs to be done to correct the problem(s)?

   Create table employee_table as:
   ```
   ( ssn              number(9)        not null,
     last_name        varchar2(20)     not null,
     first_name       varchar2(20)     not null,
     middle_name      varchar2(20)     not null,
     st address       varchar2(30)     not null,
     city             char(20)         not null,
     state            char2)           not null,
     zip              number(4)        not null,
     date hired       date)
     storage
         (initial        3k,
          next          1k);
   ```

2. Can you drop a column from a table?

3. What happens if you do not include the storage clause in the create table statement?

## Exercises

1. Go to Appendix D to get the DDL for the tables used in this book and create the tables.

# Hour 4

# The Normalization Process

In this hour you learn the process of taking a raw database and breaking it into logical units called *tables*. This process is referred to as *normalization*.

The advantages and disadvantages of both normalization and denormalization of a database are discussed, as well as data integrity versus performance issues that pertain to normalization.

The highlights of this hour include

- ☐ What is normalization?
- ☐ Benefits of normalization
- ☐ Advantages of denormalization
- ☐ Normalization techniques
- ☐ Guidelines of normalization
- ☐ The three normal forms
- ☐ Database design

# Normalizing a Database

*Normalization* is a process of reducing redundancies of data in a database. In addition to data, names, object names, and forms are also normalized in a database.

 **NEW TERM** *Normalization* is the process of reducing the redundancy of data in a relational database.

## The Raw Database

A database that is not normalized may include data that is contained in one or more different tables for no apparent reason. This could be bad for security reasons, disk space usage, speed of queries, efficiency of database updates, and maybe most importantly, data integrity. A database before normalization is one that has not been broken down logically into smaller, more manageable tables. Figure 4.1 illustrates the database used for this book before it was normalized.

**Figure 4.1.**

*The raw database.*

COMPANY_DATABASE

| | |
|---|---|
| emp_id | cust_id |
| last_name | cust_name |
| first_name | cust_address |
| middle_name | cust_city |
| address | cust_state |
| city | cust_zip |
| state | cust_phone |
| zip | cust_fax |
| phone | ord_num |
| pager | qty |
| position | ord_date |
| date_hire | prod_id |
| pay_rate | prod_desc |
| date_last_raise | cost |

## Logical Database Design

Any database should be designed with the end user in mind. Logical database design, also referred to as the *logical model*, is the process of arranging data into logical, organized groups of objects that can easily be maintained. The logical design of a database should reduce data repetition or go so far as to completely eliminate it. After all, why store the same data twice? Naming conventions used in a database should also be standard and logical.

### What Are the End User's Needs?

The needs of the end user should be one of the top considerations when designing a database. Remember that the end user is the person who ultimately uses the database. There should be ease of use through the user's *front-end tool* (a program that allows a user access to a database), but this, along with optimal performance, cannot be achieved if the user's needs are not taken into consideration.

Some user-related design considerations include

☐ What data should be stored in the database?

☐ How will the user access the database?

☐ What privileges does the user require?

☐ How should the data be grouped in the database?

☐ What data is the most commonly accessed?

☐ How is all data related in the database?

☐ What measures should be taken to ensure accurate data?

## Data Redundancy

Data should not be redundant, which means that the duplication of data should be kept to a minimum for several reasons. For example, it is unnecessary to store an employee's home address in more than one table. With duplicate data, unnecessary space is used. Confusion is always a threat when, for instance, an address for an employee in one table does not match the address of the same employee in another table. Which table is correct? Do you have documentation to verify the employee's current address? As if data management is not difficult enough, redundancy of data could prove to be a disaster.

# The Normal Forms

The next sections discuss the normal forms, an integral concept involved in the process of database normalization.

**NEW TERM** *Normal form* is a way of measuring the levels, or depth, to which a database has been normalized. A database's level of normalization is determined by the normal form.

The three most common normal forms in the normalization process are

☐ The first normal form

☐ The second normal form

☐ The third normal form

Of the three normal forms, each subsequent normal form depends upon normalization steps taken in the previous normal form. For instance, in order to normalize a database using the second normal form, the database must first be in the first normal form.

## The First Normal Form

The objective of the first normal form is to divide the base data into logical units called *tables*. When each table has been designed, a primary key is assigned to most or all tables. Examine Figure 4.2, which illustrates how the raw database, shown in the previous figure, has been redeveloped using the first normal form.

**Figure 4.2.**

*The first normal form.*

You can see that in order to achieve the first normal form, data had to be broken into logical units, each having a primary key and ensuring that there are no repeated groups in any of the tables. Instead of one large table, there are now smaller, more manageable tables: EMPLOYEE_TBL, CUSTOMER_TBL, and PRODUCTS_TBL. The primary keys are normally the first columns listed in a table, in this case, EMP_ID, CUST_ID, and PROD_ID.

## The Second Normal Form

The objective of the second normal form is to take data that is only partly dependent on the primary key and entering that data into another table. Figure 4.3 illustrates the second normal form.

According to the figure, the second normal form is derived from the first normal form by further breaking two tables down into more specific units.

EMPLOYEE_TBL split into two tables called EMPLOYEE_TBL and EMPLOYEE_PAY_TBL. Personal employee information is dependent upon the primary key, or EMP_ID, so that information remained in the EMPLOYEE_TBL (EMP_ID, LAST_NAME, FIRST_NAME, MIDDLE_NAME, ADDRESS, CITY, STATE, ZIP, PHONE, and PAGER). On the other hand, the information that is only partly dependent on the EMP_ID (each individual employee) is used to populate EMPLOYEE_PAY_TBL (EMP_ID, POSITION, POSITION_DESC, DATE_HIRE, PAY_RATE, DATE_LAST_RAISE). Notice that both tables contain the column CUST_ID. This is the primary key of each table and is used to match corresponding data between the two tables.

CUSTOMER_TBL split into two tables called CUSTOMER_TBL and ORDERS_TBL. What took place is similar to what occurred in the EMPLOYEE_TBL. Columns that were partly dependent upon the primary key were directed to another table. The order information for a customer is dependent upon each CUST_ID, but does not directly depend upon the general customer information in the original table.

**4**

**Figure 4.3.**

*The second normal form.*

FIRST NORMAL FORM        SECOND NORMAL FORM

## The Third Normal Form

The third normal form's objective is to remove data in a table that is not dependent on the primary key. Figure 4.4 illustrates the third normal form.

**Figure 4.4.**

*The third normal form.*

Another table was created to display the use of the third normal form. `EMPLOYEE_PAY_TBL` is split it into two tables, one table containing the actual employee pay information and the other containing the position descriptions, which really do not need to reside in `EMPLOYEE_PAY_TBL`. The `POSITION_DESC` column is totally independent of the primary key, `EMP_ID`.

## Naming Conventions

Naming conventions are one of the foremost considerations when you're normalizing a database. You want to give your tables names that are descriptive of the type of information they contain. A company-wide naming convention should be set, providing guidance in the naming of not only tables within the database, but users, filenames, and other related objects. Designing and enforcing naming conventions is one of a company's first steps toward a successful database implementation.

## Benefits of Normalization

Normalization provides numerous benefits to a database. Some of the major benefits include

- [ ] Greater overall database organization
- [ ] The reduction of redundant data
- [ ] Data consistency within the database
- [ ] A much more flexible database design
- [ ] A better handle on database security

Organization is brought about by the normalization process, making everyone's job easier, from the user who accesses tables to the database administrator (DBA) who is responsible for the overall management of every object in the database. Data redundancy is reduced, which simplifies data structures and conserves disk space. Because duplicate data is minimized, the possibility of inconsistent data is greatly reduced. For example, in one table an individual's name could read STEVE SMITH, where the name of the same individual reads STEPHEN R. SMITH in another table. Because the database has been normalized and broken into smaller tables, you are provided with more flexibility as far as modifying existing structures. It is much easier to modify a small table with little data than modifying one big table that holds all the vital data in the database. Lastly, security is also provided in the sense that the DBA can grant access to limited tables to certain users. Security is easier to control when normalization has occurred.

**NEW TERM**   *Data integrity* is the assurance of consistent and accurate data within a database.

### Referential Integrity

*Referential integrity* simply means that the values of one column in a table depend upon the values of a column in another table. For instance, in order for a customer to have a record in the ORDERS_TBL table, there must first be a record for that customer in the CUSTOMER_TBL table. Integrity constraints can also control the values by restricting a range of values for a column. The integrity constraint should be created upon the table creation. Referential integrity is typically controlled through the use of primary and foreign keys.

**NEW TERM**  In a table, a *foreign key*, normally a single field, directly references a field in another table to enforce referential integrity. In the preceding paragraph, the CUST_ID in ORDERS_TBL is a foreign key that references CUST_ID in CUSTOMER_TBL.

## Drawbacks of Normalization

Although most successful databases are normalized to some degree, there is one substantial drawback of a normalized database: reduced database performance. The acceptance of reduced performance requires the knowledge that when a query or transaction request is sent to the database, there are factors involved such as CPU usage, memory usage, and input/output (I/O). To make a long story short, a normalized database requires much more CPU, memory, and I/O to process transactions and database queries than does a denormalized database. A normalized database must locate the requested tables and then join the data from the tables to either get the requested information or to process the desired data. A more in-depth discussion concerning database performance occurs in Hour 18, "Managing Database Users."

## Denormalizing a Database

Denormalizing a database: Why would you ever want to do that? Attempting to improve performance is the only reason to ever denormalize a database. A denormalized database is not the same as a database that has not been normalized. *Denormalizing* a database is the process of taking the level of normalization within the database down a notch or two. Remember, normalization may actually slow performance with its frequently occurring table join operations. (Table joins are discussed during Hour 13, "Joining Tables in Queries.") Denormalization may involve recombining separate tables, or creating duplicate data within tables to reduce the number of tables that need to be joined in order to retrieve the requested data, which results in less I/O and CPU time.

**NEW TERM**  *Denormalization* is the process of taking a normalized database and modifying table structures to allow controlled redundancy for increased database performance.

There are costs to denormalization, however. Data redundancy is increased in a denormalized database, which may improve performance but requires more extraneous efforts in order to keep track of related data. Application coding renders more complications, because the data has been spread across various tables and may be more difficult to locate. In addition, referential integrity is more of a chore; related data has been divided amongst a number of tables. There is a happy medium in both normalization and denormalization, but both require a thorough knowledge of the actual data and the specific business requirements of the pertinent company.

# Summary

A difficult decision has to be made concerning database design—to normalize or not to normalize, that is the question. You will always want to normalize a database to some degree. How much do you normalize a database without destroying performance? The real decision relies on the application itself. How large is the database? What is its purpose? What types of users are going to access the data? This hour covered the three most common normal forms, the concepts behind the normalization process, and the integrity of data. The normalization process involves many steps, most of which are optional but vital to the functionality and performance of your database. Regardless of how deep you decide to normalize, there will most always be a trade-off, either between simple maintenance and questionable performance or complicated maintenance and better performance. In the end, the individual (or team of individuals) designing the database must decide, and that person or team is responsible.

## Q&A

**Q  Why should I be so concerned with the end user's needs when designing the database?**

**A**  The end users are the real data experts who use the database, and in that respect they should be the focus of any database design effort. The database designer only helps organize the data.

**Q  It seems to me that normalization is more advantageous than denormalization. Do you agree?**

**A**  It can be more advantageous. However, denormalization, to a point, could be more advantageous. Remember, there are many factors that help determine which way to go. You will probably normalize your database to reduce repetition in the database, but may turn around and denormalize to a certain extent to improve performance.

# Workshop

The following workshop is composed of a series of quiz questions and practical exercises. The quiz questions are designed to test your overall understanding of the current material. The practical exercises are intended to afford you the opportunity to apply the concepts discussed during the current hour, as well as build upon the knowledge acquired in previous hours of study. Please take time to complete the quiz questions and exercises before continuing. You may refer to the answers in Appendix C.

## Quiz

1.  True or false: Normalization is the process of grouping data into logical related groups.

2. True or false: Having no duplicate or redundant data in a database, and having everything in the database normalized, is always the best way to go.

3. True or false: If data is in the third normal form, it is automatically in the first and second normal forms.

4. What is a major advantage of a denormalized database versus a normalized database?

5. What are some major disadvantages of denormalization?

## Exercises

1. You are developing a new database for a small company. Take the following data and normalize it. Keep in mind that there would be many more items for a small company than what you are given here.

Employees:

Angela Smith, secretary, 317-545-6789, RR 1 Box 73, Greensburg, Indiana, 47890, $9.50 hour, date started January 22, 1996, SSN is 323149669.

Jack Lee Nelson, salesman, 3334 N Main St, Brownsburg, IN, 45687, 317-852-9901, salary of $35,000.00 year, SSN is 312567342, date started 10/28/95.

Customers:

Robert's Games and Things, 5612 Lafayette Rd, Indianapolis, IN, 46224, 317-291-7888, customer ID is 432A.

Reed's Dairy Bar, 4556 W 10th St, Indianapolis, IN, 46245, 317-271-9823, customer ID is 117A.

Customer Orders:

Customer ID is 117A, date of last order is February 20, 1997, product ordered was napkins and the product ID is 661.

# Hour 5

# Manipulating Data

In this hour you learn the part of SQL known as Data Manipulation Language—DML. DML is the part of SQL that is used to make changes to data and tables in a relational database.

This hour's highlights include:

- [ ] An overview of data manipulation language
- [ ] Instruction on how to manipulate data in tables
- [ ] Concepts behind table population of data
- [ ] How to delete data from tables
- [ ] How to change or modify data in tables

## Overview of Data Manipulation

Data Manipulation Language (DML) is the part of SQL that allows a database user to actually propagate changes among data in a relational database. With DML, the user can populate tables with new data, update existing data in tables, and delete data from tables. Simple database queries can also be performed within a DML command.

There are three basic DML commands in SQL:

    INSERT

    UPDATE

    DELETE

The select command, which can be used with DML commands, is discussed in more detail in Hour 7, "Introduction to the Database Query."

# Populating Tables with New Data

*Populating* a table with data is simply the process of entering new data into a table, whether through a manual process using individual commands, or through batch processes using programs or other related software.

 **NEW TERM**   *Populating* a table is the process of loading new data.

Many factors may affect what data and how much data can be put into a table when populating tables with data. Some major factors include existing table constraints, the physical table size, column datatypes, the length of columns, and other integrity constraints, such as primary and foreign keys. The following sections help you learn the basics of inserting new data into a table, in addition to offering some dos and don'ts.

**NOTE**    Do not forget that SQL statements can be in upper- or lowercase.  The data, depending upon how stored in the database is case sensitive. These examples use both lower- and uppercases just to show that it does not make any difference on the outcome.

## Inserting Data into a Table

Use the INSERT statement to insert new data into a table. There are a few options with the INSERT statement; look at the following basic syntax to begin:

```
insert into schema.table_name
VALUES ('value1', 'value2', [ NULL ] );
```

Using this INSERT statement syntax, you must include every column in the specified table in the VALUES list. Notice that each value in this list is separated by a comma. The values inserted into the table must be enclosed by quotation marks for character and date datatypes. Quotation marks are not required for numeric datatypes or NULL values using the NULL keyword. A value should be present for each column in the table.

In the following example, you insert a new record into the PRODUCTS_TBL table.

Table structure:

```
products_tbl

COLUMN Name                          Null?     DATA Type
---------------------------------- --------- ------------
PROD_ID                              NOT NULL VARCHAR2(10)
PROD_DESC                            NOT NULL VARCHAR2(25)
COST                                 NOT NULL NUMBER(6,2)
```

Sample INSERT statement:

```
insert into products_tbl
values ('7725','LEATHER GLOVES',24.99);
```

```
1 row created.
```

In this example you insert three values into a table with three columns. The inserted values are in the same order as the columns listed in the table. The first two values are inserted using quotation marks, because the datatypes of the corresponding columns are of character type. The third value's associated column, COST, is a numeric datatype and does not require quotation marks, although they are optional.

**NOTE**

The schema name, or table owner, has not been specified as part of the table name, as it was shown in the syntax. The schema name is not required if you are connected to the database as the user who owns the table.

## Inserting Data into Limited Columns of a Table

**SYNTAX**

There is a way you can insert data into a table's limited columns. For instance, suppose you only want to insert all values for an employee except a pager number. You must, in this case, specify a column list as well as a VALUES list in your INSERT statement. The syntax for inserting values into a limited number of columns in a table is as follows:

```
insert into schema.table_name ('column1', 'column2')
values ('value1', 'value2');
```

You use ORDERS_TBL, and insert values into only specified columns in the following example.

Table structure:

```
ORDERS_TBL

COLUMN NAME                        Null?     DATA TYPE
-------------------------------    -------   -----------
ORD_NUM                            NOT NULL  VARCHAR2(10)
CUST_ID                            NOT NULL  VARCHAR2(10)
PROD_ID                            NOT NULL  VARCHAR2(10)
QTY                                NOT NULL  NUMBER(4)
ORD_DATE                                     DATE
```

Sample INSERT statement:

```
insert into orders_tbl (ord_num,cust_id,prod_id,qty)
values ('23A16','109','7725',2);
```

```
1 row created.
```

You have specified a column list enclosed by parentheses after the table name in the INSERT statement. You have listed all columns in which you want to insert data. ORD_DATE is the only excluded column. You can see, if you look at the table definition, that ORD_DATE does not require data for every record in the table. You know that ORD_DATE does not require data, because NOT NULL is not specified in the table definition. NOT NULL tells us that NULL values are not allowed in the column. Furthermore, the list of values must appear in the order in which you want to insert them according to the column list.

> **NOTE**
>
> The column list in the INSERT statement does not have to reflect the same order of columns as in the definition of the associated table, but the list of values must be in the order of the associated columns in the column list.

## Inserting Data from Another Table

You may insert data into a table based on the results of a query from another table, using a combination of the insert statement and the select statement. Briefly, a *query* is an inquiry to the database that expects data to be returned. See Hour 7, "Introduction to the Database Query," for more information on queries. A query is a question that the user asks the database, and the data returned is the answer. In the case of combining the INSERT statement with the SELECT statement, you are able to insert the data retrieved from a query into a table.

The syntax for inserting data from another table is:

```
insert into schema.table_name [('column1', 'column2')]
select [*¦('column1', 'column2')]
from table_name
[where condition(s)];
```

You see three new keywords in this syntax, which are covered here briefly. These keywords are SELECT, FROM, and WHERE. SELECT is the main command used to initiate a query in SQL.

5

FROM is a clause in the query that specifies the names of tables in which the target data should be found. The WHERE clause, also part of the query, is used to place conditions on the query itself. An example condition may state: WHERE NAME = 'SMITH'. These three keywords are covered extensively during Hours 7 and 8.

**NEW TERM** A *condition* is a way of placing criteria on data affected by a SQL statement.

The following example uses a simple query to view all data in the PRODUCTS_TBL table. SELECT * tells the database server that you want information on all columns of the table. Because there is no WHERE clause, you want to see all records in the table as well.

**TYPE**
```
select * from products_tbl;
```

**OUTPUT**
```
PROD_ID     PROD_DESC                   COST
---------   ------------------------    --------
11235       WITCHES COSTUME             29.99
222         PLASTIC PUMPKIN 18 INCH      7.75
13          FALSE PARAFFIN TEETH         1.1
90          LIGHTED LANTERNS            14.5
15          ASSORTED COSTUMES           10
9           CANDY CORN                   1.35
6           PUMPKIN CANDY                1.45
87          PLASTIC SPIDERS              1.05
119         ASSORTED MASKS               4.95
1234        KEY CHAIN                    5.95
2345        OAK BOOKSHELF               59.99

11 rows selected.
```

Now insert values into the PRODUCTS_TMP table based on the preceding query. You can see that 11 rows are created in the temporary table.

**TYPE**
```
insert into products_tmp
select * from products_tbl;
```

**OUTPUT**
```
11 rows created.
```

The following query shows all data in the PRODUCTS_TMP table, which you just inserted:

**TYPE**
```
select * from products_tmp;
```

**OUTPUT**
```
PROD_ID     PROD_DESC                   COST
---------   ------------------------    --------
11235       WITCHES COSTUME             29.99
222         PLASTIC PUMPKIN 18 INCH      7.75
13          FALSE PARAFFIN TEETH         1.1
90          LIGHTED LANTERNS            14.5
15          ASSORTED COSTUMES           10
9           CANDY CORN                   1.35
6           PUMPKIN CANDY                1.45
87          PLASTIC SPIDERS              1.05
119         ASSORTED MASKS               4.95
1234        KEY CHAIN                    5.95
2345        OAK BOOKSHELF               59.99

11 rows selected.
```

5

## Inserting NULL **Values**

Inserting a NULL value into a column of a table is a simple matter. You might want to insert a NULL value into a column if the value of the column in question is unknown. For instance, not every person carries a pager, so it would be inaccurate to enter an erroneous pager number—not to mention, you would not be budgeting space. A NULL value can be inserted into a column of a table using the keyword NULL.

The syntax for inserting a NULL value follows:

```
insert into schema.table_name values
('column1', NULL, 'column3');
```

The NULL keyword should be used in the associated column exists in the table. That column will not have data in it for that row if you enter NULL. In the syntax, a NULL value is being entered in the place of COLUMN2.

Study the two following examples:

**TYPE**
```
insert into orders_tbl (ord_num,cust_id,prod_id,qty,ORD_DATE)
values ('23A16','109','7725',2,NULL);
```

**OUTPUT**  1 row created.

In the first example, all columns in which to insert values are listed, which also happens to be every column in the ORDERS_TBL table. You insert a NULL value for the column ORD_DATE, meaning that you either do not know the order date, or there is no order date at this time.

**TYPE**
```
insert into orders_tbl
values ('23A16','109','7725',2, '');
```

**OUTPUT**  1 row created.

There are two differences from the first statement in the second example, but the results are the same. Firstly, there is not a column list. Remember that a column list is not required if you are inserting data into all columns of a table. Secondly, instead of inserting the value NULL into the ORD_DATE column, you insert '' (two single quotation marks together), which also symbolizes a NULL value (because there is nothing between them).

# Updating Existing Data

Preexisting data in a table can be modified using the UPDATE command. The UPDATE command does not add new records to a table, nor does it remove records—it simply updates existing data. The update is generally used to update one table at a time in a database, but can be used to update multiple columns of a table at the same time. An individual row of data in a table can be updated, or numerous rows of data can be updated in a single statement, depending upon needs.

5

# Updating the Value of a Single Column

The most simple form of the UPDATE statement is its use to update a single column in a table. Either a single row of data or numerous records may be updated when updating a single column in a table.

**SYNTAX**

The syntax for updating a single column follows:

```
update table_name
set column_name = 'value'
[where condition];
```

The following example updates the QTY column in the ORDERS table to the new value 1 for the ORD_NUM 23A16, which you have specified using the WHERE clause.

**TYPE**
```
update orders_tbl
set qty = 1
where ord_num = '23A16';
```

**OUTPUT**   1 row updated.

The following example is identical to the previous example, except for the absence of the WHERE clause:

**TYPE**
```
update orders_tbl
set qty = 1;
```

**OUTPUT**   11 rows updated.

Notice that in this example, 11 rows of data were updated. You set the QTY to 1, which updated the quantity column in the ORDERS_TBL table for all rows of data. Is this really what you wanted to do? Perhaps in some cases, but rarely will you issue an UPDATE statement without a WHERE clause.

5

**WARNING**

> Extreme caution must be used when using the update statement without a WHERE clause. The target column is updated for all rows of data in the table if conditions are not designated using the WHERE clause.

# Updating Multiple Columns in One or More Records

Here you see how to update multiple columns with a single UPDATE statement. Study the following syntax:

**SYNTAX**

```
update table_name
set column1 = 'value',
   [column2 = 'value',]
   [column3 = 'value']
[where condition];
```

Notice the use of the SET in this syntax—there is only one SET, but multiple columns. Each column is separated by a comma. You should start to see a trend in SQL. The comma is usually used to separate different types of arguments in SQL statements.

```
update orders_tbl
set qty = 1,
    cust_id = '221'
where ord_num = '23A16';
```

**OUTPUT**  1 row updated.

A comma is used to separate the two columns being updated. Again, the WHERE clause is optional, but usually necessary.

**NOTE**

> The SET keyword is only used once for each UPDATE statement. If more than one column is to be updated, a comma is used to separate the columns to be updated.

# Deleting Data from Tables

The DELETE command is used to remove entire rows of data from a table. The DELETE command is not used to remove values from specific columns; a full record, including all columns, is removed. The DELETE statement must be used with caution—it works all too well. The next two sections discuss methods for deleting data from tables.

**SYNTAX**

To delete a single record or selected records from a table, the DELETE statement must be used with the following syntax:

```
delete from schema.table_name
[where condition];
```

**TYPE**
```
delete from orders_tbl
where ord_num = '23A16';
```

**OUTPUT**  1 row deleted.

Notice the use of the WHERE clause. The WHERE clause is an essential part of the DELETE statement if you are attempting to remove selected rows of data from a table. You rarely issue a DELETE statement without the use of the WHERE clause. If you do, your results are similar to the following example:

```
delete from orders_tbl;
```

```
11 rows deleted.
```

**5**

**WARNING**

If the where clause is omitted from the DELETE statement, then all rows of data are deleted from the table! As a general rule, always use a WHERE clause with the DELETE statement.

**NOTE**

The temporary table that was populated from the original table earlier in the hour can be very useful for testing the DELETE and UPDATE commands before issuing them against the original table.

# Summary

You have learned the three basic commands in Data Manipulation Language (DML): the INSERT, UPDATE, and DELETE statements. As you have seen, data manipulation is a very powerful part of SQL, allowing the database user to populate tables with new data, update existing data, and delete data from tables. A very important lesson when updating or deleting data from tables in a database is sometimes learned when neglecting the use of the WHERE clause. Remember that the WHERE clause places conditions on an SQL statement—particularly in the case of UDPATE and DELETE operations, when specifying specific rows of data that will be affected during a transaction. All target table data rows are affected if the WHERE clause is not used, which could be disastrous to the database. Protect your data and be cautious during data manipulation operations.

## Q&A

**Q** **With all the warnings about the DELETE and UPDATE, I'm a little afraid to use them. If I accidentally update all the records in a table because the WHERE clause was not used, can the changes be reversed?**

**A** There is no reason to be afraid, because there is not much you can do to the database that cannot be corrected, although considerable time and work may be involved. The next hour discusses the concepts of transactional control, which allows data manipulation operations to either be finalized or undone.

# Workshop

The following workshop is composed of a series of quiz questions and practical exercises. The quiz questions are designed to test your overall understanding of the current material. The practical exercises are intended to afford you the opportunity to apply the concepts discussed during the current hour, as well as build upon the knowledge acquired in previous hours of study. Please take time to complete the quiz questions and exercises before continuing. You may refer to the answers in Appendix C.

## Quiz

1. Use the `employee_tbl` with the following structure:

| COLUMN | DATATYPE | (NOT)NULL |
|---|---|---|
| LAST_NAME | VARCHAR2(20) | NOT NULL |
| FIRST_NAME | VARCHAR2(20) | NOT NULL |
| SSN | CHAR(9) | NOT NULL |
| PHONE | NUMBER(10) | NULL |

| LAST_NAME | FIRST_NAME | SSN | PHONE |
|---|---|---|---|
| SMITH | JOHN | 312456788 | 3174549923 |
| ROBERTS | LISA | 232118857 | 3175452321 |
| SMITH | SUE | 443221989 | 3178398712 |
| PIERCE | BILLY | 310239856 | 3176763990 |

What would happen if the following statements were run:

a. `insert into employee_tbl`
`('JACKSON', 'STEVE', '313546078', '3178523443');`

b. `insert into employee_tbl values`
`('JACKSON', 'STEVE', '313546078', '3178523443');`

c. `insert into employee_tbl values`
`('MILLER', 'DANIEL', '230980012', NULL);`

d. `insert into employee_tbl values`
`('TAYLOR', NULL, '445761212', '3179221331');`

e. `delete from employee_tbl;`

f. `delete from employee_tbl`
`where last_name = 'SMITH';`

g. `delete from employee_tbl`
`where last_name = 'SMITH'`
`and first_name = 'JOHN';`

h. `update employee_tbl`
`set last_name = 'CONRAD';`

i. `update employee_tbl`
`set last_name = 'CONRAD'`
`where last_name = 'SMITH';`

5

```
j. update employee_tbl
set last_name = 'CONRAD',
first_name = 'LARRY';

k. update employee_tbl
set last_name = 'CONRAD'
first_name = 'LARRY'
where ssn = '313546078';
```

# Exercises

1. Go to Appendix E of this book. Run the INSERT statements in order to populate the tables that you created in Exercise 1 of Hour 3. When this has been accomplished, you should be able to better follow the examples and exercise questions in this book.

2. Using the employee_tbl with the structure:

| COLUMN | DATATYPE | (NOT)NULL |
| --- | --- | --- |
| LAST_NAME | VARCHAR2(20) | NOT NULL |
| FIRST_NAME | VARCHAR2(20) | NOT NULL |
| SSN | CHAR(9) | NOT NULL |
| PHONE | NUMBER(10) | NULL |

| LAST_NAME | FIRST_NAME | SSN | PHONE |
| --- | --- | --- | --- |
| SMITH | JOHN | 312456788 | 3174549923 |
| ROBERTS | LISA | 232118857 | 3175452321 |
| SMITH | SUE | 443221989 | 3178398712 |
| PIERCE | BILLY | 310239856 | 3176763990 |

Write DML to do accomplish the following:

a. Correct Billy Pierce's ssn to read 310239857.

b. Add Ben Moore, phone number is 317-5649880, ssn is 313456789.

c. John Smith quit; remove his record.

5

# Hour **6**

# Managing Database Transactions

In this hour you learn the concepts behind the management of database transactions.

The highlights of this hour include

- ☐ The definition of a transaction
- ☐ The commands used to control transactions
- ☐ The syntax and examples of transaction commands
- ☐ When to use transactional commands
- ☐ The consequences of poor transactional control

## What Is a Transaction?

*Transactions* are units or sequences of work accomplished in a logical order, whether in a manual fashion by a user or automatically by some sort of a database program. In a relational database using SQL, transactions are accomplished using the DML commands that were discussed during Hour 5, "Manipulating Data" (INSERT, UPDATE, and DELETE). A transaction is the propagation of one or more changes to the database. For instance, you are performing a transaction if you performed an UPDATE statement on a table to change an individual's name.

 A *transaction* is a unit of work that is performed against a database.

A transaction can either be one DML statement or a group of statements. When managing groups of transactions, each designated group of transactions must be successful as one entity or none of them will be successful.

The following list describes the nature of transactions:

☐ All transactions have a beginning and an end.

☐ A transaction can be saved or undone.

☐ If a transaction fails in the middle, no part of the transaction can be saved to the database.

**NOTE**
> To start or execute transactions is implementation-specific. You must check your particular implementation for how to begin transactions. There is no explicit start or begin transaction in the ANSI standard.

# What Is Transactional Control?

*Transactional control* is the ability to manage various transactions that may occur within a relational database management system. When you speak of transactions, you are referring to the INSERT, UPDATE, and DELETE commands, which were covered during the last hour.

When a transaction is executed and completes successfully, the target table is not immediately changed, although it may appear so according to the output. When a transaction successfully completes, there are transactional control commands that are used to finalize the transaction, either saving the changes made by the transaction to the database or reversing the changes made by the transaction.

There are three commands used to control transactions:

☐ COMMIT

☐ ROLLBACK

☐ SAVEPOINT

Each of these is discussed in detail in the following sections.

**NOTE**

Transactional control commands are only used with DML commands (INSERT, UPDATE, DELETE). For example, you do not issue a COMMIT statement after creating a table. When the table is created, it is automatically committed to the database. Likewise, you cannot issue a ROLLBACK to replenish a table that was just dropped.

When a transaction has completed, the transactional information is stored either in an allocated area or in a temporary rollback area in the database. All changes are held in this temporary rollback area until a transactional control command is issued. When a transactional control command is issued, changes are either made to the database or discarded; then the temporary rollback area is emptied. Figure 6.1 illustrates how changes are applied to a relational database.

**Figure 6.1.**

*Rollback area.*

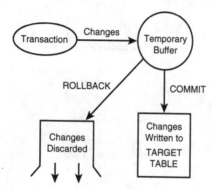

## The COMMIT Command

The COMMIT command is the transactional command used to save changes invoked by a transaction to the database. The COMMIT command saves all transactions to the database since the last COMMIT or ROLLBACK command.

**SYNTAX**

The syntax for this command is

```
commit [ work ];
```

The keyword COMMIT is the only mandatory part of the syntax, along with the character or command used to terminate a statement according to each implementation. WORK is a keyword that is completely optional; its only purpose is to make the command more user-friendly.

In the following example, you begin by selecting all data from the PRODUCT_TMP table:

```
select * from products_tmp;
```

```
PROD_ID    PROD_DESC                    COST
---------  -----------------------    ---------
11235      WITCHES COSTUME              29.99
222        PLASTIC PUMPKIN 18 INCH       7.75
13         FALSE PARAFFIN TEETH          1.1
90         LIGHTED LANTERNS             14.5
15         ASSORTED COSTUMES            10
9          CANDY CORN                    1.35
6          PUMPKIN CANDY                 1.45
87         PLASTIC SPIDERS               1.05
119        ASSORTED MASKS                4.95
1234       KEY CHAIN                     5.95
2345       OAK BOOKSHELF                59.99

11 rows selected.
```

Next, you delete all records from the table where the product cost is less than $14.00.

```
delete from products_tmp
where cost < 14;

8 rows deleted.
```

A COMMIT statement is issued to save the changes to the database, completing the transaction.

```
commit;

Commit complete.
```

**NOTE**

In some implementations, transactions are committed without issuing the commit command—instead, merely signing out of the database causes a commit to occur.

## The ROLLBACK Command

The rollback command is the transactional control command used to undo transactions that have not already been saved to the database. The rollback command can only be used to undo transactions since the last COMMIT or ROLLBACK command was issued.

The syntax for the rollback command is as follows:

```
rollback [ work ];
```

Once again, as in the COMMIT statement, the WORK keyword is an optional part of the ROLLBACK syntax.

In the following example, you begin by selecting all records from the PRODUCTS_TMP table since the previous deletion of 14 records:

**TYPE**
```
select * from products_tmp;

PROD_ID     PROD_DESC                       COST
----------  ------------------------------  ----------
11235       WITCHES COSTUME                 29.99
90          LIGHTED LANTERNS                14.5
2345        OAK BOOKSHELF                   59.99

3 rows selected.
```

Next, you update the table, changing the product cost to $39.99 for the product identification number 11235:

**TYPE**
```
update products_tmp
set cost = 39.99
where prod_id = '11235';

1 row updated.
```

If you perform a quick query on the table, the change appears to have occurred:

**TYPE**
```
select * from products_tmp;

PROD_ID     PROD_DESC                       COST
----------  ------------------------------  ----------
11235       WITCHES COSTUME                 39.99
90          LIGHTED LANTERNS                14.5
2345        OAK BOOKSHELF                   59.99

3 rows selected.
```

Now issue the ROLLBACK statement to undo the last change:

**TYPE**
```
rollback;

Rollback complete.
```

Finally, verify that the change was not committed to the database:

**TYPE**
```
select * from products_tmp;

PROD_ID     PROD_DESC                       COST
----------  ------------------------------  ----------
11235       WITCHES COSTUME                 29.99
90          LIGHTED LANTERNS                14.5
2345        OAK BOOKSHELF                   59.99

3 rows selected.
```

6

## The SAVEPOINT **Command**

A savepoint is a point in a transaction that you can roll the transaction back to without rolling back the entire transaction.

The syntax for savepoint command is

```
savepoint savepoint_name
```

This command serves only in the creation of a SAVEPOINT among transactional statements. The ROLLBACK command is used to undo a group of transactions. The SAVEPOINT is a way of managing transactions by breaking large numbers of transactions into smaller, more manageable groups.

> **NOTE**
>
> The savepoint name must be unique to the associated group of transactions. However, the SAVEPOINT can have the same name as a table or other object. Refer to specific implementation documentation for more details on naming conventions.

Syntax for rolling back to a savepoint:

```
ROLLBACK TO SAVEPOINT_NAME;
```

In this example, you plan to delete the remaining three records from the PRODUCTS_TMP table. You want to create a SAVEPOINT before each delete, so that you can ROLLBACK to any SAVEPOINT at any time to return the appropriate data to its original state:

```
savepoint sp1;
```

```
Savepoint created.
```

```
delete from products_tmp where prod_id = '11235';
```

```
1 row deleted.
```

```
savepoint sp2;
```

```
Savepoint created.
```

```
delete from products_tmp where prod_id = '90';
```

```
1 row deleted.
```

```
savepoint sp3;
```

**6**

```
Savepoint created.
```

```
delete from products_tmp where prod_id = '2345';
```

```
1 row deleted.
```

Now that the three deletions have taken place, say you have changed your mind and decided to ROLLBACK to the SAVEPOINT that you identified as SP2. Because SP2 was created after the first deletion, the last two deletions are undone:

**TYPE** `rollback to sp2;`

**OUTPUT** `Rollback complete.`

Notice that only the first deletion took place since we rolled back to SP2:

**TYPE** `select * from products_tmp;`

**OUTPUT**
```
PROD_ID    PROD_DESC                          COST
---------- ---------------------------- ----------
90         LIGHTED LANTERNS                  14.5
2345       OAK BOOKSHELF                    59.99
```

```
2 rows selected.
```

Remember, the ROLLBACK command by itself will roll back to the last COMMIT or ROLLBACK. You have not yet issued a COMMIT, so all deletions are undone, as in the following example:

```
rollback;
```

```
Rollback complete.
```

```
select * from products_tmp;
```

```
PROD_ID    PROD_DESC                          COST
---------- ---------------------------- ----------
11235      WITCHES COSTUME                  29.99
90         LIGHTED LANTERNS                  14.5
2345       OAK BOOKSHELF                    59.99
```

```
3 rows selected.
```

6

# Transactional Control and Database Performance

Poor transactional control can hurt database performance and even bring the database to a halt. Repeatedly poor database performance may be due to a lack of transactional control during large inserts, updates, or deletes. Not only are large batch processes such as these demanding on the CPU and memory themselves, but the temporary storage for rollback information continues to grow until either a COMMIT or ROLLBACK command is issued.

When a COMMIT is issued, rollback transactional information is written to the target table and the ROLLBACK information in temporary storage is cleared. When a ROLLBACK is issued, no changes are made to the database and the ROLLBACK information in the temporary storage is cleared. If neither a COMMIT or ROLLBACK is issued, the temporary storage for ROLLBACK information continues to grow until there is no more space left, thus forcing the database to stop all processes until space is freed.

## Summary

During this hour, you learned the preliminary concepts of transactional management through the use of three transactional control commands: COMMIT, ROLLBACK, and SAVEPOINT. COMMIT is used to save a transaction to the database. ROLLBACK is used to undo a transaction that was performed. SAVEPOINT is used to break a transaction or transactions into groups, allowing you to roll back to specific logical points in transaction processing. Remember that you should frequently use the COMMIT and ROLLBACK commands when running large transactional jobs to keep space free in the database. Also keep in mind that these transactional commands are only used with the three DML commands (INSERT, UPDATE, and DELETE).

## Q&A

**Q** Is it necessary to issue a commit after every insert statement?

**A** No, not necessarily. If you were inserting a few hundred thousand rows into a table, a commit would be recommended every 5,000–10,000, depending upon the size of the temporary rollback area. Remember that the database stops when the rollback area fills up.

**Q** How does the ROLLBACK command undo a transaction?

**A** The ROLLBACK command clears all changes from the rollback area.

**Q** If I issue a transaction and 99 percent of the transaction completes but the other 1 percent errors, will I be able to redo only the error part?

**A** No, the entire transaction must succeed; otherwise data integrity is compromised.

**Q** **A transaction is permanent after I issue a commit, but can't I change data with an update?**

**A** *Permanent* used in this matter means that it is now a part of the database. The UPDATE statement can always be used to make corrections to the database.

# Workshop

The following workshop is composed of a series of quiz questions and practical exercises. The quiz questions are designed to test your overall understanding of the current material. The practical exercises are intended to afford you the opportunity to apply the concepts discussed during the current hour, as well as build upon the knowledge acquired in previous hours of study. Please take time to complete the quiz questions and exercises before continuing. You may refer to the answers in Appendix C.

## Quiz

1. True or false: If you have committed several transactions, have several more transactions that have not been committed, and issue a rollback command, all your transactions for the same session are undone.

2. True or false: A savepoint actually saves transactions after a specified amount of transactions have executed.

3. Briefly describe the purpose of each one of the following commands: COMMIT, ROLLBACK, and SAVEPOINT.

## Exercises

1. Take the following transactions and create savepoints after every three transactions. Then commit the transactions.

```
transaction1;
transaction2;
transaction3;
transaction4;
transaction5;
transaction6;
transaction7;
transaction8;
transaction9;
transaction10;
transaction11;
transaction12;
```

6

# PART

# III

## Getting Effective Results From Queries

## Hour

# Hour 7

# Introduction to the Database Query

In this seventh hour you learn about database queries, which involve the use of the SELECT statement. The SELECT statement is probably the most frequently used of all SQL commands after a database's establishment.

The highlights of this hour include:

☐ What is a database query?

☐ How to use the SELECT statement

☐ Adding conditions to queries using the WHERE clause

☐ Using column aliases

☐ Selecting data from another user's table

## What Is a Query?

A *query* is an inquiry into the database using the SELECT statement. A query is used to extract data from the database in a readable format according to the user's request. For instance, if you have an employee table, you might issue a SQL statement that returns the employee who is paid the most. This request to the database for usable employee information is a typical query that may be performed in a relational database.

# Introduction to the SELECT Statement

The SELECT statement, the command that represents Data Query Language (DQL) in SQL, is the statement used to construct database queries. The SELECT statement is not a standalone statement, meaning that clauses are required. In addition to the required clauses, there are optional clauses that increase the overall functionality of the SELECT statement. The SELECT statement is by far one of the most powerful statements in SQL. The FROM clause is the mandatory clause that must always be used in conjunction with SELECT.

There are four keywords, or *clauses*, that are valuable parts of a SELECT statement. These keywords are as follows:

- [ ] SELECT
- [ ] FROM
- [ ] WHERE
- [ ] ORDER BY

Each of these keywords is covered in detail during the following sections.

## The SELECT Statement

The SELECT statement is used in conjunction with the FROM clause to extract data from the database in an organized, readable format. The SELECT part of the query is for selecting the data you want to see according to the columns in which they are stored in a table.

The syntax for a simple SELECT statement is as follows:

```
select [ * ¦ all ¦ distinct column1, column2 ]
from table1 [ , table2 ];
```

The SELECT keyword in a query is followed by a list of columns that you want displayed as part of the query output. The FROM keyword is followed by a list of one or more tables from which you want to select data. The asterisk (*) is used to denote that all columns in a table should be displayed as part of the output. Check your particular implementation for its usage. The ALL option is used to display all values for a column, including duplicates. The distinct option is used to eliminate duplicate rows. The default between DISTINCT and ALL is ALL, which does not have to be specified. Notice that the columns following the select are separated by commas, as is the table list following the FROM.

**NOTE**    Commas are used to separate arguments in a list in SQL statements. Some common lists include lists of columns in a query, lists of tables to be selected from in a query, values to be inserted into a table, and values grouped as a condition in a query's WHERE clause.

**7**

**NEW TERM**   *Arguments* are values that are either required or optional to the syntax of a SQL statement or command.

Explore the basic capabilities of the SELECT statement by studying the following examples. First perform a simple query from the PRODUCTS_TBL table.

**TYPE**

```
SELECT * FROM PRODUCTS_TBL;
```

**OUTPUT**

```
PROD_ID    PROD_DESC                    COST
---------  ------------------------  ----------
11235      WITCHES COSTUME              29.99
222        PLASTIC PUMPKIN 18 INCH       7.75
13         FALSE PARAFFIN TEETH          1.1
90         LIGHTED LANTERNS             14.5
15         ASSORTED COSTUMES            10
9          CANDY CORN                    1.35
6          PUMPKIN CANDY                 1.45
87         PLASTIC SPIDERS               1.05
119        ASSORTED MASKS                4.95

9 rows selected.
```

The asterisk represents all columns in the table, which as you can see are displayed in the form PROD_ID, PROD_DESC, and COST. Each column in the output is displayed in the order that it appears in the table. There are 9 records in this table, identified by the feedback 9 rows selected. This feedback differs among implementations; for instance, another feedback for the same query would be 9 rows affected.

Now select data from another table, CANDY_TBL. Create this table in the image of the PRODUCTS_TBL table for the following examples. List the column name after the SELECT keyword to display only one column in the table.

**TYPE**

```
SELECT PROD_DESC FROM CANDY_TBL;
```

**OUTPUT**

```
PROD_DESC
-----------------------
CANDY CORN
CANDY CORN
HERSHEYS KISS
SMARTIES

4 rows selected.
```

Four records exist in the CANDY_TBL table. You have used the ALL option in the next statement to show you that the ALL is optional and redundant. There is never a need to specify ALL; it is a default option.

**TYPE**
```
SELECT ALL PROD_DESC
FROM CANDY_TBL;
```

**OUTPUT**
```
PROD_DESC
-----------------------
CANDY CORN
CANDY CORN
HERSHEYS KISS
SMARTIES
```

```
4 rows selected.
```

The DISTINCT option is used in the following statement to suppress the display of duplicate records. Notice that the value CANDY CORN is only printed once in this example.

**TYPE**
```
SELECT DISTINCT PROD_DESC
FROM CANDY_TBL;
```

**OUTPUT**
```
PROD_DESC
-----------------------
CANDY CORN
HERSHEYS KISS
SMARTIES
```

```
3 rows selected.
```

DISTINCT and ALL can also be used with parentheses enclosing the associated column. The use of parentheses is often used in SQL—as well as many other languages—to improve readability.

**TYPE**
```
SELECT DISTINCT(PROD_DESC)
FROM CANDY_TBL;
```

**OUTPUT**
```
PROD_DESC
-----------------------
CANDY CORN
HERSHEYS KISS
SMARTIES
```

```
3 rows selected.
```

## The FROM Clause

The FROM clause is always used in conjunction with the SELECT statement. It is a required element for any query. The FROM clause's purpose is to tell the database what tables to access in order to retrieve the desired data for the query. The FROM clause can contain one or more tables.

**SYNTAX**

The syntax for the FROM clause is as follows:

```
from table1 [ , table2 ]
```

## Using Conditions to Distinguish Data

A *condition* is part of a query that is used to display selective information as specified by the user. The value of a condition is either True or False, thereby limiting the data received from the query. The WHERE clause is used to place conditions on a query by eliminating rows that would normally be returned by a query without conditions.

There can be more than one condition in the where clause. If there is more than one condition, they are connected by the AND and OR operators, which are discussed during Hour 8, "Using Operators to Categorize Data." As you also learn during the next hour, there are several conditional operators that can be used to specify conditions in a query. This hour only deals with a single condition for each query.

**NEW TERM** An *operator* is a character or keyword in SQL that is used to combine elements in a SQL statement.

**SYNTAX** The syntax for the WHERE clause is as follows:

```
select [ all ¦ * ¦ distinct column1, column2 ]
from table1 [ , table2 ]
where [ condition1 ¦ expression1 ]
[ and condition2 ¦ expression2 ]
```

The following is a simple SELECT without conditions specified by the WHERE clause:

**TYPE**
```
SELECT *
FROM PRODUCTS_TBL;
```

**OUTPUT**

| PROD_ID | PROD_DESC | COST |
|---------|-----------|------|
| 11235 | WITCHES COSTUME | 29.99 |
| 222 | PLASTIC PUMPKIN 18 INCH | 7.75 |
| 13 | FALSE PARAFFIN TEETH | 1.1 |
| 90 | LIGHTED LANTERNS | 14.5 |
| 15 | ASSORTED COSTUMES | 10 |
| 9 | CANDY CORN | 1.35 |
| 6 | PUMPKIN CANDY | 1.45 |
| 87 | PLASTIC SPIDERS | 1.05 |
| 119 | ASSORTED MASKS | 4.95 |

9 rows selected.

Now add a condition for the same query.

**TYPE**
```
SELECT *FROM PRODUCTS_TBL
WHERE COST < 5;
```

**OUTPUT**

| PROD_ID | PROD_DESC | COST |
|---------|-----------|------|
| 13 | FALSE PARAFFIN TEETH | 1.1 |
| 9 | CANDY CORN | 1.35 |
| 6 | PUMPKIN CANDY | 1.45 |
| 87 | PLASTIC SPIDERS | 1.05 |
| 119 | ASSORTED MASKS | 4.95 |

5 rows selected.

7

The only records displayed are those that cost less than $5.

In the following query, you want to display the product description and cost that matches the product identification 119.

**TYPE**

```
SELECT PROD_DESC, COST
FROM PRODUCTS_TBL
WHERE PROD_ID = '119';
```

**OUTPUT**

```
PROD_DESC                        COST
------------------------- ----------
ASSORTED MASKS                   4.95
```

1 row selected.

## Sorting Your Output

You usually want your output to have some kind of order. Data may be sorted by using the ORDER BY clause. The ORDER BY clause arranges the results of a query in a listing format you specify. The default ordering of the ORDER BY clause is an *ascending order*; the sort displays in the order A–Z if it's sorting output names alphabetically. A *descending order* for alphabetical output would be displayed in the order Z–A. Ascending order for output for numeric values between 1 and 9 would be displayed 1–9; descending order is displayed as 9–1.

The syntax for the ORDER BY is as follows:

**SYNTAX**

```
select [ all ¦ * ¦ distinct column1, column2 ]
from table1 [ , table2 ]
where [ condition1 ¦ expression1 ]
[ and condition2 ¦ expression2 ]
ORDER BY column1¦integer [ ASC¦DESC ]
```

Begin your exploration of the ORDER BY clause with an extension of one of the previous statements. Order by the product description in ascending order or alphabetical order. Note the use of the ASC option. ASC can be specified after any column in the ORDER BY clause.

**TYPE**

```
SELECT PROD_DESC, PROD_ID, COST
FROM PRODUCTS_TBL
WHERE COST < 20
ORDER BY PROD_DESC ASC;
```

**OUTPUT**

```
PROD_DESC                     PROD_ID      COST
------------------------- ---------- ----------
ASSORTED COSTUMES             15           10
ASSORTED MASKS                119          4.95
CANDY CORN                    9            1.35
FALSE PARAFFIN TEETH          13           1.1
LIGHTED LANTERNS              90           14.5
PLASTIC PUMPKIN 18 INCH       222          7.75
PLASTIC SPIDERS               87           1.05
PUMPKIN CANDY                 6            1.45
```

8 rows selected.

**NOTE**

Because ascending order for output is the default, ASC does not have to be specified.

You can use DESC, as in the following statement, if you want the same output to be sorted in reverse alphabetical order.

**TYPE**

```
SELECT PROD_DESC, PROD_ID, COST
FROM PRODUCTS_TBL
WHERE COST < 20
ORDER BY PROD_DESC DESC;
```

**OUTPUT**

| PROD_DESC | PROD_ID | COST |
|-----------|---------|------|
| PUMPKIN CANDY | 6 | 1.45 |
| PLASTIC SPIDERS | 87 | 1.05 |
| PLASTIC PUMPKIN 18 INCH | 222 | 7.75 |
| LIGHTED LANTERNS | 90 | 14.5 |
| FALSE PARAFFIN TEETH | 13 | 1.1 |
| CANDY CORN | 9 | 1.35 |
| ASSORTED MASKS | 119 | 4.95 |
| ASSORTED COSTUMES | 15 | 10 |

```
8 rows selected.
```

There are shortcuts in SQL. A column listed in the ORDER BY clause can be abbreviated with an integer. The INTEGER is a substitution for the actual column name, identifying the position of the column after the SELECT keyword.

An example of using an integer as an identifier in the ORDER BY clause follows:

**TYPE**

```
SELECT PROD_DESC, PROD_ID, COST
FROM PRODUCTS_TBL
WHERE COST < 20
ORDER BY 1;
```

**OUTPUT**

| PROD_DESC | PROD_ID | COST |
|-----------|---------|------|
| ASSORTED COSTUMES | 15 | 10 |
| ASSORTED MASKS | 119 | 4.95 |
| CANDY CORN | 9 | 1.35 |
| FALSE PARAFFIN TEETH | 13 | 1.1 |
| LIGHTED LANTERNS | 90 | 14.5 |
| PLASTIC PUMPKIN 18 INCH | 222 | 7.75 |
| PLASTIC SPIDERS | 87 | 1.05 |
| PUMPKIN CANDY | 6 | 1.45 |

```
8 rows selected.
```

In this query, the integer 1 represents the column PROD_DESC. The integer 2 represents the PROD_ID column, 3 represents the COST column, and so on.

7

You can order by multiple columns in a query, using either the column name itself or the associated number of the column in the SELECT.

```
ORDER BY 1,2,3
```

Columns in an ORDER BY clause are not required to appear in the same order as the associated columns following the SELECT, as shown by the following example:

```
ORDER BY 1,3,2
```

## Case Sensitivity

Case sensitivity is a very important concept to understand when coding with SQL. Typically, SQL commands and keywords are not case-sensitive, which allows you to enter your commands and keywords in either uppercase or lowercase—whatever your preference. The case may be mixed (both upper- and lowercase for a single word or statement). See Hour 5, "Manipulating Data," on case sensitivity.

Case sensitivity is, however, a factor when dealing with data in SQL. In most situations, data seems to be stored exclusively in uppercase in a relational database to provide data consistency.

For instance, your data would not be consistent if you arbitrarily entered your data using random case:

```
JOHN SMITH
John Smith
john smith
```

If the name was stored as john smith and you issued a query as follows, no rows would be returned.

```
SELECT *
FROM EMPLOYEE_TBL
WHERE EMPLOYEE_NAME = 'JOHN SMITH';
```

**NOTE**    You must use the same case in your query as the data is stored when referencing data in the database. When entering data, consult the rules set forth by your company for the appropriate case to be used.

# Examples of Simple Queries

This section provides several examples of queries based on the concepts that have been discussed. The chapter begins with the most simple query you can issue, and builds upon the initial query progressively. You use the table EMPLOYEE_TBL.

Selecting all records from a table and displaying all columns:

```
select * from employee_tbl;
```

Selecting all records from a table and displaying a specified column:

```
select employee_id
from employee_tbl;
```

Selecting all records from a table and displaying a specified column. You may enter code on one line or use a carriage return as desired:

```
select employee_id from employee_tbl;
```

Selecting all records from a table and displaying multiple columns separated by commas:

```
SELECT EMPLOYEE_ID, EMPLOYEE_NAME
FROM EMPLOYEE_TBL;
```

Displaying data for a given condition:

```
select employee_id, employee_name
from employee_tbl
where employee_id = '333333333';
```

Displaying data for a given condition and sorting the output:

```
select employee_id, employee_name
from employee_tbl
where CITY = 'INDIANAPOLIS'
ORDER BY EMPLOYEE_ID;
```

Displaying data for a given condition and sorting the output on multiple columns, one column sorted in reverse order:

```
select employee_id, employee_name
from employee_tbl
where CITY = 'INDIANAPOLIS'
ORDER BY EMPLOYEE_ID, EMPLOYEE_NAME DESC;
```

Displaying data for a given condition and sorting the output using an integer in the place of the spelled-out column name:

```
select employee_id, employee_name
from employee_tbl
where CITY = 'INDIANAPOLIS'
ORDER BY 1;
```

Displaying data for a given condition and sorting the output by multiple columns using integers, the order of the columns in the sort different than their corresponding order after the SELECT keyword:

```
select employee_id, employee_name
from employee_tbl
where CITY = 'INDIANAPOLIS'
ORDER BY 2, 1;
```

When selecting all rows of data from a large table, the results could render a substantial amount of data returned.

## Counting the Records in a Table

A simple query can be issued on a table to get a quick count on the number of records in the table, or on the number of values for a column in the table. A count is accomplished by the function COUNT. Although functions are not discussed until later in this book, this function should be introduced here because it is often a part of one of the simplest queries that you can create.

```
SELECT COUNT(*)
FROM TABLE_NAME;
```

The COUNT function is used with parentheses, which are used to enclose the target column to count or the asterisk to count all rows of data in the table.

Counting the number of records in the PRODUCTS_TBL table:

**TYPE**  `SELECT COUNT(*) FROM PRODUCTS_TBL;`

**OUTPUT**
```
COUNT(*)
----------
         9
```

```
1 row selected.
```

Counting the number of values for PROD_ID in the PRODUCTS_TBL table.

**TYPE**  `SELECT COUNT(PROD_ID) FROM PRODUCTS_TBL;`

**OUTPUT**
```
COUNT(PROD_ID)
--------------
             9
```

```
1 row selected.
```

**NOTE**  Counting the number of values for a column is the same as counting the number of records in a table if the column being counted is NOT NULL (a required column).

## Selecting Data from Another User's Table

**7**

Permission must be granted to a user for the table in order to access another user's table. If no permission has been granted, access is not allowed by users that do not own the table. You may select data from another user's table after access has been granted (the GRANT command is discussed in Hour 20, "Creating and Using Views and Synonyms") to select from another user's table. In order to access another user's table in a SELECT statement, you must precede the table name with the schema name or the username that owns the table, as in the following example:

```
SELECT EMP_ID
FROM SCHEMA.EMPLOYEE_TBL;
```

**NOTE**

If a synonym exists in the database for the table to which you desire access, you do not have to specify the schema name for the table. *Synonyms* are alternate names for tables, which are discussed in Hour 21, "Working with the System Catalog."

## Column Aliases

*Column aliases* are used to rename a table's columns for the purpose of a particular query. The employee_tbl illustrates the use of column aliases.

```
SELECT COLUMN_NAME ALIAS_NAME
FROM TABLE_NAME;
```

The following example displays the product description twice, giving the second column an alias named PRODUCT. Notice the column headers in the output.

**TYPE**

```
select prod_desc,
       prod_desc product
from products_tbl;
```

**OUTPUT**

```
PROD_DESC                      PRODUCT
----------------------------   ----------------------------
WITCHES COSTUME                WITCHES COSTUME
PLASTIC PUMPKIN 18 INCH        PLASTIC PUMPKIN 18 INCH
FALSE PARAFFIN TEETH           FALSE PARAFFIN TEETH
LIGHTED LANTERNS               LIGHTED LANTERNS
ASSORTED COSTUMES              ASSORTED COSTUMES
CANDY CORN                     CANDY CORN
PUMPKIN CANDY                  PUMPKIN CANDY
PLASTIC SPIDERS                PLASTIC SPIDERS
ASSORTED MASKS                 ASSORTED MASKS

9 rows selected.
```

Column aliases can be used to customize names for column headers, and can also be used to reference a column with a shorter name in some SQL implementations.

7

**NOTE**

When a column is renamed in a select statement, the name is not a permanent change. The change is for that particular select statement.

# Summary

You have been introduced to the database query, a means for obtaining useful information from a relational database. The SELECT statement, which is known as the Data Query Language (DQL) command, is used to create queries in SQL. The FROM clause must be included with every SELECT statement. You have learned how to place a condition on a query using the WHERE clause, and how to sort data using the ORDER BY clause. You have learned the fundamentals of writing queries, and after a few exercises, you should be prepared to learn more about queries during the next hour.

## Q&A

**Q  Why won't the select clause work without the FROM clause?**

**A**  The SELECT clause merely tells the database what data you want to see. The FROM clause tells the database where to get the data.

**Q  When I use the ORDER BY clause and choose the option descending, what does that really do to the data?**

**A**  Say that you use the ORDER BY clause and have selected the last_name from the employee_tbl. If you used the descending option, the order would start with the letter Z and finish with the letter A.

**Q  What advantage is there to renaming columns?**

**A**  The new column name could fit the description of the returned data more closely for that particular report.

# Workshop

The following workshop is composed of a series of quiz questions and practical exercises. The quiz questions are designed to test your overall understanding of the current material. The practical exercises are intended to afford you the opportunity to apply the concepts discussed during the current hour, as well as build upon the knowledge acquired in previous hours of study. Please take time to complete the quiz questions and exercises before continuing. You may refer to the answers in Appendix C.

# Quiz

1. Name the required parts for any SELECT statement.
2. In the WHERE clause, are single quotation marks required for all the data?
3. Under what part of the SQL language does the SELECT statement (database query) fall?
4. Can multiple conditions be used in the WHERE clause?

# Exercises

1. Look over the following SELECT statements. Determine whether the syntax is correct. If the syntax is incorrect, what would correct it? A table called employee_tbl is used here.

   a.
```
SELECT employee_id, last_name, first_name,
FROM EMPLOYEE_TBL;
```

   b.
```
SELECT EMPLOYEE_ID, LAST_NAME
ORDER BY EMPLOYEE_TBL
FROM EMPLOYEE_TBL;
```

   c.
```
SELECT EMPLOYEE_ID, LAST_NAME, FIRST_NAME
FROM EMPLOYEE_TBL
WHERE EMPLOYEE_ID = '333333333'
ORDER BY EMPLOYEE_ID;
```

   d.
```
SELECT EMPLOYEE_ID SSN, LAST_NAME
FROM EMPLOYEE_TBL
WHERE EMPLOYEE_ID = '333333333'
ORDER BY 1;
```

   e.
```
SELECT EMPLOYEE_ID, LAST_NAME, FIRST_NAME
FROM EMPLOYEE_TBL
WHERE EMPLOYEE_ID = '333333333'
ORDER BY 3, 1, 2;
```

7

# Hour **8**

# Using Operators to Categorize Data

The highlights of this hour include

☐ What is an operator?

☐ An overview of operators in SQL

☐ How are operators used singularly?

☐ How are operators used in combinations?

## What Is an Operator in SQL?

An operator is a reserved word or a character used primarily in a SQL statement's WHERE clause to perform operation(s), such as comparisons and arithmetic operations. *Operators* are used to specify conditions in a SQL statement and to serve as conjunctions for multiple conditions in a statement.

The operators discussed during this hour are

☐ Comparison operators

☐ Logical operators

☐ Operators used to negate conditions

☐ Arithmetic operators

# Comparison Operators

*Comparison operators* are used to test single values in a SQL statement. The comparison operators discussed consist of =, <>, <, and >.

These operators are used to test

☐ Equality

☐ Non-equality

☐ Less-than values

☐ Greater-than values

Examples of usage and the meanings of comparison operators are covered in the following sections.

## Equality

The *equal operator* compares single values to one another in a SQL statement. The equal sign (=) symbolizes equality. When testing for equality, the compared values must match exactly or no data is returned. If two values are equal during a comparison for equality, the returned value for the comparison is TRUE; the returned value is FALSE if equality is not found. This Boolean value (TRUE/FALSE) is used to determine whether data is returned according to the condition.

The = operator can be used by itself or combined with other operators. An example usage and the meaning of the equality operator follows:

| Usage | Meaning |
|---|---|
| WHERE SALARY = '20000' | Salary equals 20000 |

The following query returns all rows of data where the PROD_ID is equal to 2345.

```
SELECT *
FROM PRODUCTS_TBL
WHERE PROD_ID = '2345';
```

```
PROD_ID    PROD_DESC                        COST
---------  -----------------------------  ---------
2345       OAK BOOKSHELF                    59.99

1 row selected.
```

8

## Non-equality

For every equality, there is a non-equality. In SQL, the operator used to measure non-equality is <> (the less-than sign combined with the greater-than sign). The condition returns TRUE if the condition finds non-equality; FALSE is returned if equality is found.

> **NOTE** Another option comparable to <> is !=. Many of the major implementations have adopted the != to represent not-equal. Check your particular implementation for the usage.

| *Usage* | *Meaning* |
| --- | --- |
| WHERE SALARY <> '20000' | Salary is not equal 20000 |

**TYPE**
```
SELECT *
FROM PRODUCTS_TBL
WHERE PROD_ID <> '2345';
```

**OUTPUT**
```
PROD_ID    PROD_DESC                      COST
--------   ------------------------    --------
11235      WITCHES COSTUME                29.99
222        PLASTIC PUMPKIN 18 INCH         7.75
13         FALSE PARAFFIN TEETH            1.1
90         LIGHTED LANTERNS               14.5
15         ASSORTED COSTUMES              10
9          CANDY CORN                      1.35
6          PUMPKIN CANDY                   1.45
87         PLASTIC SPIDERS                 1.05
119        ASSORTED MASKS                  4.95
1234       KEY CHAIN                       5.95
7725       LEATHER GLOVES                 24.99

11 rows selected.
```

## Less-Than, Greater-Than

The symbols < (less-than) and > (greater-than) can be used by themselves, or in combination with each other or other operators.

| *Usage* | *Meaning* |
| --- | --- |
| WHERE SALARY < '20000' | Salary less than 20000 |
| WHERE SALARY > '20000' | Salary greater than 20000 |

In the first example, anything less-than and not equal to 20000 returns TRUE. Any value of 20000 or more returns FALSE. Greater-than works the opposite of less-than.

**TYPE**
```
SELECT *
FROM PRODUCTS_TBL
WHERE COST > 20;
```

**OUTPUT**
```
PROD_ID     PROD_DESC                          COST
---------   ------------------------------    ----------
11235       WITCHES COSTUME                    29.99
2345        OAK BOOKSHELF                      59.99
7725 .      LEATHER GLOVES                     24.99

3 rows selected.
```

In the next example, notice that the value 24.99 was not included in the query's result set. The less-than operator is not inclusive.

**TYPE**
```
SELECT *
FROM PRODUCTS_TBL
WHERE COST < 24.99;
```

**OUTPUT**
```
PROD_ID     PROD_DESC                          COST
---------   ------------------------------    ----------
222         PLASTIC PUMPKIN 18 INCH            7.75
13          FALSE PARAFFIN TEETH               1.1
90          LIGHTED LANTERNS                   14.5
15          ASSORTED COSTUMES                  10
9           CANDY CORN                         1.35
6           PUMPKIN CANDY                      1.45
87          PLASTIC SPIDERS                    1.05
119         ASSORTED MASKS                     4.95
1234        KEY CHAIN                          5.95

9 rows selected.
```

## Combination Examples of Comparison Operators

The equal operator can be combined with the less-than and greater-than operators, as in the following examples:

| Usage | Meaning |
|-------|---------|
| WHERE SALARY <= '20000' | Salary less-than or equal-to |
| WHERE SALARY >= '20000' | Salary greater-than or equal-to |

Less-than or equal-to 20000 includes 20000 and all values less than 20000. Any value in that range returns a TRUE; any value greater than 20000 returns FALSE. Greater-than or equal-to also includes the value 20000 in this case and works the same as the less-than or equal-to.

**TYPE**
```
SELECT *
FROM PRODUCTS_TBL
WHERE COST <= 24.99;
```

**OUTPUT**
```
PROD_ID     PROD_DESC                          COST
---------   ------------------------------    ----------
222         PLASTIC PUMPKIN 18 INCH            7.75
```

**8**

```
 13        FALSE PARAFFIN TEETH       1.1
 90        LIGHTED LANTERNS          14.5
 15        ASSORTED COSTUMES         10
 9         CANDY CORN                 1.35
 6         PUMPKIN CANDY              1.45
 87        PLASTIC SPIDERS            1.05
 119       ASSORTED MASKS             4.95
 1234      KEY CHAIN                  5.95
 7725      LEATHER GLOVES            24.99

 10 rows selected.
```

Notice that 24.99 is included in this output.

# Logical Operators

*Logical operators* are those operators that use SQL keywords to make comparison instead of symbols. The logical operators covered in the following subsections are

- [ ] IS NULL

- [ ] BETWEEN

- [ ] IN

- [ ] LIKE

- [ ] EXISTS

- [ ] UNIQUE

- [ ] ALL and ANY

## IS NULL

The NULL operator is used to compare a value with a NULL value. For instance, you might look for employees who do not have a pager by searching for NULL values in the PAGER column of the EMPLOYEE_TBL table.

The following example shows the usage of comparing a value to a NULL value:

| Usage | Meaning |
| --- | --- |
| WHERE SALARY IS NULL | Salary has no value |

The following example does not find a NULL value:

| Usage | Meaning |
| --- | --- |
| WHERE SALARY = NULL | Salary has a value containing the letters N-U-L-L |

**Type**
```
SELECT EMP_ID, LAST_NAME, FIRST_NAME, PAGER
FROM EMPLOYEE_TBL
WHERE PAGER IS NULL;
```

**Output**
```
EMP_ID     LAST_NAM FIRST_NA PAGER
--------   -------- -------- ----------
311549902 STEPHENS TINA
442346889 PLEW     LINDA
220984332 WALLACE  MARIAH
443679012 SPURGEON TIFFANY

4 rows selected.
```

Understand that the literal word "null" is different than a NULL value. Examine the following example:

**Type**
```
SELECT EMP_ID, LAST_NAME, FIRST_NAME, PAGER
FROM EMPLOYEE_TBL
WHERE PAGER = NULL;
```

**Output**  no rows selected.

## BETWEEN

The between operator is used to search for values that are within a set of values, given the minimum value and the maximum value. The minimum and maximum values are included as part of the conditional set.

| Usage | Meaning |
|---|---|
| WHERE salary between '20000' and '30000' | The salary must fall between 20000 and 30000, including the values 20000 and 30000 |

**Type**
```
SELECT *
FROM PRODUCTS_TBL
WHERE COST BETWEEN 5.95 AND 14.5;
```

**Output**
```
PROD_ID    PROD_DESC                       COST
--------   ------------------------------- ----------
222        PLASTIC PUMPKIN 18 INCH         7.75
90         LIGHTED LANTERNS                14.5
15         ASSORTED COSTUMES               10
1234       KEY CHAIN                       5.95

4 rows selected.
```

Notice that the values 5.95 and 14.5 are included in the output.

**NOTE**

The between is inclusive and therefore includes the minimum and maximum values in the query results.

## IN

The IN operator is used to compare a value to a list of literal values that have been specified. For TRUE to be returned, the compared value must match at least one of the values in the list.

| Usage | Meaning |
|---|---|
| WHERE SALARY IN ('20000', '30000', '40000') | The salary must match one of the values 20000, 30000, or 40000 |

**TYPE**

```
SELECT *
FROM PRODUCTS_TBL
WHERE PROD_ID IN ('13','9','87','119');
```

**OUTPUT**

```
PROD_ID    PROD_DESC                     COST
--------   -------------------------     --------
119        ASSORTED MASKS                4.95
87         PLASTIC SPIDERS               1.05
9          CANDY CORN                    1.35
13         FALSE PARAFFIN TEETH          1.1

4 rows selected.
```

Using the IN operator can achieve the same results as using the OR operator and can return the results quicker.

## LIKE

The LIKE operator is used to compare a value to similar values using wildcard operators. There are two wildcards used in conjunction with the LIKE operator.

☐ The percent sign (%)
☐ The underscore (_)

The percent sign represents zero, one, or multiple characters. The underscore represents a single number or character. The symbols can be used in combinations.

Examples of usage are

| | |
|---|---|
| WHERE SALARY LIKE '200%' | Finds any values that start with 200 and continues for any length, to include the value 200 |

| | |
|---|---|
| `WHERE SALARY LIKE '%200%'` | Finds any values that have 200 in any position |
| `WHERE SALARY LIKE '_00%'` | Finds any values that have 00 in the second and third positions |
| `WHERE SALARY LIKE '2_%_%'` | Finds any values that start with 2 |
| `WHERE SALARY LIKE '%2'` | Finds any values that end with 2 |
| `WHERE SALARY LIKE '_2%3'` | Finds any values that have a 2 in the second position and end with a 3 |
| `WHERE SALARY LIKE '2___3'` | Finds any values in a five-digit number that start with 2 and end with 3 |

The following example shows all product descriptions that end with the letter S:

```
SELECT PROD_DESC
FROM PRODUCTS_TBL
WHERE PROD_DESC LIKE '%S';
```

**OUTPUT**
```
PROD_DESC
-----------------------
LIGHTED LANTERNS
ASSORTED COSTUMES
PLASTIC SPIDERS
ASSORTED MASKS
LEATHER GLOVES

5 rows selected.
```

The following example shows all product descriptions whose second character is the letter S:

**TYPE**
```
SELECT PROD_DESC
FROM PRODUCTS_TBL
WHERE PROD_DESC LIKE '_S%';
```

**OUTPUT**
```
PROD_DESC
-----------------------
ASSORTED COSTUMES
ASSORTED MASKS

2 rows selected.
```

## EXISTS

The EXISTS operator is used to search for the presence of a row in a specified table that meets certain criteria.

| Usage | Meaning |
|---|---|
| WHERE EXISTS (SELECT EMPLOYEE_ID FROM EMPLOYEE_TBL WHERE EMPLOYEE_ID = '333333333') | Searching to see whether the employee_id 3333333333 is in the employee_tbl |

This example is a form of a subquery, which is further discussed during Hour 14:

**TYPE**
```
SELECT COST
FROM PRODUCTS_TBL
WHERE EXISTS ( SELECT COST
               FROM PRODUCTS_TBL
               WHERE COST > 100 );No rows selected.
```

----------

There were no rows selected, because no records existed where the cost was greater than 100.

Consider the next example:

**TYPE**
```
SELECT COST
FROM PRODUCTS_TBL
WHERE EXISTS ( SELECT COST
               FROM PRODUCTS_TBL
               WHERE COST < 100 );
```

**OUTPUT**
```
COST
----------
     29.99
      7.75
       1.1
      14.5
        10
      1.35
      1.45
      1.05
      4.95

9 rows selected.
```

The cost was displayed for records in the table, because records existed where the product cost was less than 100.

## UNIQUE

The UNIQUE operator searches every row of a specified table for uniqueness (no duplicates).

| Usage | Meaning |
|---|---|
| WHERE UNIQUE (SELECT SALARY FROM EMPLOYEE_TBL WHERE EMPLOYEE_ID = '333333333') | Testing salary to see whether there are duplicates |

## ALL and ANY OPERATORS

The ALL operator is used to compare a value to all values in another value set.

| Usage | Meaning |
|---|---|
| WHERE SALARY > ALL<br>(SELECT SALARY<br>FROM EMPLOYEE_TBL<br>WHERE CITY =<br>'INDIANAPOLIS') | Testing salary to see whether it is greater than all salaries of the employees living in Indianapolis |

**TYPE**
```
SELECT *
FROM PRODUCTS_TBL
WHERE COST > ALL ( SELECT COST
                   FROM PRODUCTS_TBL
                   WHERE COST < 10 );
```

**OUTPUT**
```
PROD_ID     PROD_DESC                       COST
--------    -----------------------    ----------
11235       WITCHES COSTUME                 29.99
90          LIGHTED LANTERNS                14.5
15          ASSORTED COSTUMES               10
2345        OAK BOOKSHELF                   59.99
7725        LEATHER GLOVES                  24.99

5 rows selected.
```

In this output, there were five records that had a cost greater than the cost of all records having a cost less than 10.

The ANY operator is used to compare a value to any applicable value in the list according to the condition.

| Usage | Meaning |
|---|---|
| WHERE SALARY > ANY<br>(SELECT SALARY FROM<br>EMPLOYEE_TBL WHERE<br>CITY = 'INDIANAPOLIS') | Testing salary to see whether it is greater than any of the salaries of employees living in Indianapolis |

**TYPE**
```
SELECT *
FROM PRODUCTS_TBL
WHERE COST > ANY ( SELECT COST
                   FROM PRODUCTS_TBL
                   WHERE COST < 10 );
```

**OUTPUT**
```
PROD_ID     PROD_DESC                       COST
--------    -----------------------    ----------
11235       WITCHES COSTUME                 29.99
```

8

```
222        PLASTIC PUMPKIN 18 INCH      7.75
13         FALSE PARAFFIN TEETH         1.1
90         LIGHTED LANTERNS             14.5
15         ASSORTED COSTUMES            10
9          CANDY CORN                   1.35
6          PUMPKIN CANDY                1.45
119        ASSORTED MASKS               4.95
1234       KEY CHAIN                    5.95
2345       OAK BOOKSHELF                59.99
7725       LEATHER GLOVES               24.99

11 rows selected.
```

In this output, more records were returned than when using ALL, because the cost only had to be greater than any of the costs that were less than 10. The one record that was not displayed had a cost of 1.05, which was not greater than any of the values less than 10 (which was, in fact, 1.05).

# Conjunctive Operators

What if you want to used multiple conditions to narrow data in a SQL statement? You must be able to combine the conditions, and you do this with what is call *conjunctive operators*. These operators are

- ☐ AND

- ☐ OR

These operators provide a means to make multiple comparisons with different operators in the same SQL statement. The following sections describe each operator's behavior.

## AND

The AND operator allows the existence of multiple conditions in a SQL statement's WHERE clause. In order for action to be taken by the SQL statement, whether it be a transaction or query, all conditions separated by the AND must be TRUE.

| Usage | Meaning |
|---|---|
| WHERE EMPLOYEE_ID = '333333333' AND SALARY = '20000' | The employee_id must match 333333333 and the salary must equal 20000 |

**TYPE**
```
SELECT *
FROM PRODUCTS_TBL
WHERE COST > 10
   AND COST < 30;
```

```
PROD_ID     PROD_DESC                        COST
--------    -------------------------    ----------
11235       WITCHES COSTUME                  29.99
90          LIGHTED LANTERNS                 14.5
7725        LEATHER GLOVES                   24.99
```

3 rows selected.

In this output, the value for cost had to be both greater than 10 and less than 30 for data to be retrieved.

**TYPE**
```
SELECT *
FROM PRODUCTS_TBL
WHERE PROD_ID = '7725'
    AND PROD_ID = '2345';
```

**OUTPUT**   no rows selected

This output retrieved no data because each row of data has only one product identification.

## OR

The OR operator is used to combine multiple conditions in a SQL statement's WHERE clause. In order for action to be taken by the SQL statement, whether it be a transaction or query, at least one of the conditions that are separated by OR must be TRUE.

| Usage | Meaning |
|-------|---------|
| WHERE SALARY = '20000' | The salary must match |
| OR SALARY = '30000' | either 20000 or 30000 |

**NOTE**   Each of the comparison and logical operators can be used singularly or in combinations with each other.

**TYPE**
```
SELECT *
FROM PRODUCTS_TBL
WHERE PROD_ID = '7725'
    OR PROD_ID = '2345'
```

**OUTPUT**
```
PROD_ID     PROD_DESC                        COST
--------    -------------------------    ----------
2345        OAK BOOKSHELF                    59.99
7725        LEATHER GLOVES                   24.99
```

2 rows selected.

In this output, either one of the conditions had to be TRUE in order for data to be retrieved. Two records that met either one or the other condition were found.

**TIP**
When using multiple conditions and operators in a SQL statement, you may find it improves overall readability if parentheses are used to separate statements into logical groups. However, be aware that the misuse of parentheses could adversely affect your output results.

In the next example, notice the use of the AND and two OR operators. In addition, notice the logical placement of the parentheses to make the statement more readable.

**TYPE**
```
SELECT *
FROM PRODUCTS_TBL
WHERE COST > 10
   AND ( PROD_ID = '222'
   OR    PROD_ID = '90'
   OR    PROD_ID = '11235' );
```

**OUTPUT**
```
PROD_ID      PROD_DESC                        COST
----------   ------------------------------   ----------
11235        WITCHES COSTUME                  29.99
90           LIGHTED LANTERNS                 14.5

2 rows selected.
```

The cost in this output had to be greater than 10 and the product identification had to be any one of the three listed. A row was not returned for PROD_ID 222, because the cost for this identification was not greater than 10.

# Negating Conditions with the NOT Operator

Of all the conditions tested by the logical operators discussed here, there is a way to negate each one of these operators in order to change the condition's viewpoint.

The NOT operator reverses the meaning of the logical operator with which it is used. The NOT can be used with the following operators in the following methods:

- [ ] NOT IN
- [ ] NOT EXISTS
- [ ] NOT BETWEEN
- [ ] NOT LIKE
- [ ] IS NOT NULL

Each method is discussed in the following sections.

## Not Equal

You have learned how to test for inequality using the <> operator. Inequality is worth mentioning in this section because in order to test for it, you are actually negating the equality operator. A second method for testing inequality available in some SQL implementations is shown here:

| Usage | Meaning |
|-------|---------|
| WHERE SALARY <> '20000' | Salary not equal 20000 |
| WHERE SALARY != '20000' | Salary not equal 20000 |

In the second example, you can see that the exclamation mark is used to negate the equality comparison. The use of the exclamation mark is allowed in some implementations in addition to the standard operator for inequality <>.

 **NOTE**

> Check your particular implementation for the use of the exclamation mark to negate the inequality operator.

## NOT BETWEEN

The between operator is negated as follows:

| Usage | Meaning |
|-------|---------|
| WHERE Salary not between '20000' and '30000' | The value for salary cannot fall between 20000 and 30000, to include the values 20000 and 30000 |

 **TYPE**

```
SELECT *
FROM PRODUCTS_TBL
WHERE COST NOT BETWEEN 5.95 AND 14.5;
```

**OUTPUT**

```
PROD_ID    PROD_DESC                    COST
---------  --------------------------  ---------
11235      WITCHES COSTUME              29.99
13         FALSE PARAFFIN TEETH          1.1
9          CANDY CORN                    1.35
6          PUMPKIN CANDY                 1.45
87         PLASTIC SPIDERS               1.05
119        ASSORTED MASKS                4.95
2345       OAK BOOKSHELF                59.99
7725       LEATHER GLOVES               24.99

8 rows selected.
```

 8

8

**NOTE**

Remember that BETWEEN is inclusive; therefore, in the previous example, any rows that equal 5.95 or 14.50 are not included in the query results.

## NOT IN

The IN operator is negated as NOT IN. All salaries in the following example that are not in the listed values, if any, are returned:

| Usage | Meaning |
|---|---|
| WHERE SALARY NOT IN ('20000', '30000', '40000') | The salary cannot be equal to any of the given values for action to be taken |

**TYPE**

```
SELECT *
FROM PRODUCTS_TBL
WHERE PROD_ID NOT IN ('13','9','87','119');
```

**OUTPUT**

| PROD_ID | PROD_DESC | COST |
|---|---|---|
| 11235 | WITCHES COSTUME | 29.99 |
| 222 | PLASTIC PUMPKIN 18 INCH | 7.75 |
| 90 | LIGHTED LANTERNS | 14.5 |
| 15 | ASSORTED COSTUMES | 10 |
| 6 | PUMPKIN CANDY | 1.45 |
| 1234 | KEY CHAIN | 5.95 |
| 2345 | OAK BOOKSHELF | 59.99 |
| 7725 | LEATHER GLOVES | 24.99 |

8 rows selected.

In this output, records were not displayed for the listed identifications after the NOT IN operator.

## NOT LIKE

The LIKE, or wildcard, operator is negated as NOT LIKE. When NOT LIKE is used, only values that are not similar are returned. Examples of usage include:

| Usage | Meaning |
|---|---|
| WHERE SALARY NOT LIKE '200%' | Finds any values that do not start with 200 |
| WHERE SALARY NOT LIKE '%200%' | Finds any values that do not have 200 in any position |

*continues*

| Usage | Meaning |
|---|---|
| WHERE SALARY NOT LIKE '_00%' | Finds any values that have 00 starting in the second position |
| WHERE SALARY NOT LIKE '2_%_%' | Does not find any values that start with 2 |

**TYPE**

```
SELECT PROD_DESC
FROM PRODUCTS_TBL
WHERE PROD_DESC NOT LIKE 'L%';
```

**OUTPUT**

```
PROD_DESC
-------------------------
WITCHES COSTUME
PLASTIC PUMPKIN 18 INCH
FALSE PARAFFIN TEETH
ASSORTED COSTUMES
CANDY CORN
PUMPKIN CANDY
PLASTIC SPIDERS
ASSORTED MASKS
KEY CHAIN
OAK BOOKSHELF

10 rows selected.
```

In this output, the product descriptions starting with the letter L were not displayed.

## IS NOT NULL

The IS NULL operator is negated as IS NOT NULL in order to test for values that are not NULL.

| Usage | Meaning |
|---|---|
| WHERE SALARY IS NOT NULL | Only NOT NULL rows are returned |

**TYPE**

```
SELECT EMP_ID, LAST_NAME, FIRST_NAME, PAGER
FROM EMPLOYEE_TBL
WHERE PAGER IS NOT NULL;
```

**OUTPUT**

```
EMP_ID     LAST_NAM FIRST_NA PAGER
---------- -------- -------- ----------
213764555 GLASS    BRANDON  3175709980
313782439 GLASS    JACOB    8887345678

2 rows selected.
```

## NOT EXISTS

EXISTS is negated as NOT EXISTS.

**8**

| Usage | Meaning |
|-------|---------|
| WHERE NOT EXISTS<br>(SELECT EMPLOYEE_ID<br>FROM EMPLOYEE_TBL<br>WHERE EMPLOYEE_ID =<br>'333333333' | Searching to see whether<br>the employee_id<br>3333333333 is not in<br>the employee_tbl |

**TYPE**

```
SELECT MAX(COST)
FROM PRODUCTS_TBL
WHERE NOT EXISTS ( SELECT COST
              FROM PRODUCTS_TBL
              WHERE COST > 100 );
```

**OUTPUT**

```
MAX(COST)
----------
    59.99
```

The maximum cost for the table is displayed in this output, because there were not any records that existed where the cost was greater than 100.

## NOT UNIQUE

The UNIQUE operator is negated as NOT UNIQUE.

| Usage | Meaning |
|-------|---------|
| WHERE NOT UNIQUE<br>(SELECT SALARY<br>FROM EMPLOYEE_TBL) | Testing to see whether there are<br>salaries in the table that<br>are not unique |

# Arithmetic Operators

*Arithmetic operators* are used to perform mathematical functions in SQL—the same as in most other languages. There are four conventional operators for mathematical functions.

- \+ (addition)
- \- (subtraction)
- \* (multiplication)
- / (division)

## Addition

Addition is performed through the use of the plus (+) symbol.

| Usage | Meaning |
|---|---|
| SELECT SALARY + BONUS<br>FROM EMPLOYEE_PAY_TBL | The salary column is added with the bonus column for a total for each row of data |
| SELECT SALARY<br>FROM EMPLOYEE_PAY_TBL<br>WHERE SALARY + BONUS<br>> '40000' | Returns all rows that are greater than the total of the salary and bonus columns |

## Subtraction

Subtraction is performed using the minus (-) symbol.

| Usage | Meaning |
|---|---|
| SELECT SALARY - BONUS<br>FROM EMPLOYEE_PAY_TBL | The bonus column is subtracted from the salary column for the difference |
| SELECT SALARY<br>FROM EMPLOYEE_PAY_TBL<br>WHERE SALARY -<br>BONUS > '40000' | Returns all rows where the salary minus the bonus is greater than 40000 |

## Multiplication

Multiplication is performed by using the asterisk (*) symbol.

| Usage | Meaning |
|---|---|
| SELECT SALARY * 10<br>FROM EMPLOYEE_PAY_TBL | The salary column is multiplied by 10 |
| SELECT SALARY<br>FROM EMPLOYEE_PAY_TBL<br>WHERE SALARY * 10<br>> '40000' | Returns all rows where the product of the salary multiplied by 10 is greater than 40000 |

The pay rate in the following example is multiplied by 1.1, which increases the current pay rate by 10 percent:

```
SELECT EMP_ID, PAY_RATE, PAY_RATE * 1.1
FROM EMPLOYEE_PAY_TBL
WHERE PAY_RATE IS NOT NULL;
```

```
EMP_ID      PAY_RATE PAY_RATE*1.1
.........  ........... ............
```

8

```
442346889      14.75      16.225
220984332         11       12.1
443679012         15       16.5

3 rows selected.
```

# Division

Division is performed through the use of the slash (/) symbol.

| Usage | Meaning |
|-------|---------|
| SELECT SALARY / 10<br>FROM EMPLOYEE_PAY_TBL | The salary column is divided by 10 |
| FROM EMPLOYEE_PAY_TBL<br>WHERE SALARY / 10<br>> '40000' | Returns all rows that are greater than the salary |
| SELECT SALARY<br>FROM EMPLOYEE_PAY_TBL<br>WHERE SALARY / 10<br>> '40000' | Returns all rows where the salary divided by 10 is greater than 40000 |

# Arithmetic Operator Combinations

The arithmetic operators may be used in combinations with one another. Remember the rules of precedence in basic mathematics. Multiplication and division operations are performed first, then addition and subtraction operations. The only way the user has control over the order of the mathematical operations is through the use of parentheses. Parentheses surrounding an expression causes that expression to be evaluated as a block.

 *Precedence* is the order in which expressions are resolved in a mathematical expression or with embedded functions in SQL.

| Expression | Result |
|------------|--------|
| 1 + 1 * 5 | 6 |
| (1 + 1) * 5 | 10 |
| 10 - 4 / 2 + 1 | 9 |
| (10 - 4) / (2 + 1) | 2 |

In the following examples, notice that the placement of parentheses in an expression does not affect the outcome if only multiplication and division are involved. Precedence is not a factor in these cases.

| Expression | Result |
|------------|--------|
| 4 * 6 / 2 | 12 |
| (4 * 6) / 2 | 12 |
| 4 * (6 / 3) | 12 |

Here are some more examples:

```
SELECT SALARY * 10 + 1000
FROM EMPLOYEE_PAY_TBL
WHERE SALARY > 20000

SELECT SALARY / 52 + BONUS
FROM EMPLOYEE_PAY_TBL

SELECT (SALARY - 1000 + BONUS) / 52 * 1.1
FROM EMPLOYEE_PAY_TBL
```

Here is a rather wild example:

```
SELECT SALARY
FROM EMPLOYEE_PAY_TBL
WHERE SALARY < BONUS * 3 + 10 / 2 - 50
```

Because parentheses are not used, mathematical precedence takes effect, altering the value for BONUS tremendously for the condition.

**WARNING**

When combining arithmetic operators, remember to consider the rules of precedence. The absence of parentheses in a statement could render inaccurate results.

# Summary

You have been introduced to various operators available in SQL. You have learned the how's and why's of operators. You have seen examples of operators being used by themselves and in various combinations with one another, using the conjunctive-type operators AND and OR. You have learned the basic arithmetic functions: addition, subtraction, multiplication, and division. Comparison operators are used to test equality, inequality, less-than values, and greater-than values. Logical operators include BETWEEN, IN, LIKE, EXIST, ANY, and ALL. You are already experiencing how elements are added to SQL statements to further specify conditions and better control the processing and retrieving capabilities provided with SQL.

## Q&A

**Q Can I have more than one AND in the where clause?**

A Yes. In fact, all the operators can be used multiple times. An example would be

```
SELECT SALARY
FROM EMPLOYEE_PAY_TBL
WHERE SALARY > 20000
AND BONUS BETWEEN 1000 AND 3000
AND POSITION = 'VICE PRESIDENT'
```

**Q What happens if I use single quotation marks around a number datatype in a WHERE clause?**

**A** Your query still processes. Quotation marks are not necessary for number fields.

# Workshop

The following workshop is composed of a series of quiz questions and practical exercises. The quiz questions are designed to test your overall understanding of the current material. The practical exercises are intended to afford you the opportunity to apply the concepts discussed during the current hour, as well as build upon the knowledge acquired in previous hours of study. Please take time to complete the quiz questions and exercises before continuing. You may refer to the answers in Appendix C.

## Quiz

1. True or false: Both conditions when using the OR operator must be TRUE.
2. True or false: All specified values must match when using the IN operator.
3. True or false: The AND operator can be used in the SELECT and the WHERE clauses.
4. What, if anything, is wrong with the following SELECT statements?

a.

```
SELECT SALARY
FROM EMPLOYEE_PAY_TBL
WHERE SALARY BETWEEN 20000, 30000
```

b.

```
SELECT SALARY + DATE_HIRE
FROM EMPLOYEE_PAY_TBL
```

c.

```
SELECT SALARY, BONUS
FROM EMPLOYEE_PAY_TBL
WHERE DATE_HIRE BETWEEN 22-SEP-97
AND 23-NOV-97
AND POSITION = 'SALES'
OR POSITION = 'MARKETING'
AND EMPLOYEE_ID LIKE '%55%'
```

## Exercises

1. Using the CUSTOMER_TBL as described here:

```
describe customer_tbl
```

| Name | Null? | Type |
| --- | --- | --- |
| CUST_ID | NOT NULL | VARCHAR2(10) |
| CUST_NAME | NOT NULL | VARCHAR2(30) |
| CUST_ADDRESS | NOT NULL | VARCHAR2(20) |
| CUST_CITY | NOT NULL | VARCHAR2(12) |
| CUST_STATE | NOT NULL | CHAR(2) |
| CUST_ZIP | NOT NULL | CHAR(5) |
| CUST_PHONE | | NUMBER(10) |
| CUST_FAX | | NUMBER(10) |

Write a SELECT statement that returns customer IDs and customer names (alpha order) for customers that live in Indiana, Ohio, Michigan, and Illinois, and the customers names begin with the letters A or B.

2. Using the PRODUCTS_TBL as described:

```
describe products_tbl
```

| Name | Null? | Type |
| --- | --- | --- |
| PROD_ID | NOT NULL | VARCHAR2(10) |
| PROD_DESC | NOT NULL | VARCHAR2(25) |
| COST | NOT NULL | NUMBER(6,2) |

Write a SELECT statement that returns the product ID, prod_desc, and the product cost. Limit the product cost to range from $1.00 and $12.50.

8

# Hour 9

# Summarizing Data Results from a Query

In this hour you learn about SQL's aggregate functions. You can perform a variety of useful functions with aggregate functions.

The highlights of this hour include

- [ ] What are functions?
- [ ] How are functions used?
- [ ] When to use functions
- [ ] Using aggregate functions
- [ ] Summarizing data with aggregate functions
- [ ] Results from using functions

## What Are Aggregate Functions?

*Functions* are keywords in SQL used to manipulate values within columns for output purposes. A function is a command always used in conjunction with a column name or expression. There are several types of functions in SQL. This hour covers aggregate functions.

Aggregate functions are functions that count, summarize, and show limits of data. COUNT, SUM, MAX, MIN, and AVG are aggregate functions.

**NEW TERM**  An *aggregate function* is used to provide summarization information for a SQL statement, such as counts, totals, and averages.

The aggregate functions discussed in this hour are

- ☐ COUNT
- ☐ SUM
- ☐ MAX
- ☐ MIN
- ☐ AVG

The following queries show the data used for most of this hour's examples:

**TYPE**
```
select *
from products_tbl;
```

**OUTPUT**

| PROD_ID | PROD_DESC | COST |
|---------|-----------|------|
| 11235 | WITCHES COSTUME | 29.99 |
| 222 | PLASTIC PUMPKIN 18 INCH | 7.75 |
| 13 | FALSE PARAFFIN TEETH | 1.1 |
| 90 | LIGHTED LANTERNS | 14.5 |
| 15 | ASSORTED COSTUMES | 10 |
| 9 | CANDY CORN | 1.35 |
| 6 | PUMPKIN CANDY | 1.45 |
| 87 | PLASTIC SPIDERS | 1.05 |
| 119 | ASSORTED MASKS | 4.95 |
| 1234 | KEY CHAIN | 5.95 |
| 2345 | OAK BOOKSHELF | 59.99 |
| 7725 | LEATHER GLOVES | 24.99 |

12 rows selected.

Some employees do not have a pager number in the results of the following query:

**TYPE**
```
select emp_id, last_name, first_name, pager
from employee_tbl;
```

**OUTPUT**

| EMP_ID | LAST_NAM | FIRST_NA | PAGER |
|--------|----------|----------|-------|
| 311549902 | STEPHENS | TINA | |
| 442346889 | PLEW | LINDA | |
| 213764555 | GLASS | BRANDON | 3175709980 |
| 313782439 | GLASS | JACOB | 8887345678 |
| 220984332 | WALLACE | MARIAH | |
| 443679012 | SPURGEON | TIFFANY | |

6 rows selected.

# The COUNT Function

SYNTAX

The COUNT function is used to count rows or values of a column that do not contain a NULL value. When used with a query, the COUNT function returns a numeric value. When the COUNT function is used with the DISTINCT command, only the distinct rows are counted. ALL (opposite of DISTINCT) is the default; it is not necessary to include ALL in the syntax. Duplicate rows are counted if DISTINCT is not specified. One other option with the COUNT function is to use the COUNT with an asterisk. The COUNT, when used with an asterisk, counts all the rows of a table including duplicates, whether a NULL value is contained in a column or not. The syntax for the COUNT function is as follows:

```
COUNT [ (*) ¦ (DISTINCT ¦ ALL ] COLUMN NAME)
```

**NOTE**

> The DISTINCT command cannot be used with COUNT(*), but only with the COUNT(column_name).

| Usage | Meaning |
|---|---|
| SELECT COUNT(EMPLOYEE_ID)<br>FROM EMPLOYEE_PAY_ID | Counts all employee IDs |
| SELECT COUNT(DISTINCT SALARY)<br>FROM EMPLOYEE_PAY_TBL | Counts only the distinct rows |
| SELECT COUNT(ALL SALARY)<br>FROM EMPLOYEE_PAY_TBL | Counts all rows for SALARY |
| SELECT COUNT(*)<br>FROM EMPLOYEE_TBL | Counts all rows of the<br>employee table |

COUNT(*) is used in the following example to get a count of all records in the EMPLOYEE_TBL table. There are six employees.

**TYPE**

```
SELECT COUNT(*)
FROM EMPLOYEE_TBL;
```

**OUTPUT**

```
COUNT(*)
----------
         6
```

COUNT(EMP_ID) is used in the next example to get a count of all of the employee identifications that exist in the table. The returned count is the same as the last query, because all employees have an identification number.

**TYPE**
```
SELECT COUNT(EMP_ID)
FROM EMPLOYEE_TBL;
```

**OUTPUT**
```
COUNT(EMP_ID)
-----------
          6
```

COUNT(PAGER) is used in this example to get a count of all of the employee records that have a pager number. Only two employees had pager numbers.

**TYPE**
```
SELECT COUNT(PAGER)
FROM EMPLOYEE_TBL;
```

**OUTPUT**
```
COUNT(PAGER)
-----------
          2
```

The ORDERS_TBL table, shown here, is used in the next COUNT example:

**TYPE**
```
SELECT *
FROM ORDERS_TBL;
```

**OUTPUT**

| ORD_NUM | CUST_ID | PROD_ID | QTY | ORD_DATE |
|---------|---------|---------|-----|----------|
| 56A901  | 232     | 11235   | 1   | 22-OCT-97 |
| 56A917  | 12      | 907     | 100 | 30-SEP-97 |
| 32A132  | 43      | 222     | 25  | 10-OCT-97 |
| 16C17   | 090     | 222     | 2   | 17-OCT-97 |
| 18D778  | 287     | 90      | 10  | 17-OCT-97 |
| 23E934  | 432     | 13      | 20  | 15-OCT-97 |
| 90C461  | 560     | 1234    | 2   |          |

```
7 rows selected.
```

This last example obtains a count of all distinct product identifications in the ORDERS_TBL table.

**TYPE**
```
SELECT COUNT(DISTINCT(PROD_ID))
FROM ORDERS_TBL;
```

**OUTPUT**
```
COUNT(DISTINCT(PROD_ID))
------------------------
                       5
```

The PROD_ID 222 has two entries in the table, thus reducing the distinct values from 6 to 5.

**NOTE**

> Because the COUNT function counts the rows, datatypes do not play a part. The rows can contain columns with any datatype.

9

## The SUM **Function**

SYNTAX

The SUM function is used to return a total on the values of a column for a group of rows. The SUM function can also be used in conjunction with DISTINCT. When SUM is used with DISTINCT, only the distinct rows are totaled, which may not have much purpose. Your total is not accurate in that case, because rows of data are omitted. The syntax for the SUM function is as follows:

```
SUM ([ DISTINCT ] COLUMN NAME)
```

**NOTE**

> The value of an argument must be numeric in order to use the SUM function. The SUM function cannot be used on columns having a datatype other than numeric, such as character or date.

| *Usage* | *Meaning* |
|---|---|
| SELECT SUM(SALARY)<br>FROM EMPLOYEE_PAY_TBL | Totals the salaries |
| SELECT SUM(DISTINCT SALARY)<br>FROM EMPLOYEE_PAY_TBL | Totals the distinct salaries |

The *sum*, or total amount of all cost values, is being retrieved from the PRODUCTS_TBL table.

**TYPE**
```
SELECT SUM(COST)
FROM PRODUCTS_TBL;
```

**OUTPUT**
```
SUM(COST)
- - - - - - - - - -
   163.07
```

## The AVG **Function**

SYNTAX

The AVG function is used to find averages for a group of rows. When used with the DISTINCT command, the AVG function returns the average of the distinct rows. The syntax for the AVG function is as follows:

```
AVG ([ DISTINCT ] COLUMN NAME)
```

**NOTE**

> The value of the argument must be numeric in order for the AVG function to work.

| *Usage* | *Meaning* |
| --- | --- |
| SELECT AVG(SALARY) <br> FROM EMPLOYEE_PAY_TBL | Returns the average salary |
| SELECT AVG(DISTINCT SALARY) <br> FROM EMPLOYEE_PAY_TBL | Returns the distinct average salary |

The average value for all values in the PRODUCTS_TBL table's COST column is being retrieved in the first example.

**TYPE**

```
SELECT AVG(COST)
FROM PRODUCTS_TBL;
```

**OUTPUT**

```
AVG(COST)
----------
13.5891667
```

This example uses two aggregate functions in the same query. Because some employees are paid hourly and others paid salary, you want to retrieve the average value for both PAY_RATE and SALARY.

**TYPE**

```
SELECT AVG(PAY_RATE), AVG(SALARY)
FROM EMPLOYEE_PAY_TBL;
```

**OUTPUT**

```
AVG(PAY_RATE) AVG(SALARY)
------------- -----------
   13.5833333       30000
```

## The MAX Function

**SYNTAX**

The MAX function is used to return the maximum value for the values of a column in a group of rows. NULL values are ignored when using the MAX function. The DISTINCT command is an option. However, because the maximum value for all the rows is the same as the distinct maximum value, it is useless.

```
MAX([ DISTINCT ] COLUMN NAME)
```

| *Usage* | *Meaning* |
| --- | --- |
| SELECT MAX(SALARY) <br> FROM EMPLOYEE_PAY_TBL | Returns the highest salary |
| SELECT MAX(DISTINCT SALARY) <br> FROM EMPLOYEE_PAY_TBL | Returns the highest salary |

The following example returns the maximum value for the COST column in the PRODUCTS_TBL table:

9

**Type**
```
SELECT MAX(COST)
FROM PRODUCTS_TBL;
```

**Output**
```
MAX(COST)
----------
    59.99
```

# The MIN Function

SYNTAX

The MIN function returns the minimum value of a column for a group of rows. NULL values are ignored when using the MIN function. The DISTINCT command is an option. However, because the minimum value for all rows is the same as the minimum value for distinct rows, it is useless.

```
MIN([ DISTINCT ] COLUMN NAME)
```

| Usage | Meaning |
|-------|---------|
| SELECT MIN(SALARY)<br>FROM EMPLOYEE_PAY_TBL | Returns the lowest salary |
| SELECT MIN(DISTINCT SALARY)<br>FROM EMPLOYEE_PAY_TBL | Returns the lowest salary |

The following example returns the maximum value for the COST column in the PRODUCTS_TBL table:

**Type**
```
SELECT MIN(COST)
FROM PRODUCTS_TBL;
```

**Output**
```
MIN(COST)
----------
     1.05
```

**WARNING**

One very important thing to keep in mind when using aggregate functions with the DISTINCT command is that your query may not return the desired results. The purpose of aggregate functions is to return summarized data based on all rows of data in a table.

The final example combines aggregate functions with the use of arithmetic operators:

**Type**
```
SELECT COUNT(ORD_NUM), SUM(QTY),
       SUM(QTY) / COUNT(ORD_NUM) AVG_QTY
FROM ORDERS_TBL;
```

**Output**
```
COUNT(ORD_NUM)   SUM(QTY)   AVG_QTY
--------------  ---------- ----------
160 22.8571429
```

You have performed a count on all order numbers, figured the sum of all quantities ordered, and by dividing the two figures, have derived the average quantity of an item per order. You also created a column alias for the computation: AVG_QTY.

# Summary

Aggregate functions can be very useful and are quite simple to use. You have learned how to count values in columns, count rows of data in a table, get the maximum and minimum values for a column, figure the sum of the values in a column, and figure the average value for values in a column. Remember that NULL values are not considered when using aggregate functions, except when using the COUNT function in the format COUNT(*). Aggregate functions are the first functions in SQL that you have learned, but more follow. Aggregate functions can also be used for group values, which is discussed the next hour. As you learn about other functions, you see that the syntax of most functions are similar to one another and that their concepts of use are relatively easy to understand.

## Q&A

**Q  Why are NULL values ignored when using the MAX or MIN functions?**

A  A NULL value means that nothing is there.

**Q  Why don't datatypes matter when using the COUNT function?**

A  The COUNT function only counts rows.

# Workshop

The following workshop is composed of a series of quiz questions and practical exercises. The quiz questions are designed to test your overall understanding of the current material. The practical exercises are intended to afford you the opportunity to apply the concepts discussed during the current hour, as well as build upon the knowledge acquired in previous hours of study. Please take time to complete the quiz questions and exercises before continuing. You may refer to the answers in Appendix C.

## Quiz

1. True or false: The AVG function returns an average of all rows from a select column including any NULL values.
2. True or false: The SUM function is used to add column totals.
3. True or false: The COUNT(*) function counts all rows in a table.
4. Will the following SELECT statements work? If not, what will fix the statements?

9

a.

```
SELECT COUNT *
FROM EMPLOYEE_PAY_TBL;
```

b.

```
SELECT COUNT(EMPLOYEE_ID), SALARY
FROM EMPLOYEE_PAY_TBL;
```

c.

```
SELECT MIN(BONUS), MAX(SALARY)
FROM EMPLOYEE_PAY_TBL
WHERE SALARY > 20000;
```

# Exercises

1. Use the EMPLOYEE_PAY_TBL:

| EMP_ID | POSITION | DATE_HIRE | PAY_RATE | DATE_LAST | SALARY | BONUS |
|--------|----------|-----------|----------|-----------|--------|-------|
| 311549902 | MARKETING | 23-MAY-89 | | 01-MAY-97 | 30000 | 2000 |
| 442346889 | TEAM LEADER | 17-JUN-90 | 14.75 | 01-JUN-97 | | |
| 213764555 | SALES MANAGER | 14-AUG-94 | | 01-AUG-97 | 40000 | 3000 |
| 313782439 | SALESMAN | 28-JUN-97 | | | 20000 | 1000 |
| 220984332 | SHIPPER | 22-JUL-96 | 11 | 01-JUL-97 | | |
| 443679012 | SHIPPER | 14-JAN-91 | 15 | 01-JAN-97 | | |

```
6 rows selected.
```

Construct SQL statements to find:

a. The average salary

b. The maximum bonus

c. The total salaries

d. The minimum pay rate

e. The total rows in the table

# Hour 10

# Sorting and Grouping Data

You have learned how to query the database and return data in an organized fashion. You have learned how to sort data from a query. During this hour you learn how to break returned data from a query into groups for improved readability.

The highlights of this hour include:

- ☐ Why group data?
- ☐ The GROUP BY clause
- ☐ Group value functions
- ☐ The how and why of group functions
- ☐ Grouping by columns
- ☐ The GROUP BY versus the ORDER BY
- ☐ The HAVING clause

# Why Group Data?

*Grouping* data is the process of combining columns with duplicate values in a logical order. For instance, a database may contain information about customers; many customers live in different cities, while some customers live in the same city. You may want to execute a query that shows customer information for each particular city. You are grouping employee information by city, and a summarized report is created.

Suppose that you wanted to figure the average salary paid to employees according to each city. You would do this by using the aggregate function AVG on the SALARY column, as you learned last hour, and by using the GROUP BY clause to group the output by city.

Grouping data is accomplished through the use of the GROUP BY clause of a SELECT statement (query). Last hour, you learned how to use aggregate functions. During this lesson you see how aggregate functions are used in conjunction with the GROUP BY clause in order for the database to display results more effectively.

## The GROUP BY Clause

The GROUP BY clause is used in collaboration with the SELECT statement to arrange identical data into groups. The GROUP BY clause follows the WHERE clause in a SELECT statement and precedes the ORDER BY clause.

The position of the GROUP BY clause in a query:

```
SELECT
FROM
WHERE
GROUP BY
ORDER BY
```

The GROUP BY clause must follow the conditions in the WHERE clause, and must proceed the ORDER BY clause if one is used.

The SELECT statement's syntax, including the GROUP BY clause, follows.

**SYNTAX**

```
SELECT COLUMN1, COLUMN2
FROM TABLE1, TABLE2
WHERE CONDITIONS
GROUP BY COLUMN1, COLUMN2
ORDER BY COLUMN1, COLUMN2
```

The following sections give examples and explanations of the GROUP BY clause's use in a variety of situations.

### Grouping Selected Data

Grouping data is a simple process. The selected columns (the column list following the SELECT keyword in a query) are the columns that may be referenced in the GROUP BY clause.

If a column is not found in the SELECT statement, it may not be used in the GROUP BY clause. It is logical if you think about it—how can you group data on a report if the data is not displayed?

If the column name has been qualified, then the qualified name must go into the GROUP BY clause. The column name can also be represented by a number, which is discussed later this hour. When grouping the data, the order of columns grouped does not have to match the column order in the SELECT clause.

## Group Functions

Typical group functions—those that are used with the GROUP BY clause to arrange data in groups—include AVG, MAX, MIN, SUM, and COUNT. These are the aggregate functions that you learned about during Hour 9, "Summarizing Data Results from a Query." Remember that the aggregate functions were used for single values in Hour 9; now you use the aggregate functions for group values.

## Creating Groups and Using Aggregate Functions

There are conditions that the SELECT clause has that must be met when using GROUP BY. Specifically, whatever columns are selected must appear in the GROUP BY clause. The columns in the GROUP BY clause do not necessarily have to be in the same order as they appear in the SELECT clause. Should the columns in the SELECT clause be qualified, the qualified names of the columns must be used in the GROUP BY clause. Here are examples of syntax for the GROUP BY clause:

*Usage*

```
SELECT EMP_ID, CITY
FROM EMPLOYEE_TBL
GROUP BY CITY, EMP_ID;
```

 The SQL statement selects the emp_id and the city from the EMPLOYEE_TBL and groups the data returned by the city and then emp_id.

 **NOTE**

> Note the order of the columns selected, versus the order of the columns in the GROUP BY clause.

*Usage*

```
SELECT EMP_ID, SUM(SALARY)
FROM EMPLOYEE_PAY_TBL
GROUP BY SALARY, EMP_ID;
```

 This SQL statement returns the EMP_ID and the total of the salary groups, as well as groups both the salaries and the employee IDs.

*Usage*

```
SELECT SUM(SALARY)
FROM EMPLOYEE_PAY_TBL;
```

**ANALYSIS**  This SQL statement returns the total of all the salaries from the EMPLOYEE_PAY_TBL.

*Usage*

```
SELECT SUM(SALARY)
FROM EMPLOYEE_PAY_TBL
GROUP BY SALARY;
```

**ANALYSIS**  This SQL statement returns the totals for the different groups of salaries.

In this example, you can see that there are three distinct cities in the EMPLOYEE_TBL table. Practical examples using real data follow.

**TYPE**
```
SELECT CITY
FROM EMPLOYEE_TBL;
```

**OUTPUT**
```
CITY
-----------
GREENWOOD
INDIANAPOLIS
WHITELAND
INDIANAPOLIS
INDIANAPOLIS
INDIANAPOLIS

6 rows selected.
```

In the following example you select the city and a count of all records for each city. You see a count on each of the three distinct cities because you are using a GROUP BY clause.

**TYPE**
```
SELECT CITY, COUNT(*)
FROM EMPLOYEE_TBL
GROUP BY CITY;
```

**OUTPUT**
```
CITY           COUNT(*)
-----------    ---------
GREENWOOD             1
INDIANAPOLIS         4
WHITELAND            1

3 rows selected.
```

The following is a query from a temporary table created based on EMPLOYEE_TBL and EMPLOYEE_PAY_TBL. You soon learn how to join two tables for a query.

**10**

**TYPE**

```
select *
from emp_pay_tmp;
```

**OUTPUT**

```
CITY          LAST_NAM FIRST_NA  PAY_RATE    SALARY
------------- -------- -------- --------- ----------
GREENWOOD     STEPHENS TINA                  30000
INDIANAPOLIS  PLEW     LINDA       14.75
WHITELAND     GLASS    BRANDON               40000
INDIANAPOLIS  GLASS    JACOB                 20000
INDIANAPOLIS  WALLACE  MARIAH      11
INDIANAPOLIS  SPURGEON TIFFANY     15

6 rows selected.
```

Now you retrieve the average pay rate and salary on each distinct city using the aggregate function AVG. There is no average pay rate for GREENWOOD or WHITELAND, because no employees living in those cities are paid hourly.

**TYPE**

```
SELECT CITY, AVG(PAY_RATE), AVG(SALARY)
FROM EMP_PAY_TMP
GROUP BY CITY;
```

**OUTPUT**

```
CITY          AVG(PAY_RATE) AVG(SALARY)
------------- ------------- -----------
GREENWOOD                      30000
INDIANAPOLIS    13.5833333     20000
WHITELAND                      40000

3 rows selected.
```

In the next example you combine the use of multiple components in a query to return grouped data. You still want to see the average pay rate and salary, but only for INDIANAPOLIS and WHITELAND. You group the data by CITY, of which you have no choice, since you are using aggregate functions on the other columns. Lastly, you want to order the report by 2, then 3, which is the average pay rate, then average salary. Study the following details and output.

**TYPE**

```
SELECT CITY, AVG(PAY_RATE), AVG(SALARY)
FROM EMP_PAY_TMP
WHERE CITY IN ('INDIANAPOLIS','WHITELAND')
GROUP BY CITY
ORDER BY 2,3;
```

**OUTPUT**

```
CITY          AVG(PAY_RATE) AVG(SALARY)
------------- ------------- -----------
INDIANAPOLIS    13.5833333     20000
WHITELAND                      40000
```

Values are sorted before NULL values; therefore, the record for INDIANAPOLIS was displayed first. GREENWOOD was not selected, but if it were, its record would have been displayed before WHITELAND's record, since GREENWOOD's average salary is $30,000 (the second sort in the ORDER BY clause was on average salary).

The next example shows the use of the MAX and MIN aggregate functions with the GROUP BY clause.

```
SELECT CITY, MAX(PAY_RATE), MIN(SALARY)
FROM EMP_PAY_TMP
GROUP BY CITY;
```

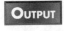

```
CITY            MAX(PAY_RATE)  MIN(SALARY)
------------    -------------  -----------
GREENWOOD                            30000
INDIANAPOLIS               15        20000
WHITELAND                            40000

3 rows selected.
```

## Representing Column Names with Numbers

Unlike the ORDER BY clause, the GROUP BY clause cannot be ordered by using an integer to represent the column name—except when using a UNION and the column names are different. Here is an example of representing column names with numbers:

```
SELECT EMP_ID, SUM(SALARY)
FROM EMPLOYEE_PAY_TBL
UNION
SELECT EMP_ID, SUM(PAY_RATE)
FROM EMPLOYEE_PAY_TBL
GROUP BY 2, 1;
```

 This SQL statement returns the employee ID and the group totals for the salaries. The order for the groupings is 2 representing salary, and 1 representing emp_id.

# GROUP BY Versus ORDER BY

You should understand that the GROUP BY clause works the same as the ORDER BY clause in that both are used to sort data. The ORDER BY clause is specifically used to sort data from a query; the GROUP BY clause must sort data from a query in order to properly group the data. Therefore, the GROUP BY clause can be used to sort data the same as the ORDER BY.

There are some disadvantages of using GROUP BY for sorting operations.

- [ ] All non-aggregate columns selected must be listed in the GROUP BY clause.
- [ ] Integers may not be used in the GROUP BY to represent columns after the SELECT keyword, similar to using the ORDER BY clause.
- [ ] The GROUP BY clause is generally not necessary unless using aggregate functions.

An example of performing sort operations utilizing the GROUP BY clause in place of the ORDER BY clause is shown here:

**TYPE**
```
SELECT LAST_NAME, FIRST_NAME, CITY
FROM EMPLOYEE_TBL
GROUP BY LAST_NAME;
```

**OUTPUT**
```
SELECT LAST_NAME, FIRST_NAME, CITY
                  *
ERROR at line 1:
ORA-00979: not a GROUP BY expression
```

In this example, an error was received from the database server stating that FIRST_NAME is not a GROUP BY expression. Remember that all columns and expressions in the SELECT must be listed in the GROUP BY clause, with the exception of aggregate columns (those columns targeted by an aggregate function).

In the next example, the previous problem is solved by adding all expressions in the SELECT to the GROUP BY clause:

**TYPE**
```
SELECT LAST_NAME, FIRST_NAME, CITY
FROM EMPLOYEE_TBL
GROUP BY LAST_NAME, FIRST_NAME, CITY;
```

**10**

**OUTPUT**
```
LAST_NAM FIRST_NA CITY
-------- -------- ------------
GLASS    BRANDON  WHITELAND
GLASS    JACOB    INDIANAPOLIS
PLEW     LINDA    INDIANAPOLIS
SPURGEON TIFFANY  INDIANAPOLIS
STEPHENS TINA     GREENWOOD
WALLACE  MARIAH   INDIANAPOLIS

6 rows selected.
```

In this example, the same columns were selected from the same table, but all columns in the GROUP BY clause are listed as they appeared after the SELECT keyword. The results were ordered by LAST_NAME first, FIRST_NAME second, and CITY third. These results could have been accomplished easier with the ORDER BY clause; however, it may help you better understand how the GROUP BY works if you can visualize how it must first sort data in order to group data results.

The following example shows a SELECT from EMPLOYEE_TBL and uses the GROUP BY to order by CITY, which leads into the next example.

**TYPE**
```
SELECT CITY, LAST_NAME
FROM EMPLOYEE_TBL
GROUP BY CITY, LAST_NAME;
```

**OUTPUT**
```
CITY         LAST_NAM
------------ --------
GREENWOOD    STEPHENS
INDIANAPOLIS GLASS
INDIANAPOLIS PLEW
INDIANAPOLIS SPURGEON
INDIANAPOLIS WALLACE
WHITELAND    GLASS

6 rows selected.
```

Notice the order of data in the previous results, as well as the LAST_NAME of the individual for each CITY. All employee records in the EMPLOYEE_TBL table are now counted, the results are grouped by CITY, but order by the count on each city first.

```
SELECT CITY, COUNT(*)
FROM EMPLOYEE_TBL
GROUP BY CITY
ORDER BY 2,1;
```

```
CITY            COUNT(*)
------------    ---------
GREENWOOD              1
WHITELAND             1
INDIANAPOLIS          4
```

Notice the order of the results. The results were first sorted by the count on each city (1-4), then by city. The count for the first two cities in the output is 1. Since the count is the same, which is the first expression in the ORDER BY clause, the city is then sorted; GREENWOOD is placed before WHITELAND.

Although the GROUP BY and the ORDER BY perform a similar function, there is one major difference. The GROUP BY is designed to group identical data, while the ORDER BY is designed merely to put data into a specific order. The GROUP BY and the ORDER BY can be used in the same SELECT statement, but must follow a specific order. The GROUP BY is always placed before the ORDER BY in the SELECT statement.

> **TIP**
> The GROUP BY can be used in the CREATE VIEW statement to sort data where the ORDER BY is not allowed in the CREATE VIEW statement. The CREATE VIEW statement is discussed in depth in Hour 20, "Creating and Using Views and Synonyms."

# The HAVING Clause

The HAVING clause, when used in conjunction with the GROUP BY in a SELECT statement, tells the GROUP BY which groups to include in the output. HAVING is to GROUP BY as WHERE is to SELECT. In other words, the WHERE clause places conditions on the selected columns, whereas the HAVING clause places conditions on groups created by the GROUP BY clause.

Here is the position of the HAVING clause in a query:

```
SELECT
FROM
WHERE
GROUP BY
HAVING
ORDER BY
```

The HAVING clause must follow the GROUP BY clause in a query, but must also precede the ORDER BY clause if used.

The syntax of the SELECT statement, including the HAVING clause, follows:

```
SELECT COLUMN1, COLUMN2
FROM TABLE1, TABLE2
WHERE CONDITIONS
GROUP BY COLUMN1, COLUMN2
HAVING CONDITIONS
ORDER BY COLUMN1, COLUMN2
```

In the following example, you select the average pay rate and salary for all cities except GREENWOOD. You group the output by CITY, but only want to display those groups (cities) that have an average salary greater than $20,000. You sort the results by average salary for each city.

```
SELECT CITY, AVG(PAY_RATE), AVG(SALARY)
FROM EMP_PAY_TMP
WHERE CITY <> 'GREENWOOD'
GROUP BY CITY
HAVING AVG(SALARY) > 20000
ORDER BY 3;
```

**OUTPUT**

```
CITY            AVG(PAY_RATE) AVG(SALARY)
------------    ------------- -----------
WHITELAND                           40000

    1 row selected.
```

Why was only one row returned by this query?

☐ The city GREENWOOD was eliminated from the WHERE clause.

☐ INDIANAPOLIS was deducted from the output because the average salary was 20000, which is not greater than 20000, but equal.

# Summary

You have learned how to group the results of a query using the GROUP BY clause. The GROUP BY clause is primarily used with aggregate SQL functions like SUM, AVG, MAX, MIN, and COUNT. The nature of GROUP BY is like that of the ORDER BY in that both sort query results. The GROUP BY clause must sort data in order to group results logically, but can also be used exclusively to sort data, although an ORDER BY is much simpler for this purpose. The HAVING clause, an extension to the GROUP BY clause, is used to place conditions on the established groups of a query; the WHERE clause is used to place conditions on a query's SELECT clause. During the next hour you learn a new arsenal of functions that allow you to further manipulate query results.

# Q&A

**Q Is using the GROUP BY clause mandatory when using the ORDER BY clause in a SELECT statement?**

**A** No. Using the GROUP BY clause is strictly optional, but can be very useful when used with ORDER BY.

**Q  What is a group value?**

**A**  Take the CITY column from the EMPLOYEE_TBL. If you select the employee's name and city, then grouped the output by city, all the cities that are identical are arranged together.

# Workshop

The following workshop is composed of a series of quiz questions and practical exercises. The quiz questions are designed to test your overall understanding of the current material. The practical exercises are intended to afford you the opportunity to apply the concepts discussed during the current hour, as well as build upon the knowledge acquired in previous hours of study. Please take time to complete the quiz questions and exercises before continuing. You may refer to the answers in Appendix C.

## Quiz

1. Will the following SQL statements work?

   a.
   ```
   SELECT SUM(SALARY), EMP_ID
   FROM EMPLOYEE_PAY_TBL
   GROUP BY 1 and 2;
   ```

   b.
   ```
   SELECT EMP_ID, MAX(SALARY)
   FROM EMPLOYEE_PAY_TBL
   GROUP BY SALARY, EMP_ID;
   ```

   c.
   ```
   SELECT EMP_ID, COUNT(SALARY)
   FROM EMPLOYEE_PAY_TBL
   ORDER BY EMP_ID
   GROUP BY SALARY;
   ```

2. True or false: You must also use the GROUP BY clause when using the HAVING clause.

3. True or false: This SQL statement returns a total of the salaries by groups:
   ```
   SELECT SUM(SALARY)
   FROM EMPLOYEE_PAY_TBL;
   ```

4. True or false: The columns selected must appear in the GROUP BY clause in the same order.

5. True or false: The HAVING clause tells the GROUP BY which groups to include.

## Exercises

1. Write a SQL statement that returns the employee ID, employee name, and city from the EMPLOYEE_TBL. Group by the city column first.

2. Write a SQL statement that returns the city and a count of all employees per city from EMPLOYEE_TBL. Add a HAVING clause to display only those cities that have a count of more than two employees.

**10**

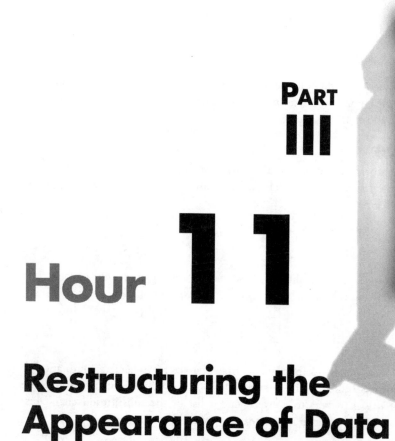

# Hour 11

# Restructuring the Appearance of Data

During this hour you learn how to restructure the appearance of output results using a wide array of functions, some ANSI standard functions, and other functions based on the standard and several variations used by some major SQL implementations.

This hour's highlights include:

☐ Introduction to character functions
☐ How and when to use character functions
☐ Examples of ANSI SQL functions
☐ Examples of common implementation-specific functions
☐ Overview of conversion functions
☐ How and when to use conversion functions

## The Concepts of ANSI Character Functions

*Character functions* are functions used to represent strings in SQL in formats alternate to how they are stored in the table. The first part of this chapter discusses the concepts for character functions as covered by ANSI. The second part of this hour shows real-world examples using functions that are specific to various SQL implementations. ANSI functions discussed in this chapter include concatenation, substring, TRANSLATE, CONVERT, and POSITION.

## Concatenation

*Concatenation* is the process of combining two separate strings into one string. For example, you may want to concatenate an individual's first and last names into a single string for the complete name.

JOHN concatenated with SMITH = JOHN SMITH

## Substring

The concept of *substring* is the capability to extract part of a string, or a "sub" of the string. For example, the following values are substrings of JOHNSON:

J       JOHN       JO       ON       SON       ...

## TRANSLATE

The TRANSLATE function is used to translate a string, character by character, into another string. There are normally three arguments with the TRANSLATE function: the string to be converted, a list of the characters to convert, and a list of the substitution characters. Implementation examples are shown in the next part of this hour.

## CONVERT

The CONVERT function is used to convert entire strings in a certain format to a string with the same length in another format, which is provided by the programmer. The functionality of CONVERT is much like that of the TRANSLATE function. As a matter of fact, conversions usually occur through the use of the TRANSLATE function, or another, similar function that may be provided with a specific SQL implementation.

## POSITION

The POSITION function is used to return the actual position of a string within another string. For instance, you may want to return the position of the character "M" in the string SMITH. A POSITION function type can be used to return the value 2, which is the position in the target string for the searched character (or string).

# Various Common Character Functions

Character functions are used mainly to compare, join, search, and extract a segment of a string or a value in a column. There are several character functions available to the SQL programmer.

11

The following sections illustrate the application of ANSI concepts in some of the leading implementations of SQL, such as in Oracle, Sybase, SQLBase, Informix, and SQL Server.

**NOTE**

> The ANSI concepts discussed in this book are just that—concepts. Standards provided by ANSI are simply guidelines for how the use of SQL in a relational database should be implemented. With that thought, keep in mind that the specific functions discussed in this chapter are not necessarily the exact functions that you may use in your particular implementation. Yes, the concepts are the same and the way the functions work are generally the same, but function names and actual syntax may differ.

## Concatenation

Concatenation, along with most other functions, is represented slightly different among various implementations. The following examples show the use of concatenation in Oracle and SQL Server.

*In Oracle*

```
SELECT 'JOHN' ¦¦ 'SON'                    returns          JOHNSON
```

*In SQL Server*

```
SELECT 'JOHN' + 'SON'                     returns          JOHNSON
```

**SYNTAX**

The syntax for Oracle is

```
column_name ¦¦ [ '' ¦¦ ] column_name [ column_name ]
```

The syntax for SQL Server is

```
column_name + [ '' + ] column_name [ column_name ]
```

| Usage | Meaning |
|---|---|
| SELECT CITY + STATE FROM EMPLOYEE_TBL; | This SQL Server statement concatenates the values for city and state into one value. |

*continues*

11

| Usage | Meaning |
|-------|---------|
| `SELECT CITY ||',` <br> `'||STATEFROM` <br> `EMPLOYEE_TBL;` | This Oracle statement concatenates the values for city and state into one value, placing a comma between the values for city and state. |
| `SELECT CITY + '` <br> `' + STATE` <br> `FROM EMPLOYEE_TBL;` | This SQL Server statement concatenates the values for city and state into one value, placing a space between the two original values. |

Example:

```
SELECT LAST_NAME || ', ' || FIRST_NAME NAME
FROM EMPLOYEE_TBL;
```

```
NAME
------------------
STEPHENS, TINA
PLEW, LINDA
GLASS, BRANDON
GLASS, JACOB
WALLACE, MARIAH
SPURGEON, TIFFANY

6 rows selected.
```

> **NOTE**
>
> Notice the use of single quotation marks and a comma in the preceding SQL statement. Most characters and symbols are allowed if enclosed by single quotations marks. Some implementations may use double quotation marks for literal strings values.

## TRANSLATE

The TRANSLATE function searches a string of characters and checks for a specific character, makes note of the position found, and it searches the replacement string at the same position, then it replaces that character with the new value. The syntax is

`TRANSLATE(CHARACTER SET, VALUE1, VALUE2)`

| Usage | Meaning |
|-------|---------|
| `SELECT TRANSLATE` <br> `(CITY,'IND','ABC'` | This SQL statement substitutes every |

11

| Usage | Meaning |
|---|---|
| `FROM EMPLOYEE_TBL;` | occurrence of I in the string with A, replaces all occurrences of N with B, and D with C. |

The following example illustrates the use of the TRANSLATE with real data:

**TYPE**
```
SELECT CITY, TRANSLATE(CITY,'IND','ABC')
FROM EMPLOYEE_TBL;
```

**OUTPUT**
```
CITY          TRANSLATE(CI
------------  ------------
GREENWOOD     GREEBWOOC
INDIANAPOLIS  ABCAABAPOLAS
WHITELAND     WHATELABC
INDIANAPOLIS  ABCAABAPOLAS
INDIANAPOLIS  ABCAABAPOLAS
INDIANAPOLIS  ABCAABAPOLAS

6 rows selected.
```

Notice that in this example that all occurrences of I were replaced with A, N with B, and D with C. In the city INDIANAPOLIS, IND was replaced with ABC, but in GREENWOOD, D was replaced with C. Also notice how the value WHITELAND was translated.

## REPLACE

**SYNTAX**
The REPLACE function is used to replace every occurrence of a character(s) with specified character(s). The use of this function is similar to the TRANSLATE function, only one specific character or string is replaced within another string. The syntax is

```
REPLACE('VALUE', 'VALUE', [ NULL ] 'VALUE')
```

| Usage | Meaning |
|---|---|
| `SELECT REPLACEFIRST_`<br>`NAME, 'T', 'B')`<br>`FROM EMPLOYEE_TBL` | This statement returns all the first names and changes any occurrence of T to a B. |

**TYPE**
```
SELECT CITY, REPLACE(CITY,'I','Z')
FROM EMPLOYEE_TBL;
```

**OUTPUT**
```
CITY          REPLACE(CITY
------------  ------------
GREENWOOD     GREENWOOD
INDIANAPOLIS  ZNDZANAPOLZS
WHITELAND     WHZTELAND
INDIANAPOLIS  ZNDZANAPOLZS
INDIANAPOLIS  ZNDZANAPOLZS
INDIANAPOLIS  ZNDZANAPOLZS

6 rows selected.
```

11

## UPPER

Most implementations have a way to control the case of data by using functions. The UPPER function is used to convert lowercase letters to uppercase letters for a specific string.

The syntax is as follows:

```
UPPER(character string)
```

| Usage | Meaning |
|-------|---------|
| SELECT UPPER(LAST_NAME)<br>FROM EMPLOYEE_TBL; | This SQL statement converts all characters in the column LAST_NAME to uppercase. |

**TYPE**

```
SELECT UPPER(CITY)
FROM EMPLOYEE_TBL;
```

**OUTPUT**

```
UPPER(CITY)
-----------
GREENWOOD
INDIANAPOLIS
WHITELAND
INDIANAPOLIS
INDIANAPOLIS
INDIANAPOLIS

6 rows selected.
```

## LOWER

Converse of the UPPER function, the LOWER function is used to convert uppercase letters to lowercase letters for a specific string.

The syntax is as follows:

```
LOWER(character string)
```

| Usage | Meaning |
|-------|---------|
| SELECT LOWER(LAST_NAME)<br>FROM EMPLOYEE_TBL; | This SQL statement converts all characters in the column LAST_NAME to lowercase. |

11

```
SELECT LOWER(CITY)
FROM EMPLOYEE_TBL;
```

```
LOWER(CITY)
-----------
greenwood
indianapolis
whiteland
indianapolis
indianapolis
indianapolis

6 rows selected.
```

## SUBSTR

Taking an expression's substring is common in most implementations of SQL, but the function name may differ, as shown in the following Oracle and SQL Server examples.

The syntax for Oracle is

```
SUBSTR(COLUMN NAME, STARTING POSITION, LENGTH)
```

The syntax for SQL Server is

```
SUBSTRING(COLUMN NAME, STARTING POSITION, LENGTH)
```

The only difference between the two implementations is the spelling of the function name.

| Usage | Meaning |
| --- | --- |
| SELECT SUBSTRING<br>(EMP_ID,1,3)<br>FROM EMPLOYEE_TBL | This SQL statement returns the first three characters of EMP_ID. |
| SELECT SUBSTRING<br>(EMP_ID,4,2)<br>FROM EMPLOYEE_TBL | This SQL statement returns the fourth and fifth characters of EMP_ID. |
| SELECT SUBSTRING<br>(EMP_ID,6,4)<br>FROM EMPLOYEE_TBL | This SQL statement returns the sixth through the tenth characters of EMP_ID. |

An example using Microsoft SQL Server:

**TYPE**

```
SELECT EMP_ID, SUBSTRING(EMP_ID,1,3)
FROM EMPLOYEE_TBL
```

**OUTPUT**

```
EMP_ID     SUB
---------  ---
311549902  311
442346889  442
213764555  213
313782439  313
220984332  220
443679012  443

6 rows affected.
```

An example using Oracle7:

**TYPE**

```
SELECT EMP_ID, SUBSTRING(EMP_ID,1,3)
FROM EMPLOYEE_TBL
```

**OUTPUT**

```
EMP_ID     SUB
---------  ---
311549902  311
442346889  442
213764555  213
313782439  313
220984332  220
443679012  443

6 rows selected.
```

**NOTE**

Notice the difference between the feedback of the two queries. The first example returns the feedback 6 rows affected and the second returns 6 rows selected. You see differences such as this between implementations.

## INSTR

**SYNTAX**

The INSTR function is a variation of the POSITION function; it is used to search a string of characters for a specific set of characters and report the position of those characters.

```
INSTR(COLUMN NAME, 'SET',
[ START POSITION [ , OCCURRENCE ] ]);
```

11

| Usage | Meaning |
|-------|---------|
| SELECT INSTR(STATE<br>,'I',1,1)<br>FROM EMPLOYEE_TBL; | This SQL statement returns the position of the first occurrence of the letter I for each state in EMPLOYEE_TBL. |

**TYPE**

```
SELECT PROD_DESC,
       INSTR(PROD_DESC,'A',1,1)
FROM PRODUCTS_TBL;
```

**OUTPUT**

```
PROD_DESC                    INSTR(PROD_DESC,'A',1,1)
--------------------         ------------------------
WITCHES COSTUME                                     0
PLASTIC PUMPKIN 18 INCH                             3
FALSE PARAFFIN TEETH                                2
LIGHTED LANTERNS                                   10
ASSORTED COSTUMES                                   1
CANDY CORN                                          2
PUMPKIN CANDY                                      10
PLASTIC SPIDERS                                     3
ASSORTED MASKS                                      1

9 rows selected.
```

Notice that if the searched character A was not found in a string, the value 0 was returned for the position.

## LTRIM

**SYNTAX**

The LTRIM function is another way of clipping part of a string. This function and SUBSTRING are in the same family. LTRIM is used to trim characters from the left of a string. The syntax is

```
LTRIM(CHARACTER STRING [ ,'set' ])
```

| Usage | Meaning |
|-------|---------|
| SELECT LTRIM(FIRST_<br>NAME,'LES')<br>FROM CUSTOMER_TBL<br>WHERE FIRST_NAME =<br>'LESLIE'; | This SQL statement trims the characters LES from the left of all names that are LESLIE. |

**TYPE**
```
SELECT POSITION, LTRIM(POSITION,'SALES')
FROM EMPLOYEE_PAY_TBL;
```

**OUTPUT**
```
POSITION          LTRIM(POSITION,
--------------    ---------------
MARKETING         MARKETING
TEAM LEADER       TEAM LEADER
SALES MANAGER     MANAGER
SALESMAN          MAN
SHIPPER           HIPPER
SHIPPER           HIPPER
```

6 rows selected.

The S in SHIPPER was trimmed off, even though SHIPPER does not contain the string SALES. The first four characters of SALES were ignored. The searched characters must appear in the same order of the search string and must be on the far left of the string.

## RTRIM

**SYNTAX**

Like the LTRIM, the RTRIM function is used to trim characters from the right of a string. The syntax is

```
RTRIM(CHARACTER STRING [ ,'set' ])
```

| Usage | Meaning |
| --- | --- |
| SELECT RTRIM(FIRST_<br>NAME, 'ON'<br>FROM EMPLOYEE_TBL<br>WHERE FIRST_NAME =<br>'BRANDON'; | This SQL statement returns the first name BRANDON and trims the ON, leaving BRAND as a results. |

**TYPE**
```
SELECT POSITION, RTRIM(POSITION,'ER')
FROM EMPLOYEE_PAY_TBL;
```

**OUTPUT**
```
POSITION          RTRIM(POSITION,
--------------    ---------------
MARKETING         MARKETING
TEAM LEADER       TEAM LEAD
SALES MANAGER     SALES MANAG
SALESMAN          SALESMAN
SHIPPER           SHIPP
SHIPPER           SHIPP
```

6 rows selected.

The string ER was trimmed from the right of all applicable strings.

## DECODE

**SYNTAX**

The DECODE function is not ANSI—at least not at the time of this writing—but its use is shown here because of its great power. This function is used in SQLBase, Oracle, and possibly other implementations. DECODE is used to search a string for a value or string, and if the string is found, an alternate string is displayed as part of the query results. The syntax is

```
DECODE(COLUMN NAME, 'SEARCH1', 'RETURN1',[ 'SEARCH2', 'RETURN2' ,'DEFAULT
➡VALUE'])
```

| Usage | Meaning |
|-------|---------|
| SELECT DECODE(LAST_NAME, 'SMITH', 'JONES', 'OTHER') FROM EMPLOYEE_ TBL; | This query searches the value of all last names in EMPLOYEE_TBL; if the value SMITH is found, JONES is displayed in its place. Any other names are displayed as OTHER, which is called the *default value*. |

In the following example, DECODE is used on the values for CITY in EMPLOYEE_TBL:

**TYPE**
```
SELECT CITY,
       DECODE(CITY,'INDIANAPOLIS','INDY',
                   'GREENWOOD','GREEN', 'OTHER')
FROM EMPLOYEE_TBL;
```

**OUTPUT**
```
CITY          DECOD
------------  ----
GREENWOOD     GREEN
INDIANAPOLIS  INDY
WHITELAND     OTHER
INDIANAPOLIS  INDY
INDIANAPOLIS  INDY
INDIANAPOLIS  INDY

6 rows selected.
```

The output shows the value INDIANAPOLIS displayed as INDY, GREENWOOD displayed as GREEN, and all other cities displayed as OTHER.

# Miscellaneous Character Functions

The following sections show a few other character functions worth mentioning. Once again, these are functions that are fairly common among major implementations.

**11**

## Finding a Value's Length

**SYNTAX**

The LENGTH function is a common function used to find the length of a string, number, date, or expression in bytes. The syntax is

LENGTH(CHARACTER STRING)

| Usage | Meaning |
|---|---|
| SELECT LENGTH<br>(LAST_NAME)<br>FROM EMPLOYEE_TBL; | This SQL statement returns the length of the last name for each employee. |

**TYPE**
```
select prod_desc, length(prod_desc)
from products_tbl;
```

**OUTPUT**

| PROD_DESC | LENGTH(PROD_DESC) |
|---|---|
| WITCHES COSTUME | 15 |
| PLASTIC PUMPKIN 18 INCH | 23 |
| FALSE PARAFFIN TEETH | 19 |
| LIGHTED LANTERNS | 16 |
| ASSORTED COSTUMES | 17 |
| CANDY CORN | 10 |
| PUMPKIN CANDY | 13 |
| PLASTIC SPIDERS | 15 |
| ASSORTED MASKS | 14 |

9 rows selected.

## NVL (NULL Value)

**SYNTAX**

The NVL function is used to return data from one expression if another expression is NULL. NVL can be used with most datatypes; however, the value and the substitute must be the same datatype. The syntax is

NVL('VALUE', 'SUBSTITUTION')

| Usage | Meaning |
|---|---|
| SELECT NVL(SALARY,<br>'00000') FROM<br>EMPLOYEE_PAY_TBL; | This SQL statement NULLs values and substitutes 00000 for any NULL values. |

**TYPE**
```
SELECT PAGER, NVL(PAGER,9999999999)
FROM EMPLOYEE_TBL;
```

**OUTPUT**

| PAGER | NVL(PAGER, |
|---|---|
| | 9999999999 |
| | 9999999999 |

**11**

```
3175709980 3175709980
8887345678 8887345678
           9999999999
           9999999999
```

6 rows selected.

Only NULL values were represented as 9999999999.

## LPAD

LPAD (left pad) is used to add characters or spaces to the left of a string. The syntax is

```
LPAD(CHARACTER SET)
```

The following example pads periods to the left of each product description, totaling 30 characters between the actual value and padded periods.

**TYPE**
```
SELECT LPAD(PROD_DESC,30,'.') PRODUCT
FROM PRODUCTS_TBL;
```

**OUTPUT**
```
PRODUCT
------------------------------
..............WITCHES COSTUME
.......PLASTIC PUMPKIN 18 INCH
..........FALSE PARAFFIN TEETH
.............LIGHTED LANTERNS
............ASSORTED COSTUMES
...................CANDY CORN
................PUMPKIN CANDY
...............PLASTIC SPIDERS
...............ASSORTED MASKS
```

9 rows selected.

## RPAD

The RPAD (right pad) is used to add characters or spaces to the right of a string. The syntax is

```
RPAD(CHARACTER SET)
```

The following example pads periods to the right of each product description, totaling 30 characters between the actual value and padded periods.

**TYPE**
```
SELECT RPAD(PROD_DESC,30,'.') PRODUCT
FROM PRODUCTS_TBL;
```

**OUTPUT**
```
PRODUCT
------------------------------
WITCHES COSTUME...............
PLASTIC PUMPKIN 18 INCH.......
FALSE PARAFFIN TEETH..........
LIGHTED LANTERNS..............
```

```
ASSORTED COSTUMES.............
CANDY CORN...................
PUMPKIN CANDY................
PLASTIC SPIDERS..............
ASSORTED MASKS...............

9 rows selected.
```

## What Does It Sound Like?

The SOUNDEX function is used to return expressions that sound like another expression. This function is used when searching for a value for which you do not know the exact spelling, or like values that have been entered inconsistently. The syntax is:

```
WHERE SOUNDEX(EXPRESSION) = SOUNDEX(EXPRESSION)
```

**TYPE**
```
SELECT LAST_NAME
FROM EMPLOYEE_TBL
WHERE SOUNDEX(LAST_NAME) = SOUNDEX('STEVENS')
```

**OUTPUT**
```
LAST_NAM
--------
STEPHENS
```

```
1 row selected.
```

## ASCII

The ASCII function is used to return the ASCII (American Standard Code for Information Interchange) representation of the leftmost character of a string. The syntax is

```
ASCII(CHARACTER SET)
```

Examples:

```
ASCII('A') returns 65
ASCII('B') returns 66
ASCII('C') returns 67
```

For more information, refer to the ASCII chart in Appendix B of this book.

# Mathematical Functions

Mathematical functions are fairly standard across implementations. These are functions that allow you to manipulate numeric values in a database according to mathematical rules.

The most common functions include:

| | |
|---|---|
| Absolute value | (ABS) |
| Rounding | (ROUND) |
| Square root | (SQRT) |

| | |
|---|---|
| Sign values | (SIGN) |
| Power | (POWER) |
| Ceiling and floor values | (CEIL, FLOOR) |
| Exponential values | (EXP) |
| SIN, COS, TAN | |

The general syntax of most mathematical functions is:

```
FUNCTION(EXPRESSION)
```

# Conversion Functions

*Conversion functions* are used to convert a datatype into another datatype. For instance, there may be times when you want to convert character data into numeric data. You may have data that is normally stored in character format, but occasionally you want to convert the character format to numeric for the purpose of making calculations. Mathematical functions and computations are not allowed on data that is represented in character format.

General types of data conversions:

- ☐ Character to numeric
- ☐ Numeric to character
- ☐ Character to date
- ☐ Date to character

The first two types of conversions are discussed in this hour. The remaining conversion types are discussed during Hour 12, "Understanding Dates and Time," after date and time storage is discussed in more detail.

**NOTE**

Some implementations may implicitly convert datatypes when necessary.

## Converting Character Strings to Numbers

There are two things you should notice regarding the differences between numeric datatypes and character string datatypes.

1. Arithmetic expressions and functions may be used on numeric values.
2. Numeric values are right-justified, whereas character string datatypes are left-justified in output results.

When a character string is converted to a numeric value, the value takes on the two attributes just mentioned.

Some implementations may not have functions to convert character strings to numbers, while some have conversion functions such as this. In either case, consult your implementation documentation for specific syntax and rules for conversions.

**NOTE**

Characters in a character string being converted to a number must typically be 0 through 9; the addition symbol, minus symbol, and period can also be used to represent positive numbers, negative numbers, and decimals. For instance, the string STEVE cannot be converted to a number, whereas an individual's social security number could be stored as a character string, but could easily be converted to a numeric value via use of a conversion function.

An example of a numeric conversion using an Oracle conversion function:

**TYPE**

```
SELECT EMP_ID, TO_NUMBER(EMP_ID)
FROM EMPLOYEE_TBL;
```

**OUTPUT**

```
EMP_ID              TO_NUMBER(EMP_ID)
--------            -----------------
311549902           311549902
442346889           442346889
213764555           213764555
313782439           313782439
220984332           220984332
443679012           443679012

6 rows selected.
```

The employee identification is right-justified following the conversion.

**TIP**

The justification of data is the simplest way to identify a column's datatype.

## Converting Numbers to Strings

The conversion of numeric values to character strings is precisely the opposite of converting characters to numbers.

An example of converting a numeric value to a character string using a Transact-SQL conversion function for Microsoft SQL Server follows:

**TYPE**
```
SELECT PAY = PAY_RATE, NEW_PAY = STR(PAY_RATE)
FROM EMPLOYEE_PAY_TBL
WHERE PAY_RATE IS NOT NULL;
```

**OUTPUT**
```
       PAY NEW_PAY
---------- --------------------------------------------
      17.5 17.5
     14.75 14.75
     18.25 18.25
      12.8 12.8
        11 11
        15 15

6 rows affected.
```

Here's the same example using an Oracle conversion function:

**TYPE**
```
SELECT PAY_RATE, TO_CHAR(PAY_RATE)
FROM EMPLOYEE_PAY_TBL
WHERE PAY_RATE IS NOT NULL;
```

**OUTPUT**
```
  PAY_RATE TO_CHAR(PAY_RATE)
---------- --------------------------------------------
      17.5 17.5
     14.75 14.75
     18.25 18.25
      12.8 12.8
        11 11
        15 15

6 rows selected.
```

# The Concept of Combining Character Functions

Most functions can be combined in a single SQL statement. SQL would be far too limited if function combinations were not allowed. The following examples show how some functions may be combined with one another in a query:

**TYPE**
```
SELECT LAST_NAME || ', ' || FIRST_NAME NAME,
       SUBSTR(EMP_ID,1,3) || '-' ||
       SUBSTR(EMP_ID,4,2) || '-' ||
       SUBSTR(EMP_ID,6,4) ID
FROM EMPLOYEE_TBL;
```

**OUTPUT**
```
NAME                 ID
-------------------- ----------
STEPHENS, TINA       311-54-9902
PLEW, LINDA          442-34-6889
GLASS, BRANDON       213-76-4555
GLASS, JACOB         313-78-2439
WALLACE, MARIAH      220-98-4332
SPURGEON, TIFFANY    443-67-9012

6 rows selected.
```

This example combines two functions in the query (concatenation with substring). By pulling the EMP_ID column apart into three pieces, you can concatenate those pieces with dashes in order to render a readable social security number.

**TYPE**

```
SELECT SUM(LENGTH(LAST_NAME) + LENGTH(FIRST_NAME)) TOTAL
FROM EMPLOYEE_TBL;
```

**OUTPUT**

```
      TOTAL
  ----------
         71
```

1 row selected.

This example uses the LENGTH function and the arithmetic operator (+) to add the length of the first name to the length of the last name for each column; the sum function then finds the total length of all first and last names.

**NOTE**

> When embedding functions within functions in a SQL statement, remember that the innermost function is resolved first, then each function is subsequently resolved from the inside out.

# Summary

You have been introduced to various functions used in a SQL statement—usually a query—to modify or enhance the way output is represented. Those functions include character, mathematical, and conversion functions. It is very important to realize that the ANSI standard is a guideline for how SQL should be implemented by vendors, but does not dictate the exact syntax or necessarily place limits on vendors' innovations. Most vendors have standard functions and conform to the ANSI concepts, but each vendor has his or her own, specific list of available functions. The function name may differ and the syntax may differ, but the concepts with all functions are the same.

## Q&A

**Q Are all the functions in the ANSI standard?**

**A** No, not all functions are exactly ANSI SQL. Functions, like datatypes, are often implementation-dependent. Several examples of functions from selected implementations are included, however, because so many implementations use similar functions (although they may slightly differ). Check your particular implementation for available functions and their usage.

**Q Is the data actually changed in the database when using functions?**

**A** No. Data is not changed in the database when using functions. Functions are typically used in queries in order to manipulate the output's appearance.

**11**

# Workshop

The following workshop is composed of a series of quiz questions and practical exercises. The quiz questions are designed to test your overall understanding of the current material. The practical exercises are intended to afford you the opportunity to apply the concepts discussed during the current hour, as well as build upon the knowledge acquired in previous hours of study. Please take time to complete the quiz questions and exercises before continuing. You may refer to the answers in Appendix C.

## Quiz

Match the Descriptions with the possible Functions.

| | DESCRIPTIONS | FUNCTIONS |
|---|---|---|
| a. | Used to select a portion of a character string. | \|\|<br>RPAD<br>LPAD |
| b. | Used to trim characters from either the right or left of a string. | LENGTH<br>UPPER<br>SOUNDEX |
| c. | Used to change all letters to lowercase. | LTRIM<br>RTRIM<br>LOWER |
| d. | Used to find the length of a string. | SUBSTR |
| e. | Used to combine strings. | |

1. True or false: The SOUNDEX function is used to compare strings that may sound alike.
2. True or false: The outermost function is always resolved first when functions are embedded within other functions in a query.

## Exercises

1. Use the appropriate function to convert the string hello to all uppercase letters.
2. Use the appropriate function to print only the first four characters of the string JOHNSON.
3. Use the function to concatenate the strings JOHN and SON.

11

# Hour 12

# Understanding Dates and Time

In this hour you learn about the nature of dates and time in SQL. Not only does this chapter discuss the DATETIME data type in more detail; you see how some implementations use dates, some of the common rules, and how to extract the date and time in a desired format. The highlights of this hour include:

- ☐ Understanding dates and time
- ☐ How the date and time are stored
- ☐ Typical date and time formats
- ☐ How to use date functions
- ☐ How to use date conversions

**NOTE**

> As you know by now, there are many different SQL implementations. This book shows the ANSI standard and the most common non-standard functions, commands, and operators. Oracle is used for the examples. Even in Oracle, the date can be stored in different formats. You must check your particular implementation for the date storage. No matter how it is stored, your implementation should have functions that convert date formats.

# How Is a Date Stored?

Each implementation has a default storage format for the date and time. This default storage often varies among different implementations as does other datatypes for each implementation. The following sections begin by reviewing the standard format of the `datetime` datatype and its elements. Then you see the datatypes for date and time in some popular implementations of SQL, including Oracle, Sybase, and Microsoft SQL Server.

## Standard Data Types for Date and Time

There are three standard SQL datatypes for date and time (`DATETIME`) storage:

| Datatype | Usage |
|---|---|
| DATE | Stores date literals |
| TIME | Stores time literals |
| TIMESTAMP | Stores date and time literals |

Format and range of valid values for each datatype:

**DATE**

Format: YYYY-MM-DD
Range: 0001-01-01 to 9999-12-31

**TIME**

Format: HH:MI:SS.*nn*...
Range: 00:00:00... to 23:59:61.999...

**TIMESTAMP**

Format: YYYY-MM-DD HH:MI:SS.*nn*...
Range: 0001-01-01 00:00:00... to 9999-12-31 23:59:61.999...

### DATETIME **Elements**

DATETIME elements are those elements pertaining to date and time that are included as part of a DATETIME definition. Following, we have listed the constrained DATETIME elements and a valid range of values for each element.

| | |
|---|---|
| YEAR | 0001 to 9999 |
| MONTH | 01 to 12 |
| DAY | 01 to 31 |
| HOUR | 00 to 23 |
| MINUTE | 00 to 59 |
| SECOND | 00.000… to 61.999… |

Seconds can be represented as a decimal, allowing the expression of tenths of a second, hundredths of a second, milliseconds, and so on. Each of these elements are self explanatory and are elements of time that we deal with on a daily basis.

## Implementation Specific Datatypes

As with other datatypes, each implementation provides its own representation and syntax. This section shows how three products (Oracle, Sybase, SQLBase) have been implemented with date and time.

| Product | Datatype | Use |
|---|---|---|
| Oracle | DATE | Stores both date and time information. |
| Sybase | DATETIME | Stores both date and time information. |
| | SMALLDATETIME | Stores both date and time information, but includes a smaller date range than DATETIME. |
| SQLBase | DATETIME | Stores both date and time information. |
| | TIMESTAMP | Stores both date and time information. |
| | DATE | Stores a date value. |
| | TIME | Stores a time value. |

12

**NOTE**

> Each implementation has its own specific datatype(s) for date and time information. However, most implementations comply with the ANSI standard in the fact that all elements of the date and time are included in their associated datatypes. The way the date is internally stored is implementation dependent.

# Date Functions

Date functions are available in SQL depending on the options with each specific implementation. *Date functions*, similar to character string functions, are used to manipulate the representation of date and time data. Available date functions are often used to format the output of dates and time in an appealing format, compare date values with one another, compute intervals between dates, and so on.

## The Current Date

You may have already raised the question: How do I get the current date from the database? The need to retrieve the current date from the database may originate from several situations, but the current date is normally returned either to compare to a stored date or to return the value of the current date as some sort of timestamp.

The current date is ultimately stored on the host computer for the database, and is called the *system date*. The database, which interfaces with the appropriate operating system, has the capability to retrieve the system date for its own purpose or to resolve database requests, such as queries.

Take a look at a couple of methods of attaining the system date based on commands from two different implementations.

Sybase uses a function called GETDATE() to return the system date. This function is used in a query as follows. The output is what would return if today's current date was New Year's Eve for 1998.

```
SELECT GETDATE()
```

Dec 31, 1997

 **NOTE**
> Most options discussed in this book for Sybase's and Microsoft's implementations are applicable to both implementations, because both use SQL Server for their database server. Both implementations also use an extension to standard SQL known as Transact-SQL.

Oracle uses what is calls a *pseudocolumn*, SYSDATE, to retrieve the current date. SYSDATE acts as any other column in a table, and can be selected from any table in the database, although it is not actually part of the table's definition.

To return the system date in Oracle, the following statement returns the output if today was New Year's Eve before 1998:

**TYPE**    `SELECT SYSDATE FROM TABLE_NAME`

**OUTPUT**    31-DEC-97

## Time Zones

The use of time zones may be a factor when dealing with date and time information. For instance, a time of 6:00 p.m. in the central United States does not equate to the same time in Australia, although the actual point in time is the same. Some of us who live within the daylight savings time zone are used to adjusting our clocks twice a year. If time zones are considerations when maintaining data in your case, you may find it necessary to consider time zones and perform time conversions if available with your SQL implementation.

Some common time zones and their abbreviations:

| Abbreviation | Definition |
| --- | --- |
| AST, ADT | Atlantic standard, daylight time |
| BST, BDT | Bering standard, daylight time |
| CST, CDT | Central standard, daylight time |
| EST, EDT | Eastern standard, daylight time |
| GMT | Greenwich mean time |
| HST, HDT | Alaska/Hawaii standard, daylight time |
| MST, MDT | Mountain standard, daylight time |
| NST | Newfoundland standard, daylight time |
| PST, PDT | Pacific standard, daylight time |
| YST, YDT | Yukon standard, daylight time |

**NOTE**

Some implementations have functions that allow you to deal with different time zones; however, not all implementations may support the use of time zones. Be sure to verify the use of time zones in your particular implementation, as well as the need in the case of your database.

**12**

## Adding Time to Dates

Days, months, and other parts of time can be added to dates for the purpose of comparing dates to one another, or to provide more specific conditions in the WHERE clause of a query.

Intervals can be used to add periods of time to a DATETIME value. As defined by the standard, intervals are used to manipulate the value of a DATETIME value as in the following examples:

```
DATE '1997-12-31' + INTERVAL '1' DAY
```

```
'1998-01-01'
```

```
DATE '1997-12-31' + INTERVAL '1' MONTH
```

```
'1998-01-31'
```

Example using the SQL Server function DATEADD:

**TYPE**
```
SELECT DATEADD(MONTH, 1, DATE_HIRE)
FROM EMPLOYEE_PAY_TBL
```

**OUTPUT**
```
DATE_HIRE ADD_MONTH
......... .........
23-MAY-89 23-JUN-89
17-JUN-90 17-JUL-90
14-AUG-94 14-SEP-94
28-JUN-97 28-JUL-97
22-JUL-96 22-AUG-96
14-JAN-91 14-FEB-91

6 rows affected.
```

Example using the Oracle function ADD_MONTHS:

**TYPE**
```
SELECT DATE_HIRE, ADD_MONTHS(DATE_HIRE,1)
FROM EMPLOYEE_PAY_TBL;
```

**OUTPUT**
```
DATE_HIRE ADD_MONTH
......... .........
23-MAY-89 23-JUN-89
17-JUN-90 17-JUL-90
14-AUG-94 14-SEP-94
28-JUN-97 28-JUL-97
22-JUL-96 22-AUG-96
14-JAN-91 14-FEB-91

6 rows selected.
```

Adding one day to a date in Oracle:

**TYPE**
```
SELECT DATE_HIRE, DATE_HIRE + 1
FROM EMPLOYEE_PAY_TBL
WHERE EMP_ID = '311549902';
```

**OUTPUT**
```
DATE_HIRE DATE_HIRE
......... .........
23-MAY-89 24-MAY-89

1 row selected.
```

Notice that these examples in SQL Server and Oracle, though they differ syntactically from the ANSI examples, derive their results based on the same concept as described by the SQL standard.

## Comparing Dates and Time Periods

OVERLAPS is a powerful standard SQL conditional operator for DATETIME values. The overlaps operator is used to compare two timeframes and return the Boolean value TRUE or FALSE, depending on whether the two timeframes overlap. The following comparison returns the value TRUE:

**12**

```
(TIME '01:00:00' , TIME '05:59:00')
OVERLAPS
(TIME '05:00:00' , TIME '07:00:00')
```

The following comparison returns the value FALSE:

```
(TIME '01:00:00' , TIME '05:59:00')
OVERLAPS
(TIME '06:00:00 , TIME '07:00:00')
```

## Miscellaneous Date Functions

The following list shows some powerful date functions that exist in the implementations for SQL Server and Oracle.

### SQL SERVER

| | |
|---|---|
| DATEPART | Returns the integer value of a datepart for a date |
| DATENAME | Returns the text value of a datepart for a date |
| GETDATE() | Returns the system date |
| DATEDIFF | Returns the difference between two dates for specified date parts, such as days, minutes, and seconds |

### ORACLE

| | |
|---|---|
| NEXT_DAY | Returns the next day of the week as specified (for example, FRIDAY) since a given date |
| MONTHS_BETWEEN | Returns the number of months between two given dates |

# Date Conversions

The conversion of dates takes place for any number of reasons. Conversions are mainly used to alter the datatype of values defined as a DATETIME value, or any other valid datatype of a particular implementation.

Typical reasons for date conversions:

☐ To compare date values of different datatypes

☐ To format a date value as a character string

☐ To convert a character string into a date format

The ANSI CAST operator is used to convert datatypes into other datatypes.

The basic syntax is as follows:

```
CAST ( EXPRESSION AS NEW_DATA_TYPE )
```

Specific examples according to the syntax of some implementations are illustrated in the following subsections, covering

☐ The representation of parts of a DATETIME value

☐ Conversions of dates to character strings

☐ Conversions of character strings to dates

## Date Pictures

A *date picture* is composed of formatting elements used to extract date and time information from the database in a desired format. Date pictures may not be available in all SQL implementations.

Without the use of a date picture and some type of conversion function, the date and time information is retrieved from the database in a default format, such as:

```
1997-12-31
31-DEC-97
1997-12-31 23:59:01.11
...
```

What if you wanted the date displayed as the following? You have to convert the date from a DATETIME format into a character string format.

```
December 31, 1997
```

This is accomplished by implementation-specific functions for this very purpose, which is further illustrated in the following sections.

*Sybase date pictures:*

| | |
|---|---|
| yy | year |
| qq | quarter |
| mm | month |
| dy | day of year |
| wk | week |
| dw | weekday |
| hh | hour |
| mi | minute |
| ss | second |
| ms | millisecond |

*Oracle date pictures:*

| | |
|---|---|
| AD | anno Domini |
| AM | ante meridian |
| BC | Before Christ |
| CC | Century |
| D | Number of the day in the week |

**12**

*Oracle date pictures:*

| | |
|---|---|
| DD | Number of the day in the month |
| DDD | Number of the day in the year |
| DAY | The day spelled out (MONDAY) |
| Day | The day spelled out (Monday) |
| day | The day spelled out (monday) |
| DY | The three-letter abbreviation of day (MON) |
| Dy | The three-letter abbreviation of day (Mon) |
| dy | The three-letter abbreviation of day (mon) |
| HH | Hour of the day |
| HH12 | Hour of the day |
| HH24 | Hour of the day for a 24-hour clock |
| J | Julian days since 12-31-4713 B.C. |
| MI | Minute of the hour |
| MM | The number of the month |
| MON | The three-letter abbreviation of the month (JAN) |
| Mon | The three-letter abbreviation of the month (Jan) |
| mon | The three-letter abbreviation of the month (jan) |
| MONTH | The month spelled out (JANUARY) |
| Month | The month spelled out (January) |
| month | The month spelled out (january) |
| PM | post meridian |
| Q | The number of the quarter |
| RM | The Roman numeral for the month |
| RR | The two digits of the year |
| SS | The second of a minute |
| SSSSS | The seconds since midnight |
| SYYYY | The signed year, if B.C. 500, then B.C. = -500 |
| W | The number of the week in a month |
| WW | The number of the week in a year |
| Y | The last digit of the year |
| YY | The last two digits of the year |
| YYY | The last three digits of the year |
| YYYY | The year |
| YEAR | The year spelled out (NINETEEN-NINETY-SEVEN) |
| Year | The year spelled out (Nineteen-Ninety-Seven) |
| year | The year spelled out (nineteen-ninety-seven) |

## Converting Dates to Character Strings

Particularly, DATETIME values are converted to character strings to alter the appearance of output from a query. A conversion function is used to achieve this. Two examples of converting date and time data into a character string as designated by a query follow:

**TYPE**
```
SELECT DATE_HIRE = DATENAME(MONTH, DATE_HIRE)
FROM EMPLOYEE_PAY_TBL
```

**OUTPUT**
```
DATE_HIRE
- - - - - - - -
May
June

August

June

July

Jan

6 rows affected.
```

An Oracle date conversion using the TO_CHAR function:

**TYPE**
```
SELECT DATE_HIRE, TO_CHAR(DATE_HIRE,'Month dd, yyyy') HIRE
FROM EMPLOYEE_PAY_TBL;
```

**OUTPUT**
```
DATE_HIRE HIRE
- - - - - - - -  - - - - - - - - - - - - - - - - - - - -
23-MAY-89 May        23, 1989
17-JUN-90 June       17, 1990
14-AUG-94 August     14, 1994
28-JUN-97 June       28, 1997
22-JUL-96 July       22, 1996
14-JAN-91 January    14, 1991

6 rows selected.
```

## Converting Character Strings to Dates

The following example illustrates a method from one implementation of converting a character string into a date format. When the conversion is complete, the data can be stored in a column defined as having some form of a DATETIME datatype.

**TYPE**
```
SELECT TO_DATE('JANUARY 01 1998','MONTH DD YYYY')
FROM EMPLOYEE_PAY_TBL;
```

**OUTPUT**
```
TO_DATE('
- - - - - - - -
01-JAN-98
01-JAN-98
01-JAN-98
01-JAN-98
01-JAN-98
01-JAN-98

6 rows selected.
```

**12**

You may be wondering why six rows were selected from this query when only one date value was provided. The reason is because the conversion of the literal string was selected from the EMPLOYEE_PAY_TBL, which has six rows of data. Hence, the conversion of the literal string was selected against each record in the table.

# Summary

You have an understanding of DATETIME values based on the fact that ANSI has provided a standard. However, as with many SQL elements, most implementations have deviated from the exact functions and syntax of standard SQL commands although the concepts always remain the same as far as the basic representation and manipulation of date and time information. Last hour, you saw how functions greatly varied depending upon each implementation, and this hour, you have seen some of the differences between date and time datatypes, functions, and operators. Keep in mind that not all examples discussed in this chapter work with your particular implementation, but the concepts of dates and times are the same and should be applicable to any implementation.

## Q&A

**Q Why do implementations choose to deviate from a single standard set of datatypes and functions?**

A Implementations differ as far as the representation of datatypes and functions mainly because of the way each vendor has chosen to internally store data and provide the most efficient means of data retrieval. However, all implementations should provide the same means for the storage of date and time values based on the required elements prescribed by ANSI, such as the year, month, day, hour, minute, second, and so on.

**Q What if I want to store date and time information differently than what is available in my implementation?**

A Dates can be stored in nearly any type of format if you choose to define the column for a date as a variable length character. The main thing to remember is that when comparing date values to one another, it is usually required to first convert the character string representation of the date to a valid DATETIME format for your implementation; that is, if appropriate conversion functions are available.

# Workshop

The following workshop is composed of a series of quiz questions and practical exercises. The quiz questions are designed to test your overall understanding of the current material. The practical exercises are intended to afford you the opportunity to apply the concepts discussed during the current hour, as well as build upon the knowledge acquired in previous hours of study. Please take time to complete the quiz questions and exercises before continuing. You may refer to the answers in Appendix C.

12

## Quiz

1. From where is the system date and time normally derived?

2. List the standard internal elements of a DATETIME value.

3. What could be a major factor concerning the representation and comparison of date and time values if your company is an international organization?

4. Can a character string date value be compared to a date value defined as a valid DATETIME datatype?

## Exercises

1. Provide SQL code for the exercises given the following information:

   Use SYSDATE to represent the current date and time.

   Use the table called DATES.

   Use the TO_CHAR function to convert dates to character strings, with syntax:

   ```
   TO_CHAR('EXPRESSION','DATE_PICTURE')
   ```

   Use the TO_DATE function to convert character strings to dates, with syntax:

   ```
   TO_DATE('EXPRESSION','DATE_PICTURE')
   ```

Date picture information:

| DATE PICTURE | MEANING |
| --- | --- |
| MONTH | Month spelled out |
| DAY | Day spelled out |
| DD | Day of month, number |
| MM | Month of year, number |
| YY | Two-digit year |
| YYYY | Four-digit year |
| MI | Minutes of the hour |
| SS | Seconds of the minute |

1. Assuming today is 1997-12-31, convert the current date to the format December 31 1997.

2. Convert the following string to DATE format:

   ```
   'DECEMBER 31 1997'
   ```

3. Write the code to return the day of the week that New Year's Eve of 1998 falls upon. Assume that the date is stored in the format 31-DEC-97, which is a valid DATETIME datatype.

12

# PART IV

## Building Sophisticated Database Queries

## Hour

# Hour 13

# Joining Tables in Queries

To this point, all database queries you have executed have extracted data from a single table. During this hour you learn how to join tables in a query so that data may be retrieved from multiple tables.

The highlights of this hour include:

- [ ] An introduction to the table join
- [ ] The different types of joins
- [ ] How and when joins are used
- [ ] Numerous practical examples of table joins
- [ ] The effects of improperly joined tables
- [ ] Renaming tables in a query using an alias

## Selecting Data From Multiple Tables

Having the capability to select data from multiple tables is one of SQL's most powerful features. Without this capability, the entire relational database concept would not be feasible. Single-table queries are sometimes quite informative, but in the real world, the most practical queries are those whose data is acquired from multiple tables within the database.

As you witnessed in the hour on normalization, a relational database is broken up into smaller, more manageable tables for simplicity and the sake of overall management ease. As tables are divided into smaller tables, the related tables are created with common columns—*primary keys*. These keys are used to join related tables to one another.

**NEW TERM**    A *join* combines two or more tables in order to retrieve data from multiple tables.

You might ask why you should normalize tables if, in the end, you are only going to rejoin the tables in order to retrieve the data you want. You rarely select all data from all tables, so it is better to pick and choose according to the needs of each individual query. Although performance may suffer slightly due to a normalized database, overall coding and mainte-nance is much simpler.

# Types of Joins

While different implementations have many ways of joining tables, you concentrate on the most common joins in this lesson. The types of joins that you learn are

```
EQUIJOINS
NATURAL JOINS
NON-EQUIJOINS
OUTER JOINS
SELF JOINS
```

## Component Locations of a Join Condition

As you have learned from previous hours, the SELECT and FROM clauses are both required SQL statement elements; the WHERE clause is a required element of a SQL statement when joining tables. The tables being joined are listed in the FROM clause. The join is performed in the WHERE clause. Several operators can be used to join tables, such as =, <, >, <>, <=, >=, !=, between, like, and not; they can all be used to join tables. However, the most common operator is the equal symbol.

## Joins of Equality

Perhaps the most used and important of the joins is the EQUIJOIN, also referred to as an INNER JOIN. The EQUIJOIN joins two tables with a common column, in which each is usually the primary key. The syntax for an EQUIJOIN is:

```
SELECT TABLE1.COLUMN1, TABLE2.COLUMN2…
FROM TABLE1, TABLE2 [, TABLE3 ]
WHERE TABLE1.COLUMN_NAME = TABLE2.COLUMN_NAME
[ AND TABLE1.COLUMN_NAME = TABLE3.COLUMN_NAME ]
```

**NOTE**

> Take note of the example SQL statements. Indentation is used in the SQL statements to improve overall readability. Indentation is not required, but is recommend.

*Usage*

```
SELECT EMPLOYEE_TBL.EMP_ID,
       EMPLOYEE_PAY_TBL.DATE_HIRE
FROM EMPLOYEE_TBL,
     EMPLOYEE_PAY_TBL
WHERE EMPLOYEE_TBL.EMP_ID = EMPLOYEE_PAY_TBL.EMP_ID;
```

**ANALYSIS**    The preceding SQL statement returns the employee identification and the employee's date of hire. The employee identification is selected from the EMPLOYEE_TBL (although it exists in both tables, you must specify one table), while the hire date is selected from the EMPLOYEE_PAY_TBL. Because the employee identification exists in both tables, both columns must be justified with the table name. By justifying the columns with the table names, you tell the database server where to get the data.

Data in the following example is selected from the tables EMPLOYEE_TBL and EMPLOYEE_PAY_TBL, because desired data resides in each of the two tables. An equality join is used.

**TYPE**
```
SELECT EMPLOYEE_TBL.EMP_ID, EMPLOYEE_TBL.LAST_NAME,
       EMPLOYEE_PAY_TBL.POSITION
FROM EMPLOYEE_TBL, EMPLOYEE_PAY_TBL
WHERE EMPLOYEE_TBL.EMP_ID = EMPLOYEE_PAY_TBL.EMP_ID;
```

**OUTPUT**
```
EMP_ID     LAST_NAM POSITION
--------   -------- ---------------
311549902 STEPHENS MARKETING
442346889 PLEW     TEAM LEADER
213764555 GLASS    SALES MANAGER
313782439 GLASS    SALESMAN
220984332 WALLACE  SHIPPER
443679012 SPURGEON SHIPPER

6 rows selected.
```

Notice that each column in the SELECT clause is proceeded by the associated table name in order to identify each column. This is called *qualifying columns in a query*. Qualifying columns is only necessary for columns that exist in more than one table referenced by a query. You usually qualify all columns for consistency and to avoid any questions when debugging or modifying SQL code.

## Natural Joins

A NATURAL JOIN is nearly the same as the EQUIJOIN; however, the NATURAL JOIN differs from the EQUIJOIN by eliminating duplicate columns in the joining columns. The JOIN condition is the same, but the columns selected differ.

**13**

The syntax is as follows:

SYNTAX

```
SELECT TABLE1.*, TABLE2.COLUMN_NAME
       [ TABLE3.COLUMN_NAME ]
FROM TABLE1, TABLE2 [ TABLE3 ]
WHERE TABLE1.COLUMN_NAME = TABLE2.COLUMN_NAME
[ AND TABLE1.COLUMN_NAME = TABLE3.COLUMN ]
```

*Usage*

```
SELECT E.*, EP.SALARY
FROM EMPLOYEE_TBL E,
     EMPLOYEE_PAY_TBL EP
WHERE E.EMP_ID = EP.EMP_ID
```

The preceding SQL statement returns all columns from EMPLOYEE_TBL and SALARY from the EMPLOYEE_PAY_TBL. The EMP_ID is in both tables, but is retrieved only from the EMPLOYEE_TBL, because both contain the same information and do not need to be selected.

The following example selects all columns from the EMPLOYEE_TBL table and only one column from the EMPLOYEE_PAY_TBL table. Remember that the asterisk (*) represents all columns of a table.

**TYPE**

```
SELECT EMPLOYEE_TBL.*, EMPLOYEE_PAY_TBL.POSITION
FROM EMPLOYEE_TBL, EMPLOYEE_PAY_TBL
WHERE EMPLOYEE_TBL.EMP_ID = EMPLOYEE_PAY_TBL.EMP_ID;
```

**OUTPUT**

```
EMP_ID     LAST_NAM FIRST_NA M ADDRESS        CITY          ST ZIP   PHONE
--------   -------- -------- - -------------- ------------- -- ----- ----------
PAGER        POSITION
----------   --------------
311549902 STEPHENS TINA     D RR 3 BOX 17A   GREENWOOD     IN 47890 3178784465
             MARKETING

442346889 PLEW     LINDA    C 3301 BEACON    INDIANAPOLIS  IN 46224 3172978990
             TEAM LEADER

213764555 GLASS    BRANDON  S 1710 MAIN ST   WHITELAND     IN 47885 3178984321
3175709980 SALES MANAGER

313782439 GLASS    JACOB      3789 RIVER BLVD INDIANAPOLIS IN 45734 3175457676
8887345678 SALESMAN

220984332 WALLACE  MARIAH     7889 KEYSTONE   INDIANAPOLIS IN 46741 3173325986
             SHIPPER

443679012 SPURGEON TIFFANY  5 GEORGE COURT   INDIANAPOLIS  IN 46234 3175679007
             SHIPPER


6 rows selected.
```

**13**

## Using Table Aliases

The use of *table aliases* means to rename a table in a particular SQL statement. The renaming is a temporary change. The actual table name does not change in the database. As you learned for the SELF JOIN, giving the tables aliases is a necessity. Giving tables aliases is most often used to save keystrokes, which results in the SQL statement being shorter and easier to read. In addition, fewer keystrokes means fewer keystroke errors. Giving tables aliases also means that the columns being selected must be qualified with the table alias. Here are some examples of table aliases and the corresponding columns:

**OUTPUT**

```
SELECT E.EMP_ID, EP.SALARY, EP.DATE_HIRE, E.LAST_NAME
FROM EMPLOYEE_TBL E,
     EMPLOYEE_PAY_TBL EP
WHERE E.EMP_ID = EP.EMP_ID
AND EP.SALARY > 20000
```

**ANALYSIS**

The tables have been given aliases in the preceding SQL statement. The EMPLOYEE_TBL has been renamed E. The EMPLOYEE_PAY_TBL has been renamed EP. The choice of what to rename the tables is arbitrary. The letter E is chosen because the EMPLOYEE_TBL starts with E. Because the EMPLOYEE_PAY_TBL also begins with the letter E, you could not use E again. Instead, the first letter (E) and the first letter of the second word in the name (PAY) are used as the alias. The selected columns were justified with the corresponding table alias. Note that SALARY was used in the WHERE clause and must also be justified with the table alias.

## Joins of Non-Equality

**SYNTAX**

NON-EQUIJOIN joins two or more tables based on a specified column value not equaling a specified column value in another table. The syntax for the NON-EQUIJOIN is

```
FROM TABLE1, TABLE2 [, TABLE3 ]
WHERE TABLE1.COLUMN_NAME != TABLE2.COLUMN_NAME
[ AND TABLE1.COLUMN_NAME != TABLE2.COLUMN_NAME ]
```

**OUTPUT**

```
SELECT EMPLOYEE_TBL.EMP_ID, EMPLOYEE_PAY_TBL.DATE_HIRE
FROM EMPLOYEE_TBL,
     EMPLOYEE_PAY_TBL
WHERE EMPLOYEE_TBL.EMP_ID != EMPLOYEE_PAY_TBL.EMP_ID
```

**ANALYSIS**

The preceding SQL statement returns the employee identification and the date of hire for all employees who do not have a corresponding record in both tables. The following example is a join of non-equality:

**TYPE**

```
SELECT E.EMP_ID, E.LAST_NAME, P.POSITION
FROM EMPLOYEE_TBL E,
     EMPLOYEE_PAY_TBL P
WHERE E.EMP_ID <> P.EMP_ID;
```

**OUTPUT**

```
EMP_ID     LAST_NAM POSITION
--------   -------- ------------
442346889  PLEW     MARKETING
213764555  GLASS    MARKETING
313782439  GLASS    MARKETING
```

```
220984332  WALLACE   MARKETING
443679012  SPURGEON  MARKETING
311549902  STEPHENS  TEAM LEADER
213764555  GLASS     TEAM LEADER
313782439  GLASS     TEAM LEADER
220984332  WALLACE   TEAM LEADER
443679012  SPURGEON  TEAM LEADER
311549902  STEPHENS  SALES MANAGER
442346889  PLEW      SALES MANAGER
313782439  GLASS     SALES MANAGER
220984332  WALLACE   SALES MANAGER
443679012  SPURGEON  SALES MANAGER
311549902  STEPHENS  SALESMAN
442346889  PLEW      SALESMAN
213764555  GLASS     SALESMAN
220984332  WALLACE   SALESMAN
443679012  SPURGEON  SALESMAN
311549902  STEPHENS  SHIPPER
442346889  PLEW      SHIPPER
213764555  GLASS     SHIPPER
313782439  GLASS     SHIPPER
443679012  SPURGEON  SHIPPER
311549902  STEPHENS  SHIPPER
442346889  PLEW      SHIPPER
213764555  GLASS     SHIPPER
313782439  GLASS     SHIPPER
220984332  WALLACE   SHIPPER

30 rows selected.
```

You may be curious why 30 rows were retrieved when only 6 rows exist in each table. For every record in EMPLOYEE_TBL, there is a corresponding record in EMPLOYEE_PAY_TBL. Because non-equality was tested in the join of the two tables, each row in the first table is paired with all rows from the second table, except for its own corresponding row. This means that each of the six rows are paired with five unrelated rows in the second table; 6 rows multiplied by 5 rows equals 30 rows total.

In the previous section's test for equality example, each of the six rows in the first table were paired with only one row in the second table (each row's corresponding row); six rows multiplied by one row yields a total of six rows.

**WARNING**

When using NON-EQUIJOINs, you may receive several rows of data that are of no use to you. Check your results carefully.

## Outer Joins

An OUTER JOIN is used to return all rows that exist in one table, even though corresponding rows do not exist in the joined table. The (+) symbol is used to denote an OUTER JOIN in a query. The (+) is placed at the end of the table name in the WHERE clause. The table with the (+) should be the table that does not have matching rows. In many implementations, the OUTER JOIN is broken down into joins called LEFT OUTER JOIN, RIGHT OUTER JOIN, and FULL OUTER JOIN. The OUTER JOIN in these implementations is normally optional.

**13**

**NOTE**

You must check your particular implementation for exact usage and syntax of the OUTER JOIN. The (+) symbol is used by some major implementations, but is non-standard.

**SYNTAX**

The general syntax is

```
FROM TABLE1
{RIGHT ¦ LEFT ¦ FULL} [OUTER] JOIN
ON TABLE2
```

The Oracle syntax is

```
FROM TABLE1, TABLE2 [, TABLE3 ]
WHERE TABLE1.COLUMN_NAME[(+)] = TABLE2.COLUMN_NAME[(+)]
[ AND TABLE1.COLUMN_NAME[(+)] = TABLE3.COLUMN_NAME[(+)]
```

**NOTE**

The OUTER JOIN can only be used on one side of a join condition; however, you can use an OUTER JOIN on more than one column of the same table in the join condition.

The concept of the OUTER JOIN is explained in the next two examples. In the first example, the product description and the quantity ordered are selected; both values are extracted from two separate tables. One important factor to keep in mind is that there may not be a corresponding record in the ORDERS_TBL table for every product. A regular join of equality is performed:

**TYPE**

```
SELECT P.PROD_DESC, O.QTY
FROM PRODUCTS_TBL P,
        ORDERS_TBL O
WHERE P.PROD_ID = O.PROD_ID;
```

**OUTPUT**

```
PROD_DESC                         QTY
------------------------     ----------
WITCHES COSTUME                     1
PLASTIC PUMPKIN 18 INCH             25
PLASTIC PUMPKIN 18 INCH              2
LIGHTED LANTERNS                    10
FALSE PARAFFIN TEETH                20

5 rows selected.
```

Only 5 rows were selected, but there are 10 distinct products. You want to display all products, whether the products have been placed on order or not.

The next example accomplishes the desired output through the use of an outer join. Oracle's syntax is used for the outer join.

**13**

```
SELECT P.PROD_DESC, O.QTY
FROM PRODUCTS_TBL P,
     ORDERS_TBL O
WHERE P.PROD_ID = O.PROD_ID(+);
```

```
PROD_DESC                          QTY
- - - - - - - - - - - - - - - -    - - - - - - - - -
WITCHES COSTUME                      1
ASSORTED MASKS
FALSE PARAFFIN TEETH                20
ASSORTED COSTUMES
PLASTIC PUMPKIN 18 INCH             25
PLASTIC PUMPKIN 18 INCH              2
PUMPKIN CANDY
PLASTIC SPIDERS
CANDY CORN
LIGHTED LANTERNS                    10

10 rows selected.
```

All products were returned by the query, even though they may not have had a quantity ordered. The outer join is inclusive of all rows of data in the PRODUCTS_TBL table, whether a corresponding row exists in the ORDERS_TBL table or not.

## Self Joins

The SELF JOIN is used to join a table to itself, as if the table were two tables temporarily renaming a table in the SQL statement.

```
SELECT A.COLUMN_NAME, B.COLUMN_NAME, [ C.COLUMN_NAME ]
FROM TABLE1 A, TABLE2 B [, TABLE3 C ]
WHERE A.COLUMN_NAME = B.COLUMN_NAME
[ AND A.COLUMN_NAME = C.COLUMN_NAME ]
```

```
SELECT A.LAST_NAME, B.LAST_NAME, A.FIRST_NAME
FROM EMPLOYEE_TBL A,
     EMPLOYEE_TBL B
WHERE A.LAST_NAME = B.LAST_NAME
```

The preceding SQL statement returns the employees' first name for all the employees with the same last name from the EMPLOYEE_TBL.

# Join Considerations

Several things should be considered before using joins. Some considerations include what columns(s) to join on, if there is no common column to join on, and performance issues. Performance issues are discussed in Hour 18, "Managing Database Users."

## Using a BASE TABLE

What to join on? Should you have the need to retrieve data from two tables that do not have a common column to join, you must use another table that has a common column or columns

13

to both tables to join on. That table becomes the BASE TABLE. A BASE TABLE is used to join one or more tables that have common columns, or to join tables that do not have common columns. Use the following three tables for an example of a base table:

**CUSTOMER_TBL**

| | | | |
|---|---|---|---|
| cust_id | varchar2(10) | not null | primary key |
| cust_name | varchar2(30) | not null | |
| cust_address | varchar2(20) | not null | |
| cust_city | varchar2(15) | not null | |
| cust_state | char(2) | not null | |
| cust_zip | number(5) | not null | |
| cust_phone | number(10) | | |
| cust_fax | number(10) | | |

**ORDERS_TBL**

| | | | |
|---|---|---|---|
| ord_num | varchar2(10) | not null | primary key |
| cust_id | varchar2(10) | not null | |
| prod_id | varchar2(10) | not null | |
| qty | number(6) | not null | |
| ord_date | date | | |

**PRODUCTS_TBL**

| | | | |
|---|---|---|---|
| prod_id | varchar2(10) | not null | primary key |
| prod_desc | varchar2(40) | not null | |
| cost | number(6,2) | not null | |

You have a need to use the CUSTOMERS_TBL and the PRODUCTS_TBL. There is no common column in which to join the tables. Now look at the ORDERS_TBL. The ORDERS_TBL has cust_id to join with the CUSTOMERS_TBL, which also has CUST_ID. The PRODUCTS_TBL has PROD_ID, which is also in the ORDERS_TBL. The JOIN conditions and results look like this:

**TYPE**

```
SELECT C.CUST_NAME, P.PROD_DESC
FROM CUSTOMER_TBL C,
     PRODUCTS_TBL P,
     ORDERS_TBL O
WHERE C.CUST_ID = O.CUST_ID
  AND P.PROD_ID = O.PROD_ID;
```

**OUTPUT**

```
CUST_NAME                        PROD_DESC
-------------------------------  -------------------------
LESLIE GLEASON                   WITCHES COSTUME
SCHYLERS NOVELTIES               PLASTIC PUMPKIN 18 INCH
WENDY WOLF                       PLASTIC PUMPKIN 18 INCH
GAVINS PLACE                     LIGHTED LANTERNS
SCOTTYS MARKET                   FALSE PARAFFIN TEETH

5 rows selected.
```

13

**NOTE**
Note the use of table aliases and their use on the columns in the WHERE clause.

## The Cartesian Product

The *Cartesian Product* is a result of a CARTESIAN JOIN or "no join." If you select from two or more tables and do not JOIN the tables, your output is all possible rows from all the tables selected from. If your tables were large, the result could be hundreds of thousands of rows, or even millions of rows of data. A WHERE clause is highly recommended for SQL statements retrieving data from two or more tables. The Cartesian Product is also known as a cross join. The syntax is

```
FROM TABLE1, TABLE2 [, TABLE3 ]
WHERE TABLE1, TABLE2 [, TABLE3 ]
```

An example of a cross join, or the dreaded Cartesian Product, is shown here:

**TYPE**
```
SELECT E.EMP_ID, E.LAST_NAME, P.POSITION
FROM EMPLOYEE_TBL E,
     EMPLOYEE_PAY_TBL P;
```

**OUTPUT**

```
EMP_ID    LAST_NAM POSITION
--------- -------- --------------
311549902 STEPHENS MARKETING
442346889 PLEW     MARKETING
213764555 GLASS    MARKETING
313782439 GLASS    MARKETING
220984332 WALLACE  MARKETING
443679012 SPURGEON MARKETING
311549902 STEPHENS TEAM LEADER
442346889 PLEW     TEAM LEADER
213764555 GLASS    TEAM LEADER
313782439 GLASS    TEAM LEADER
220984332 WALLACE  TEAM LEADER
443679012 SPURGEON TEAM LEADER
311549902 STEPHENS SALES MANAGER
442346889 PLEW     SALES MANAGER
213764555 GLASS    SALES MANAGER
313782439 GLASS    SALES MANAGER
220984332 WALLACE  SALES MANAGER
443679012 SPURGEON SALES MANAGER
311549902 STEPHENS SALESMAN
442346889 PLEW     SALESMAN
213764555 GLASS    SALESMAN
313782439 GLASS    SALESMAN
220984332 WALLACE  SALESMAN
443679012 SPURGEON SALESMAN
311549902 STEPHENS SHIPPER
442346889 PLEW     SHIPPER
```

**13**

```
213764555 GLASS    SHIPPER
313782439 GLASS    SHIPPER
220984332 WALLACE  SHIPPER
443679012 SPURGEON SHIPPER
311549902 STEPHENS SHIPPER
442346889 PLEW     SHIPPER
213764555 GLASS    SHIPPER
313782439 GLASS    SHIPPER
220984332 WALLACE  SHIPPER
443679012 SPURGEON SHIPPER

36 rows selected.
```

Data is being selected from two separate tables, yet no join operation is performed. Because you have not specified how to join rows in the first table with rows in the second table, the database server pairs every row in the first table with every row in the second table. Because each table has 6 rows of data each, the product of 36 rows selected is achieved from 6 rows multiplied by 6 rows.

**WARNING**

> Be careful to always join all tables in a query. If two tables in a query have not been joined and each table contains 1,000 rows of data, the Cartesian Product consists of 1,000 rows multiplied by 1,000 rows, which results in a total of 1,000,000 rows of data returned.

# Summary

You have been introduced to one of the most robust features of SQL—the table join. Imagine the limits if you were not able to extract data from more than one table in a single query. You were shown several types of joins, each serving its own purpose depending upon conditions placed on the query. Joins are used to link data from tables based on equality and non-equality. Outer joins are very powerful, allowing data retrieved from one table, even though associated data is not found in a joined table. Self joins are used to join a table to itself. Beware of the cross join, more commonly known as the Cartesian Product. The Cartesian Product is the result set of a multiple table query without a join, often yielding a multitude of unwanted output. When selecting data from more than one table, be sure to properly join the tables according to the related columns (normally primary keys). Failure to properly join tables could result in incomplete or inaccurate output.

**13**

## Q&A

**Q** When joining tables, must they be joined in the same order that they appear in the FROM clause?

**A** No, they do not have to appear in the same order; however, performance benefits may be experienced depending on the order of tables in the FROM clause and the order that tables are joined.

**Q** **When using a base table to join unrelated tables, must I select any columns from the base table?**

**A** No, the use of a base table to join unrelated tables does not mandate columns for selection from the base table.

**Q** **Can I join on more than one column between tables?**

**A** Yes, some queries may require you to join on more than one column per table in order to provide a complete relationship between rows of data in the joined tables.

# Workshop

The following workshop is composed of a series of quiz questions and practical exercises. The quiz questions are designed to test your overall understanding of the current material. The practical exercises are intended to afford you the opportunity to apply the concepts discussed during the current hour, as well as build upon the knowledge acquired in previous hours of study. Please take time to complete the quiz questions and exercises before continuing. You may refer to the answers in Appendix C.

## Quiz

1. What type of join would you use to return records from one table, regardless of the existence of associated records in the related table?

2. The JOIN conditions are located in what part of the SQL statement?

3. What type of JOIN do you use to evaluate equality among rows of related tables?

4. What happens if you select from two different tables but fail to join the tables?

5. Use the following tables:

ORDERS_TBL

| | | | |
|---|---|---|---|
| ord_num | varchar2(10) | not null | primary key |
| cust_id | varchar2(10) | not null | |
| prod_id | varchar2(10) | not null | |
| qty | number(6) | not null | |
| ord_date | date | | |

PRODUCTS_TBL

| | | | |
|---|---|---|---|
| prod_id | varchar2(10) | not null | primary key |
| prod_desc | varchar2(40) | not null | |
| cost | number(6,2) | not null | |

Is the following syntax correct for using an OUTER JOIN?

```
SELECT C.CUST_ID, C.CUST_NAME, O.ORD_NUM
FROM CUSTOMER_TBL C, ORDERS_TBL O
WHERE C.CUST_ID(+) = O.CUST_ID(+)
```

# Exercises

Perform the exercises using the following tables:

**EMPLOYEE_TBL**

| emp_id | varchar2(9) | not null | PRIMARY KEY |
|---|---|---|---|
| last_name | varchar2(15) | not null | |
| first_name | varchar2(15) | not null | |
| middle_name | varchar2(15) | | |
| address | varchar2(30) | not null | |
| city | varchar2(15) | not null | |
| state | char(2) | not null | |
| zip | number(5) | not null | |
| phone | char(10) | | |
| pager | char(10) | | |

**EMPLOYEE_PAY_TBL**

| emp_id | varchar2(9) | not null | primary key |
|---|---|---|---|
| position | varchar2(15) | not null | |
| date_hire | date | | |
| pay_rate | number(4,2) | not null | |
| date_last_raise | date | | |
| salary | number(6,2) | | |
| bonus | number(4,2) | | |

constraint emp_fk foreign key (emp_id) references
   employee_tbl (emp_id)

**CUSTOMER_TBL**

| cust_id | varchar2(10) | not null | primary key |
|---|---|---|---|
| cust_name | varchar2(30) | not null | |
| cust_address | varchar2(20) | not null | |
| cust_city | varchar2(15) | not null | |
| cust_state | char(2) | not null | |
| cust_zip | number(5) | not null | |
| cust_phone | number(10) | | |
| cust_fax | number(10) | | |

**13**

**ORDERS_TBL**

| | | | |
|---|---|---|---|
| ord_num | varchar2(10) | not null | primary key |
| cust_id | varchar2(10) | not null | |
| prod_id | varchar2(10) | not null | |
| qty | number(6) | not null | |
| ord_date | date | | |

**PRODUCTS_TBL**

| | | | |
|---|---|---|---|
| prod_id | varchar2(10) | not null | primary key |
| prod_desc | varchar2(40) | not null | |
| cost | number(6,2) | not null | |

1. Write a SQL statement to return the emp_id, last_name, and first_name from the EMPLOYEE_TBL and salary, bonus from the EMPLOYEE_PAY_TBL.

2. Select from the CUSTOMERS_TBL the columns: CUST_ID, CUST_NAME. Select from the PRODUCTS_TBL the columns: PROD_ID, COST. Select from the ORDERS_TBL the ORD_NUM and QTY columns. Join all three of the tables into one SQL statement.

# Hour **14**

# Using Subqueries to Define Unknown Data

During this hour you are presented with the concepts of using subqueries in order to return results from a database query more effectively.

The highlights of this hour include:

- ☐ What is a subquery?
- ☐ The justifications of using subqueries
- ☐ Examples of subqueries in regular database queries
- ☐ Using subqueries with data manipulation commands
- ☐ Embedded subqueries

## What Is a Subquery?

A *subquery* is a query within another query. This is also known as a *nested query*. A subquery is used to return data that will be used in the main query as a condition to further restrict the data to be retrieved. Subqueries are used with the SELECT, INSERT, UPDATE, and DELETE statements.

A *subquery* is a query embedded within the WHERE clause of another query to further restrict data returned by the query.

A subquery can be used in some cases in the place of a join operation by indirectly linking data between the tables based on one or more conditions. When a subquery is used in a query, the subquery is resolved first, then the main query is resolved according to the condition(s) as resolved by the subquery. The results of the subquery are used to process expressions in the WHERE clause of the main query. The subquery can either be used in the WHERE clause or the HAVING clause of the main query. Logical and relational operators such as =, >, <, <>, IN, NOT IN, AND, OR, and so on, can be used within the subquery as well as to evaluate a subquery in the WHERE or HAVING clause.

> **NOTE**
>
> The same rules that apply to standard queries also apply to subqueries. Join operations, functions, conversions, and other options may be used within a subquery.

There are a few rules that subqueries must follow:

- [ ] Subqueries must be enclosed within parentheses.

- [ ] A subquery may have only one column in the SELECT clause, unless multiple columns are in the main query for the subquery to compare its selected columns.

- [ ] An ORDER BY cannot be used in a subquery, although the main query can use an ORDER BY. The GROUP BY can be used to perform the same function as the ORDER BY in a subquery.

- [ ] Subqueries that return more than one row can only be used with multiple value operators, such as the IN operator.

- [ ] The BETWEEN operator cannot be used with a subquery; however, the BETWEEN can be used within the subquery.

**SYNTAX**

The basic syntax for a subquery:

```
SELECT COLUMN_NAME
FROM TABLE
WHERE COLUMN_NAME = (SELECT COLUMN_NAME
                     FROM TABLE
                     WHERE CONDITIONS);
```

The following examples show how the BETWEEN operator may and may not be used with a subquery:

Correct use of BETWEEN in the subquery:

```
SELECT COLUMN_NAME
FROM TABLE
```

**14**

```
WHERE COLUMN_NAME OPERATOR (SELECT COLUMN_NAME
                                  FROM TABLE)
                           WHERE VALUE BETWEEN VALUE)
```

Illegal use of BETWEEN with a subquery:

```
SELECT COLUMN_NAME
FROM TABLE
WHERE COLUMN_NAME BETWEEN VALUE AND (SELECT COLUMN_NAME
                                           FROM TABLE)
```

# Subqueries with the SELECT Statement

Subqueries are most frequently used with the SELECT statement, although they may be used within a data manipulation statement as well. The subquery, when used with the SELECT statement, retrieves data for the main query to use to solve the main query.

The basic syntax is as follows:

```
SELECT COLUMN_NAME [, COLUMN_NAME ]
FROM TABLE1 [, TABLE2 ]
WHERE COLUMN_NAME OPERATOR
                 (SELECT COLUMN_NAME [, COLUMN_NAME ]
                  FROM TABLE1 [, TABLE2 ]
                  [ WHERE ]

SELECT E.EMP_ID, E._LAST_NAME, E.FIRST_NAME, EP.PAY_RATE
FROM EMPLOYEE_TBL E, EMPLOYEE_PAY_TBL EP
WHERE E.EMP_ID = EP.EMP_ID
AND EP.PAY_RATE > (SELECT PAY_RATE
                   FROM EMPLOYEE_PAY_TBL
                   WHERE EMP_ID = '313782439')
```

**ANALYSIS**  The preceding SQL statement returns the employee identification, last name, first name, and pay rate for all employees who have a pay rate greater than that of the employee with the identification 313782439. In this case, you do not necessarily know (or care) what the exact pay rate is for this particular employee; you only care about the pay rate for the purpose of getting a list of employees who bring home more than the employee specified in the subquery.

The first query selects the pay rate for a particular employee. This query is used as the subquery in the next example.

**TYPE**
```
SELECT PAY_RATE
FROM EMPLOYEE_PAY_TBL
WHERE EMP_ID = '313782439';
```

**OUTPUT**
```
PAY_RATE
----------
     12.8
```

```
1 row selected.
```

The previous query is used as a subquery in the WHERE clause of the following query.

**TYPE**

```
SELECT E.EMP_ID, E.LAST_NAME, E.FIRST_NAME, EP.PAY_RATE
FROM EMPLOYEE_TBL E, EMPLOYEE_PAY_TBL EP
WHERE E.EMP_ID = EP.EMP_ID
  AND EP.PAY_RATE > (SELECT PAY_RATE
                     FROM EMPLOYEE_PAY_TBL
                     WHERE EMP_ID = '313782439');
```

**OUTPUT**

```
EMP_ID     LAST_NAM FIRST_NA   PAY_RATE
--------   -------- --------   --------
311549902  STEPHENS TINA          17.5
442346889  PLEW     LINDA        14.75
213764555  GLASS    BRANDON      18.25
443679012  SPURGEON TIFFANY         15

4 rows selected.
```

The result of the subquery is 12.8 (shown in the last example), so the last condition of the WHERE clause is evaluated as:

```
AND EP.PAY_RATE > 12.8
```

You did not know the value of the pay rate for the given individual when you executed the query. However, the main query was able to compare each individual's pay rate to the subquery results.

**NOTE**

> Subqueries are frequently used to place conditions on a query when the exact conditions are unknown. The salary for 313782439 was unknown, but the subquery was designed to do the footwork for you.

## Subqueries with the INSERT Statement

Subqueries may also be used in conjunction with data manipulation language (DML) statements. The INSERT statement is the first you examine. The INSERT statement uses the data returned from the subquery to insert into another table. The selected data in the subquery can be modified with any of the character, date, or number functions.

**SYNTAX**

The basic syntax is as follows:

```
INSERT INTO TABLE_NAME [ (COLUMN1 [ COLUMN2 ]) ]
SELECT [ *|COLUMN1 [ COLUMN2 ])
FROM TABLE1 [, TABLE2 ]
[ WHERE VALUE OPERATOR ]
```

An example of the INSERT statement with a subquery:

**TYPE**

```
INSERT INTO RICH_EMPLOYEES
SELECT E.EMP_ID, E.LAST_NAME, E.FIRST_NAME, EP.PAY_RATE
FROM EMPLOYEE_TBL E, EMPLOYEE_PAY_TBL EP
WHERE E.EMP_ID = EP.EMP_ID
```

**14**

```
AND EP.PAY_RATE > (SELECT PAY_RATE
                   FROM EMPLOYEE_PAY_TBL
                   WHERE EMP_ID = '313782439');
```

**OUTPUT** 4 rows created.

This INSERT statement inserts the EMP_ID, LAST_NAME, FIRST_NAME, and PAY_RATE into a table called RICH_EMPLOYEES for all records of employees who have a pay rate greater than the pay rate of the employee with identification 313782439.

 **NOTE** Remember to use the COMMIT and ROLLBACK commands when using DML commands such as the INSERT statement.

## Subqueries with the UPDATE Statement

The subquery can be used in conjunction with the UPDATE statement. Either single or multiple columns in a table may be updated when using a subquery with the UPDATE statement.

**SYNTAX** The basic syntax is as follows:

```
UPDATE TABLE
SET [(}COLUMN_NAME [, COLUMN_NAME) ] =
    (SELECT [(]COLUMN_NAME [, COLUMN_NAME) ]
    FROM TABLE
    [ WHERE ]
```

Examples showing the use of the UPDATE statement with a subquery follow. The first query returns the employee identification of all employees that reside in Indianapolis. You can see that there are four individuals who meet this criteria.

**TYPE**
```
SELECT EMP_ID
FROM EMPLOYEE_TBL
WHERE CITY = 'INDIANAPOLIS';
```

**OUTPUT**
```
EMP_ID
--------
442346889
313782439
220984332
443679012

4 rows selected.
```

The first query is used as the subquery in the following UPDATE statement. The first query proves how many employee identifications are returned by the subquery. Now, the UPDATE with the subquery:

**TYPE**
```
UPDATE EMPLOYEE_PAY_TBL
SET PAY_RATE = PAY_RATE * 1.1
WHERE EMP_ID IN (SELECT EMP_ID
```

14

```
                       FROM EMPLOYEE_TBL
                       WHERE CITY = 'INDIANAPOLIS');
```

**OUTPUT**    4 rows updated.

As expected, four rows are updated. One very important thing to notice is that, unlike the example in the first section, this subquery returns multiple rows of data. Because you expect multiple rows to be returned, you have used the IN operator instead of the equal sign. Remember that IN is used to compare an expression to values in a list. If the equal sign was used, an error would have been returned.

**WARNING**

> Be sure to use the correct operator when evaluating a subquery. For instance, an operator used to compare an expression to one value, such as the equal sign, cannot be used to evaluate a subquery that returns more than one row of data.

## Subqueries with the DELETE Statement

The subquery may also be used in conjunction with the DELETE statement.

**SYNTAX**

The basic syntax is as follows:

```
DELETE FROM TABLE_NAME
[ WHERE OPERATOR [ VALUE ]
                [ (SELECT COLUMN_NAME
                FROM TABLE_NAME) ]
                [ WHERE) ]
```

In this example, you delete BRANDON GLASS's record from the EMPLOYEE_PAY_TBL table for one reason or another. You do not know what Brandon's employee identification number, but you can use a subquery to get his identification from the EMPLOYEE_TBL table, which contains the FIRST_NAME and LAST_NAME columns.

**TYPE**

```
DELETE FROM EMPLOYEE_PAY_TBL
WHERE EMP_ID = (SELECT EMP_ID
                FROM EMPLOYEE_TBL
                WHERE LAST_NAME = 'GLASS'
                  AND FIRST_NAME = 'BRANDON');
```

**OUTPUT**    1 row deleted.

**WARNING**

> Do not forget the use of the WHERE clause with the UPDATE and DELETE statements. All rows are updated or deleted from the target table if the WHERE clause is not used.

14

# Embedding a Subquery within a Subquery

A subquery may be embedded within another subquery, just as you can if the subquery were embedded within a regular query. When a subquery is used, that subquery is resolved before the main query. Likewise, the lowest level subquery is resolved first in embedded, or nested, subqueries, working out to the main query.

**NOTE**
You must check your particular implementation for limits on the amount of subqueries, if any, that may be used in a single statement. It may differ between vendors.

**SYNTAX**

The basic syntax for embedded subqueries is as follows:

```
SELECT COLUMN_NAME [, COLUMN_NAME ]
FROM TABLE1 [, TABLE2 ]
WHERE COLUMN_NAME OPERATOR (SELECT COLUMN_NAME
                           FROM TABLE
                           WHERE COLUMN_NAME OPERATOR
                                 (SELECT COLUMN_NAME
                                 FROM TABLE
                                 [ WHERE ]))
```

The following example uses two subqueries, one embedded within the other. You want to find out what customers have placed orders where the quantity multiplied by the cost of a single order is greater than the sum of the cost of all products.

**TYPE**

```
select cust_id, cust_name
from customer_tbl
where cust_id in (select o.cust_id
                  from orders_tbl o, products_tbl p
                  where o.prod_id = p.prod_id
                  and o.qty * p.cost > (select sum(cost)
                                        from products_tbl));
```

**OUTPUT**

```
CUST_ID    CUST_NAME
---------- ------------------------------
287        GAVINS PLACE
43         SCHYLERS NOVELTIES

2 rows selected.
```

Two rows that met the criteria of both subqueries were selected.

The following two examples show the results of each of the subqueries, to aid your understanding of how the main query was resolved.

**14**

**TYPE**
```
select sum(cost) from products_tbl;
```

**OUTPUT**
```
SUM(COST)
----------
     72.14
```

```
1 row selected.
```

**TYPE**
```
select o.cust_id
from orders_tbl o, products_tbl p
where o.prod_id = p.prod_id
  and o.qty * p.cost > 72.14;
```

**OUTPUT**
```
CUST_ID
----------
43
287
```

```
2 rows selected.
```

In essence, the main query (after the resolution of the subqueries) is evaluated as shown in the following example. The substitution of the second subquery:

**TYPE**
```
select cust_id, cust_name
from customer_tbl
where cust_id in (select o.cust_id
                  from orders_tbl o, products_tbl p
                  where o.prod_id = p.prod_id
                    and o.qty * p.cost > 72.14;
```

The substitution of the first subquery:

**TYPE**
```
select cust_id, cust_name
from customer_tbl
where cust_id in ('287','43');
```

The final results:

**OUTPUT**
```
CUST_ID     CUST_NAME
----------  ----------------------------
287         GAVINS PLACE
43          SCHYLERS NOVELTIES
```

```
2 rows selected.
```

> **WARNING**
>
> The use of multiple subqueries results in slower response time and accuracy of the results due to mistakes in the statement coding.

## Correlated Subqueries

Correlated subqueries are common in many SQL implementations. The concept of correlated subqueries is discussed as an ANSI standard SQL topic, and is covered briefly in

14

this hour. A *correlated subquery* is a subquery that is dependent upon information in the main query.

In the following example, the table join between CUSTOMER_TBL and ORDERS_TBL in the subquery is dependent upon the alias for CUSTOMER_TBL (C) in the main query. This query returns the name of all customers that have ordered more than 10 units of one or more items.

```
select c.cust_name
from customer_tbl c
where 10 < (select sum(o.qty)
            from orders_tbl o
            where o.cust_id = c.cust_id);
```

```
CUST_NAME
----------------------------
MARYS GIFT SHOP
SCOTTYS MARKET
SCHYLERS NOVELTIES
```

**NOTE**

> In the case of a correlated subquery, the reference to the table in the main query must be accomplished before the subquery can be resolved.

The subquery is slightly modified in the next statement to show you the total quantity of units ordered for each customer, allowing the previous results to be verified.

```
select c.cust_name, sum(o.qty)
from customer_tbl c,
     orders_tbl o
where c.cust_id = o.cust_id
group by c.cust_name;
```

**OUTPUT**

```
CUST_NAME                        SUM(O.QTY)
-----------------------------    ----------
ANDYS CANDIES                             2
GAVINS PLACE                             10
LESLIE GLEASON                            1
MARYS GIFT SHOP                         100
SCHYLERS NOVELTIES                       25
SCOTTYS MARKET                           20
WENDY WOLF                                2

7 rows selected.
```

The GROUP BY clause in this example is required, because another column is being selected with the aggregate function SUM. This gives you a sum for each customer. In the original subquery, a GROUP BY clause is not required, because the sum is used to achieve a total for the entire query, which is run against the record for each individual customer.

**14**

# Summary

By simple definition and general concept, a subquery is a query that is performed within another query in order to further place conditions on a query. A subquery may be used in a SQL statement's WHERE clause or HAVING clause. Queries are typically used within other queries (Data Query Language), but may also be used in the resolution of Data Manipulation Language statements such as the INSERT, UPDATE, and DELETE. All basic rules for DML apply when using subqueries with DML commands. The subquery's syntax is virtually the same as that of a standalone query, with a few minor restrictions. One of these restrictions is that the ORDER BY clause may not be used within a subquery; a GROUP BY clause can be used, however, which renders virtually the same effect. Subqueries are used to place conditions that are not necessarily known for a query, providing more power and flexibility with SQL.

## Q&A

**Q** **In the examples of subqueries, I noticed quite a bit of indentation. Is this necessary in the syntax of a subquery?**

**A** Absolutely not. The indentation is used merely to break the statement into separate parts, making the statement more readable and easier to follow.

**Q** **Is there a limit on the number of embedded subqueries that may be used in a single query?**

**A** Limitations such as the number of embedded subqueries allowed and the number of tables joined in a query are specific to each implementation. Some implementations may not have limits, although the use of too many embedded subqueries could drastically hinder SQL statement performance. Most limitations are affected by the actual hardware, CPU speed, and system memory available, although there are many other considerations.

**Q** **It seems that debugging a query with subqueries can prove to be very confusing, especially with embedded subqueries. What is the best way to debug a query with subqueries?**

**A** The best way to debug a query with subqueries is to evaluate the query in sections. First, evaluate the lowest-level subquery, then work your way to the main query (the same way the database evaluates the query). When you evaluate each subquery individually, you can substitute the returned values for each subquery in order to check your main query's logic. An error with a subquery is often the use of the operator used to evaluate the subquery, such as (=), IN, >, <, and so on.

**14**

# Workshop

The following workshop is composed of a series of quiz questions and practical exercises. The quiz questions are designed to test your overall understanding of the current material. The practical exercises are intended to afford you the opportunity to apply the concepts discussed during the current hour, as well as build upon the knowledge acquired in previous hours of study. Please take time to complete the quiz questions and exercises before continuing. You may refer to the answers in Appendix C.

## Quiz

1. What is the function of a subquery when used with a SELECT statement?

2. Can you update more than one column when using the UPDATE statement in conjunction with a subquery?

3. Are the following syntaxes correct? If not, what is the correct syntax?

   a.
   ```
   SELECT CUST_ID, CUST_NAME
           FROM CUSTOMER_TBL
           WHERE CUST_ID =
                         (SELECT CUST_ID
                              FROM ORDERS_TBL
                              WHERE ORD_NUM = '16C17')
   ```

   b.
   ```
   SELECT EMP_ID, SALARY
           FROM EMPLOYEE_PAY_TBL
           WHERE SALARY BETWEEN '20000'
                         AND (SELECT SALARY
                                  FROM EMPLOYEE_ID
                                  WHERE SALARY = '40000')
   ```

   c.
   ```
   UPDATE PRODUCTS_TBL
      SET COST = 1.15
      WHERE CUST_ID =
                    (SELECT CUST_ID
                     FROM ORDERS_TBL
                     WHERE ORD_NUM = '32A132')
   ```

4. What would happen if the following statement were run?

   ```
   DELETE FROM EMPLOYEE_TBL
   WHERE EMP_ID IN
                  (SELECT EMP_ID
                   FROM EMPLOYEE_PAY_TBL)
   ```

**14**

## Exercises

Use the following tables to complete the exercises:

EMPLOYEE_TBL

| emp_id | varchar2(9) | not null | primary key |
|---|---|---|---|
| last_name | varchar2(15) | not null | |
| first_name | varchar2(15) | not null | |
| middle_name | varchar2(15) | | |
| address | varchar2(30) | not null | |
| city | varchar2(15) | not null | |
| state | char(2) | not null | |
| zip | number(5) | not null | |
| phone | char(10) | | |
| pager | char(10) | | |

EMPLOYEE_PAY_TBL

| emp_id | varchar2(9) | not null | primary key |
|---|---|---|---|
| position | varchar2(15) | not null | |
| date_hire | date | | |
| pay_rate | number(4,2) | not null | |
| date_last_raise | date | | |

constraint emp_fk foreign key  (emp_id) references
   employee_tbl (emp_id)

CUSTOMER_TBL

| cust_id | varchar2(10) | not null | primary key |
|---|---|---|---|
| cust_name | varchar2(30) | not null | |
| cust_address | varchar2(20) | not null | |
| cust_city | varchar2(15) | not null | |
| cust_state | char(2) | not null | |
| cust_zip | number(5) | not null | |
| cust_phone | number(10) | | |
| cust_fax | number(10) | | |

ORDERS_TBL

| ord_num | varchar2(10) | not null | primary key |
|---|---|---|---|
| cust_id | varchar2(10) | not null | |
| prod_id | varchar2(10) | not null | |
| qty | number(6) | not null | |
| ord_date | date | | |

14

```
PRODUCTS_TBL
```
```
prod_id          varchar2(10)        not null         primary key
prod_desc        varchar2(40)        not null
cost             number(6,2)         not null
```

1. Using a subquery, write a SQL statement to update the CUSTOMER_TBL table, changing the customer name to DAVIDS MARKET, who has an order with order number 23E934.

2. Using a subquery, write a query that returns all the names of all employees who have a pay rate greater than JOHN DOE, whose employee identification number is 343559876.

3. Using a subquery, write a query that lists all products that cost more than the average cost of all products.

14

# Hour **15**

# Combining Multiple Queries into One

During this hour you learn how to combine SQL queries into one by using the UNION, UNION ALL, INTERSECT, and EXCEPT operators. Once again, you must check your particular implementation for any variations in the use of the UNION, UNION ALL, INTERSECT, and EXCEPT operators.

The highlights of this hour include

- ☐ An overview of the operators used to combine queries
- ☐ When to use the commands to combine queries
- ☐ Using the GROUP BY with the compound operators
- ☐ Using the ORDER BY with the compound operators
- ☐ How to retrieve accurate data

## Single Queries Versus Compound Queries

The single query is one SELECT statement, while the compound query includes two or more SELECT statements.

Compound queries are formed by using some type of operator, which is used to join the two queries. The UNION operator in the following examples is used to join two queries.

A single SQL statement could be written as follows:

```
SELECT EMP_ID, SALARY, PAY_RATE
FROM EMPLOYEE_PAY_TBL
WHERE SALARY IS NOT NULL OR
PAY_RATE IS NOT NULL
```

This is the same statement using the UNION operator:

```
SELECT EMP_ID, SALARY
FROM EMPLOYEE_PAY_TBL
WHERE SALARY IS NOT NULL
UNION
SELECT EMP_ID, PAY_RATE
FROM EMPLOYEE_PAY_TBL
WHERE PAY_RATE IS NOT NULL
```

The previous statements return pay information for all employees who are either paid hourly or a salary.

**NOTE**

> If you executed the second query, the output has two column headings: EMP_ID and SALARY. Each individual's pay rate is listed under the SALARY column. When using the UNION operator, column headings are determined by column names or column aliases used in the first SELECT of the UNION.

# Why Would I Ever Want to Use a Compound Query?

Compound operators are used to combine and restrict the results of two SELECT statements. These operators can be used to return or suppress the output of duplicate records. Compound operators can bring together similar data that is stored in different fields.

Compound queries allow you to combine the results of more than one query in order to return a single set of data. Compound queries are often simpler to write than a single query with complex conditions. Compound queries also allow for more flexibility regarding the never-ending task of data retrieval.

# Compound Query Operators

The compound query operators vary among database vendors. The ANSI standard includes the following operators: UNION, UNION ALL, EXCEPT, and INTERSECT, all of which are discussed in the following sections.

# The UNION **Operator**

The UNION operator is used to combine the results of two or more SELECT statements without returning any duplicate rows. In other words, if a row of output exists in the results of one query, the same row is not returned even though it exists in the second query that combined with a UNION operator. To use UNION, each SELECT must have the same number of columns selected, the same number of column expressions, the same datatype, and have them in the same order—but they do not have to be the same length. The syntax is as follows:

**SYNTAX**

```
SELECT COLUMN1 [, COLUMN2 ]
FROM TABLE1 [, TABLE2 ]
[ WHERE ]
UNION
SELECT COLUMN1 [, COLUMN2 ]
FROM TABLE1 [, TABLE2 ]
[ WHERE ]
```

Usage:

```
SELECT EMP_ID FROM EMPLOYEE_TBL
UNION
SELECT EMP_ID FROM EMPLOYEE_PAY_TBL
```

**ANALYSIS**    Those employee IDs that are in both tables appear only once in the results.

This hour's examples begin with a simple select from two tables:

**TYPE**

```
Select prod_desc from products_tbl;
```

**OUTPUT**

```
PROD_DESC
- - - - - - - - - - - - - - - - - - - - - -
WITCHES COSTUME
PLASTIC PUMPKIN 18 INCH
FALSE PARAFFIN TEETH
LIGHTED LANTERNS
ASSORTED COSTUMES
CANDY CORN
PUMPKIN CANDY
PLASTIC SPIDERS
ASSORTED MASKS

9 rows selected.
```

**TYPE**

```
select prod_desc from products_tmp;
```

**OUTPUT**

```
PROD_DESC
- - - - - - - - - - - - - - - - - - - - - -
ASSORTED COSTUMES
ASSORTED MASKS
WITCHES COSTUME
FALSE PARAFFIN TEETH
LIGHTED LANTERNS
CANDY CORN

6 rows selected.
```

Now you combine the same two queries with the UNION operator, making a compound query.

**TYPE**

```
select prod_desc from products_tbl
UNION
select prod_desc from products_tmp;
```

**OUTPUT**

```
PROD_DESC
-----------------------
ASSORTED COSTUMES
ASSORTED MASKS
CANDY CORN
FALSE PARAFFIN TEETH
LIGHTED LANTERNS
PLASTIC PUMPKIN 18 INCH
PLASTIC SPIDERS
PUMPKIN CANDY
WITCHES COSTUME

9 rows selected.
```

In the first query, nine rows of data were returned, and six rows of data were returned from the second query. Nine rows of data are returned when the UNION operator combines the two queries. Only nine rows are returned because duplicate rows of data are not returned when using the UNION operator.

The next example shows an example of combining two unrelated queries with the UNION operator:

**TYPE**

```
select prod_desc from products_tbl
union
select last_name from employee_tbl;
```

**OUTPUT**

```
PROD_DESC
-----------------------
ASSORTED COSTUMES
ASSORTED MASKS
CANDY CORN
FALSE PARAFFIN TEETH
GLASS
LIGHTED LANTERNS
PLASTIC PUMPKIN 18 INCH
PLASTIC SPIDERS
PLEW
PUMPKIN CANDY
SPURGEON
STEPHENS
WALLACE
WITCHES COSTUME

14 rows selected.
```

The PROD_DESC and LAST_NAME values are listed together, and the column heading taken is from the column name in the first query.

**15**

# The UNION ALL **Operator**

The UNION ALL operator is used to combine the results of two SELECT statements including duplicate rows. The same rules that apply to the UNION apply to the UNION ALL. The UNION and UNION ALL operators are the same, although one returns duplicate rows of data where the other does not. The syntax is as follows:

```
SELECT COLUMN1 [ , COLUMN2 ]
FROM TABLE1 [ , TABLE2 ]
[ WHERE ]
UNION ALL
SELECT COLUMN1 [ , COLUMN2 ]
FROM TABLE1 [ , TABLE2 ]
[ WHERE ]
```

Usage:

```
SELECT EMP_ID FROM EMPLOYEE_TBL
UNION ALL
SELECT EMP_ID FROM EMPLOYEE_PAY_TBL
```

**ANALYSIS**  The preceding SQL statement returns all employee IDs from both tables and shows duplicates.

Here is the same compound query in the previous section with the UNION ALL operator:

**TYPE**
```
select prod_desc from products_tbl
union all
select prod_desc from products_tmp;
```

**OUTPUT**
```
PROD_DESC
-----------------------
WITCHES COSTUME
PLASTIC PUMPKIN 18 INCH
FALSE PARAFFIN TEETH
LIGHTED LANTERNS
ASSORTED COSTUMES
CANDY CORN
PUMPKIN CANDY
PLASTIC SPIDERS
ASSORTED MASKS
ASSORTED COSTUMES
ASSORTED MASKS
WITCHES COSTUME
FALSE PARAFFIN TEETH
LIGHTED LANTERNS
CANDY CORN

15 rows selected.
```

Notice that there were 15 rows returned in this query (9+6), since duplicate records are retrieved with the UNION ALL operator.

# The INTERSECT **Operator**

The INTERSECT operator is used to combine two SELECT statements, but returns rows only from the first SELECT statement that are identical to a row in the second SELECT statement. Just as with the UNION, the same rules apply when using the INTERSECT operator. The syntax is as follows:

**SYNTAX**

```
SELECT COLUMN1 [, COLUMN2 ]
FROM TABLE1 [, TABLE2 ]
[ WHERE ]
INTERSECT
SELECT COLUMN1 [, COLUMN2 ]
FROM TABLE1 [, TABLE2 ]
[ WHERE ]
```

Usage:

```
SELECT CUST_ID FROM CUSTOMER_TBL
INTERSECT
SELECT CUST_ID FROM ORDERS_TBL;
```

**ANALYSIS**  The preceding SQL statement returns the customer identification for those customers who have placed an order.

The following example illustrates the INTERSECT using the two original queries in this hour:

**TYPE**

```
select prod_desc from products_tbl
intersect
select prod_desc from products_tmp;
```

**OUTPUT**

```
PROD_DESC
-------------------------
ASSORTED COSTUMES
ASSORTED MASKS
CANDY CORN
FALSE PARAFFIN TEETH
LIGHTED LANTERNS
WITCHES COSTUME

6 rows selected.
```

Only six rows are returned, because only six rows were identical between the output of the two single queries.

## The EXCEPT Operator

The EXCEPT operator combines two SELECT statements and returns rows from the first SELECT statement that are not returned by the second SELECT statement. Once again, the same rules that apply to the UNION operator also apply to the EXCEPT operator. The syntax is as follows:

**SYNTAX**

```
SELECT COLUMN1 [, COLUMN2 ]
FROM TABLE1 [, TABLE2 ]
[ WHERE ]
EXCEPT
SELECT COLUMN1 [, COLUMN2 ]
FROM TABLE1 [, TABLE2 ]
[ WHERE ]
```

**15**

Study the following example:

```
select prod_desc from products_tbl
EXCEPT
select prod_desc from products_tmp;
```

```
PROD_DESC
------------------------
PLASTIC PUMPKIN 18 INCH
PLASTIC SPIDERS
PUMPKIN CANDY

3 rows selected.
```

According to the results, there were three rows of data returned by the first query that were not returned by the second query.

**NOTE**

> The EXCEPT operator is known as the MINUS operator in some implementations. Check your implementation for the operator name that performs the EXCEPT operator's function.

```
select prod_desc from products_tbl
minus
select prod_desc from products_tmp;
```

```
PROD_DESC
------------------------
PLASTIC PUMPKIN 18 INCH
PLASTIC SPIDERS
PUMPKIN CANDY

3 rows selected.
```

# Using an ORDER BY with a Compound Query

The ORDER BY clause may be used with a compound query. However, the ORDER BY can only be used to order the results of both queries. Therefore, there can only be one ORDER BY clause in a compound query, even though the compound query may consist of multiple individual queries or SELECT statements. The ORDER BY must reference the columns being ordered by an alias or by the number of column order. The syntax is as follows:

```
SELECT COLUMN1 [, COLUMN2 ]
FROM TABLE1 [, TABLE2 ]
[ WHERE ]
OPERATOR{UNION ¦ EXCEPT ¦ INTERSECT ¦ UNION ALL}
SELECT COLUMN1 [, COLUMN2 ]
FROM TABLE1 [, TABLE2 ]
[ WHERE ]
[ ORDER BY ]
```

Usage:

```
SELECT EMP_ID FROM EMPLOYEE_TBL
UNION
SELECT EMP_ID FROM EMPLOYEE_PAY_TBL
ORDER BY 1;
```

 **ANALYSIS** The results of the compound query are sorted by the first column of each individual query. Duplicate records can easily be recognized by sorting compound queries.

 **NOTE**

> The column in the ORDER BY clause is referenced by the number 1 instead of the actual column name.

**ANALYSIS** The preceding SQL statement returns the employee ID from the EMPLOYEE_TBL and the EMPLOYEE_PAY_TBL, but does not show duplicates and orders by the employee ID.

The following example shows the use of the ORDER BY clause with a compound query. The column name can be used in the ORDER BY clause if the column sorted by has the same name in all individual queries of the statement.

 **TYPE**
```
select prod_desc from products_tbl
union
select prod_desc from products_tbl
order by prod_desc;
```

**OUTPUT**
```
PROD_DESC
-----------------------
ASSORTED COSTUMES
ASSORTED MASKS
CANDY CORN
FALSE PARAFFIN TEETH
LIGHTED LANTERNS
PLASTIC PUMPKIN 18 INCH
PLASTIC SPIDERS
PUMPKIN CANDY
WITCHES COSTUME

9 rows selected.
```

The following query uses a numeric value in place of the actual column name in the ORDER BY clause:

 **TYPE**
```
select prod_desc from products_tbl
union
select prod_desc from products_tbl
order by 1;
```

**OUTPUT**
```
PROD_DESC
-----------------------
ASSORTED COSTUMES
ASSORTED MASKS
```

**15**

```
CANDY CORN
FALSE PARAFFIN TEETH
LIGHTED LANTERNS
PLASTIC PUMPKIN 18 INCH
PLASTIC SPIDERS
PUMPKIN CANDY
WITCHES COSTUME

9 rows selected.
```

# Using a GROUP BY with a Compound Query

Unlike the ORDER BY, the GROUP BY can be used in each SELECT statement of a compound query, but may also be used following all individual queries. In addition, the HAVING clause (sometimes used with the GROUP BY clause) may be used in each SELECT statement of a compound statement. The syntax is as follows:

**SYNTAX**

```
SELECT COLUMN1 [, COLUMN2 ]
FROM TABLE1 [, TABLE2 ]
[ WHERE ]
[ GROUP BY ]
[ HAVING ]
OPERATOR {UNION ¦ EXCEPT ¦ INTERSECT ¦ UNION ALL}
SELECT COLUMN1 [, COLUMN2 ]
FROM TABLE1 [, TABLE2 ]
[ WHERE ]
[ GROUP BY ]
[ HAVING ]
[ ORDER BY ]
```

In the following example, you select a literal string to represent customer records, employee records, and product records. Each individual query is simply a count of all records in each appropriate table. The GROUP BY clause is used to group the results of the entire report by the numeric value 1, which represents the first column in each individual query.

**TYPE**

```
select 'CUSTOMERS' TYPE, COUNT(*)
FROM CUSTOMER_TBL
UNION
SELECT 'EMPLOYEES' TYPE, COUNT(*)
FROM EMPLOYEE_TBL
UNION
SELECT 'PRODUCTS' TYPE, COUNT(*)
FROM PRODUCTS_TBL
GROUP BY 1;
```

**OUTPUT**

```
TYPE         COUNT(*)
--------  ----------
CUSTOMERS        15
EMPLOYEES         6
PRODUCTS          9

3 rows selected.
```

The following query is identical to the previous query, except that the ORDER BY clause is used as well:

```
select 'CUSTOMERS' TYPE, COUNT(*)
FROM CUSTOMER_TBL
UNION
SELECT 'EMPLOYEES' TYPE, COUNT(*)
FROM EMPLOYEE_TBL
UNION
SELECT 'PRODUCTS' TYPE, COUNT(*)
FROM PRODUCTS_TBL
GROUP BY 1
ORDER BY 2;
```

**OUTPUT**
```
TYPE            COUNT(*)
--------        ----------
EMPLOYEES              6
PRODUCTS              9
CUSTOMERS            15

3 rows selected.
```

This is sorted by column 2, which was the count on each table. Hence, the final output is sorted by the count from least to greatest.

## Retrieving Accurate Data

Be cautious when using the compound operators. For instance, incorrect or incomplete data may be returned if you were using the INTERSECT operator and you used the wrong SELECT statement as the first individual query. In addition, consider whether duplicate records are wanted when using the UNION and UNION ALL operators. What about EXCEPT? Do you need any of the rows that were not returned by the second query? As you can see, the wrong compound query operator or the wrong order of individual queries in a compound query can easily cause misleading data to be returned.

**NOTE**

> Incomplete data returned by a query qualifies as incorrect data.

## Summary

You have been introduced to compound queries. All SQL statements previous to this hour have consisted of a single query. Compound queries allow multiple individual queries to be used together as a single query to achieve the data result set desired as output. The compound query operators discussed include UNION, UNION ALL, INTERSECT, and EXCEPT (MINUS). UNION returns the output of two single queries without displaying duplicate rows of data. UNION ALL simply displays all output of single queries, regardless of existing duplicate rows. INTERSECT is used to return identical rows between two queries. EXCEPT (the same as MINUS) is used to return the results of one query that do not exist in another query. Compound queries provide greater flexibility when trying to satisfy the requirements of various queries, which, without the use of compound operators, could result in very complex queries.

**15**

## Q&A

**Q** How are the columns referenced in the GROUP BY clause when using the GROUP BY clause with a compound query?

**A** The columns may be referenced by the actual column name or by the number of the column placement in the query if the column names are not identical in the two queries.

**Q** I realize what the EXCEPT operator does, but would the outcome change if I were to reverse the SELECT statements?

**A** Yes. The order of the individual queries is very important when using the EXCEPT or MINUS operators. Remember that all rows are returned from the first query that are not returned by the second query. Changing the order of the two individual queries in the compound query could definitely affect the results.

**Q** Must the datatype and the length of columns in a compound query be the same in both queries?

**A** No. Only the datatype must be the same. The length can differ.

# Workshop

The following workshop is composed of a series of quiz questions and practical exercises. The quiz questions are designed to test your overall understanding of the current material. The practical exercises are intended to afford you the opportunity to apply the concepts discussed during the current hour, as well as build upon the knowledge acquired in previous hours of study. Please take time to complete the quiz questions and exercises before continuing. You may refer to the answers in Appendix C.

## Quiz

1. Is the syntax correct for the following compound queries? If not, what would correct the syntax? Use the EMPLOYEE_TBL and the EMPLOYEE_PAY_TBL shown as follows:

```
EMPLOYEE_TBL

emp_id            varchar2(9)          not null,
last_name         varchar2(15)         not null,
first_name        varchar2(15)         not null,
middle_name       varchar2(15),
address           varchar2(30)         not null,
city              varchar2(15)         not null,
state             char(2)              not null,
zip               number(5)            not null,
phone             char(10),
pager             char(10),
constraint emp_pk primary key (emp_id)
```

```
EMPLOYEE_PAY_TBL
emp_id                       varchar2(9)                not null,
primary key,
position                     varchar2(15)    not null,
date_hire                    date,
pay_rate                     number(4,2)     not null,
date_last_raise              date,
salary                       number(8,2),
bonus                        number(8,2),
constraint emp_fk foreign key (emp_id)
references employee_tbl (emp_id)
```

a.

```
SELECT EMP_ID, LAST_NAME, FIRST_NAME
FROM EMPLOYEE_TBL
UNION
SELECT EMP_ID, POSITION, DATE_HIRE
FROM EMPLOYEE_PAY_TBL
```

b.

```
SELECT EMP_ID FROM EMPLOYEE_TBL
UNION ALL
SELECT EMP_ID FROM EMPLOYEE_PAY_TBL
ORDER BY EMP_ID
```

c.

```
SELECT EMP_ID FROM EMPLOYEE_PAY_TBL
INTERSECT
SELECT EMP_ID FROM EMPLOYEE_TBL
ORDER BY 1
```

2. Match the correct operator to the following statements.

|  | STATEMENT | OPERATOR |
|---|---|---|
| a. | Show duplicates | UNION |
|  |  | INTERSECT |
| b. | Return only rows from the first query that match those in the second query | UNION ALL |
|  |  | EXCEPT |
| c. | Return no duplicates |  |
| d. | Return only rows from the first query not returned by the second |  |

15

# Exercises

1. Using the CUSTOMER_TBL and the ORDERS_TBL as listed:

CUSTOMER_TBL

| | | | |
|---|---|---|---|
| cust_id | varchar2(10) | not null | primary key, |
| cust_name | varchar2(30) | not null, | |
| cust_address | varchar2(20) | not null, | |
| cust_city | varchar2(15) | not null, | |
| cust_state | char(2) | not null, | |
| cust_zip | number(5) | not null, | |
| cust_phone | number(10), | | |
| cust_fax | number(10) | | |

ORDERS_TBL

| | | | |
|---|---|---|---|
| ord_num | varchar2(10) | not null | primary key, |
| cust_id | varchar2(10) | not null, | |
| prod_id | varchar2(10) | not null, | |
| qty | number(6) | not null, | |
| ord_date | date | | |

a. Write a compound query to find the customers that have placed an order.

b. Write a compound query to find the customers that have not placed an order.

# PART

# V

# SQL Performance Tuning

## Hour

**PART V**

# Hour 16

# Using Indexes to Improve Performance

During this hour you learn how to improve SQL statement performance by creating and using indexes.

You begin with the CREATE INDEX command and learn how to use indexes that have been created on tables.

The highlights of this hour include

- ☐ How to create an index
- ☐ How do indexes work?
- ☐ The different types of indexes
- ☐ When to use indexes
- ☐ When not to use indexes

## What Is an Index?

Simply put, an *index* is a pointer to data in a table. An index in a database is very similar to an index in the back of a book. For example, if you want to reference all pages in a book that discuss a certain topic, you first refer to the index, which lists all topics alphabetically, and are then referred to one or more specific page numbers. An index in a database works the same way in that a query is pointed to the exact physical location of data in a table. You are actually being directed to the data's location in an underlying file of the database, but as far as you are concerned, you are referring to a table.

Which would be faster, looking through a book page by page for some information, or searching the book's index and getting a page number? Of course, using the book's index is the most efficient method. A lot of time can be saved if that book is large. Say you have a small book of just a few pages. In this case it may be much faster to check the pages for the information than to flip back and forth between the index and pages of the book. When a database does not use an index, it is performing what is typically called a *full table scan*, the same as flipping through a book page by page. Full table scans are discussed later this hour.

An index is stored separately from the table for which the index was created. An index's main purpose is to improve the performance of data retrieval. Indexes can be created or dropped with no effect on the data. However, once dropped, performance of data retrieval may be slowed. An index does take up physical space, and often grows larger than the table itself.

## How Do Indexes Work?

When an index is created, it records the location of values in a table that are associated with the column that is indexed. Entries are added to the index when new data is added to the table. When a query is executed against the database and a condition is specified on a column in the WHERE clause that is indexed, the index is first searched for the values specified in the WHERE clause. If the value is found in the index, the index returns the exact location of the searched data in the table. Figure 16.1 illustrates how an index functions.

**Figure 16.1.**

*Table access using an index.*

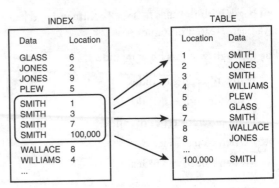

Suppose the following query was issued:

```
SELECT *
FROM TABLE_NAME
WHERE NAME = 'SMITH';
```

16

As shown in Figure 16.1, the name index is referenced to resolve the location of all names equal to 'SMITH'. Once the location is determined, the data can be quickly retrieved from the table. The data, in this case names, is alphabetized in the index.

A full table scan would occur if there were no index on the table and the same query was executed, which means that every row of data in the table would be read in order to retrieve information pertaining to all individuals with the name SMITH.

# The CREATE INDEX Command

The CREATE INDEX statement, as with many other statements in SQL, varies greatly among different relational database vendors. Most relational database implementations use the CREATE INDEX statement.

```
CREATE INDEX INDEX_NAME ON TABLE_NAME
```

The syntax is where the vendors start varying greatly on the CREATE INDEX statement options. Some implementations allow the specification of a storage clause (as with the CREATE TABLE statement), ordering (DESC¦¦ASC), and the use of clusters. You must check your particular implementation for its correct syntax.

# Types of Indexes

There are different types of indexes that can be created on tables in a database, all of which serve the same goal: to improve database performance by expediting data retrieval. This hour discusses single-column indexes, composite indexes, and unique indexes.

**NOTE**

Indexes can be created during table creation in some implementations. Most implementations accommodate a command, aside from the CREATE TABLE command, used to create indexes. You must check your particular implementation for the exact syntax for the command, if any, that is available to create an index.

## Single-Column Indexes

Indexing on a single column of a table is the simplest and most common manifestation of an index. Obviously, a single-column index is one that is created based on only one table column. The basic syntax is as follows:

```
CREATE INDEX INDEX_NAME
ON TABLE_NAME (COLUMN_NAME)
```

For example, if you want to create an index on the EMPLOYEE_TBL table for employees' last names, the command used to create the index would look like this:

```
CREATE INDEX NAME_IDX
ON EMPLOYEE_TBL (LAST_NAME);
```

**NOTE**

You should plan your tables and indexes. Do not assume that because an index has been created that all performance issues are resolved. The index may not help at all (it may actually hinder performance), and may just take up disk space.

**TIP**

Single-column indexes are most effective when used on columns that are frequently used alone in the WHERE clause as query conditions. Good candidates for a single-column index are an individual identification number, a serial number, or a system-assigned key.

## Unique Indexes

*Unique indexes* are used not only for performance, but also for data integrity. A unique index does not allow any duplicate values to be inserted into the table. Otherwise, the unique index performs the same way a regular index performs. The syntax is as follows:

```
CREATE UNIQUE INDEX INDEX_NAME
ON TABLE_NAME (COLUMN_NAME)
```

If you want to create a unique index on the EMPLOYEE_TBL table for an employee's last name, the command used to create the unique index would look like this:

```
CREATE UNIQUE INDEX NAME_IDX
ON EMPLOYEE_TBL (LAST_NAME);
```

The only problem with this index is that every individual's last name in the EMPLOYEE_TBL table must be unique—pretty impractical. However, a unique index should be created for a column, such as an individual's social security number, since each of these numbers for each individual is unique.

You may be wondering, "What if an employee's SSN were the primary key for a table?" An index is usually implicitly created when you define a primary key for a table. However, a company may use a fictitious number for an employee ID, but maintain each employees' SSN for tax purposes. You probably want to index this column, and yet ensure that all entries into this column are unique values.

**NOTE**

The unique index can only be created on a column in a table whose values are unique. In other words, you cannot create a unique index on an existing table with data that already contains records on the indexed key.

## Composite Indexes

**SYNTAX**

A *composite index* is an index on two or more columns of a table. You should consider performance when creating a composite index, as the order of columns in the index has a measurable effect on data retrieval speed. Generally, the most restrictive value should be placed first for optimum performance. However, the columns that will always be specified should be placed first. The syntax is as follows:

```
CREATE INDEX INDEX_NAME
ON TABLE_NAME (COLUMN1, COLUMN2)
```

An example of a composite index follows:

```
CREATE INDEX ORD_IDX
ON ORDERS_TBL (CUST_ID, PROD_ID);
```

In this example, you create a composite index based on two columns in the ORDERS_TBL table: CUST_ID and PROD_ID. You assume that these two columns are frequently used together as conditions in the WHERE clause of a query.

**TIP**

Composite indexes are most effective on table columns that are used together frequently as conditions in a query's WHERE clause.

## Single-Column Versus Composite Indexes

In deciding whether to create a single-column index or a composite index, take into consideration the column(s) that you may use very frequently in a query's WHERE clause as filter conditions. Should there be only one column used, a single-column index should be the choice. Should there be two or more columns that are frequently used in the WHERE clause as filters, the composite index would be the best choice.

# When Should Indexes Be Considered?

Unique indexes are implicitly used in conjunction with a primary key in order for the primary key to work. Foreign keys are also excellent candidates for an index, as they are often used to join the parent table. Most, if not all, columns used for table joins should be indexed.

Columns that are frequently referenced in the ORDER BY and GROUP BY clauses should be considered for indexes. For instance, if you are sorting on an individual's name, it would be quite beneficial to have any index on the name column. It renders an automatic alphabetical order on every name, thus simplifying the actual sort operation and expediting the output results.

Furthermore, indexes should be created on columns with a high number of unique values, or columns when used as filter conditions in the WHERE clause return a low percentage of rows of data from a table. This is where trial and error may come into play. Just as production code and database structures should always be tested before their implementation into production, so should indexes. This testing is time that should be spent trying different combinations of indexes, no indexes, single-column indexes, and composite indexes. There is no cut and dried rule for using indexes. The effective use of indexes requires a thorough knowledge of table relationships, query and transaction requirements, and the data itself.

## When Should Indexes Be Avoided?

Although indexes are intended to enhance a database's performance, there are times when they should be avoided. The following guidelines indicate when the use of an index should be reconsidered:

- [ ] Indexes should not be used on small tables.
- [ ] Indexes should not be used on columns that return a high percentage of data rows when used as a filter condition in a query's WHERE clause. For instance, you would not have an entry for the word "the" or "and" in the index of a book.
- [ ] Tables that have frequent, large batch update jobs run can be indexed. However, the batch job's performance is slowed considerably by the index. The conflict of having an index on a table that is frequently loaded or manipulated by a large batch process can be corrected by dropping the index before the batch job, then recreating the index after the job has completed.
- [ ] Indexes should not be used on columns that contain a high number of NULL values.
- [ ] Columns that are frequently manipulated should not be indexed. Maintenance on the index can be come excessive.

**WARNING**

Caution should be taken when creating indexes on a table's extremely long keys, as performance is inevitably slowed by high I/O costs.

**16**

You can see in Figure 16.2 that an index on a column such as sex may not prove beneficial. For instance, suppose the following query was submitted to the database:

```
SELECT *
FROM TABLE_NAME
WHERE GENDER = 'FEMALE';
```

**Figure 16.2.**

*When to avoid using an index.*

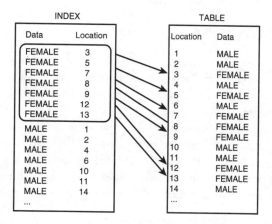

By referring to Figure 16.2, which is based on the previous query, you can see that there is constant activity between the table and its index. Since a high number of data rows is returned WHERE GENDER = 'FEMALE' (or MALE), the database server constantly has to read the index, then the table, then the index, then the table, and so on. In this case it may be more efficient for a full table scan to occur, since a high percentage of the table must be read anyway.

As a general rule, you do not want to use an index on a column used in a query's condition that will return a high percentage of data rows from the table. In other words, do not create an index on a column such as sex, or any column that contains very few distinct values.

**TIP**

Indexes can be very good for performance, but in some cases may actually hurt performance. Refrain from creating indexes on columns that will contain few unique values, such as sex, state of residence, and so on.

## Dropping an Index

An index can be dropped rather simply. Check your particular implementation for the exact syntax, but most major implementations use the DROP command. Care should be taken when dropping an index, as performance may be slowed drastically (or improved!). The syntax is as follows:

```
DROP INDEX INDEX_NAME
```

The most common reason for dropping an index is in attempt to improve performance. Remember that if you drop an index, you can also recreate it. Indexes may need to be rebuilt sometimes, to reduce fragmentation. It is often necessary to experiment with the use of indexes in a database to determine the route to best performance, which may involve creating an index, dropping it, and eventually recreating it, with or without modifications.

## Summary

You have learned that indexes can be used to improve the overall performance of queries and transactions performed within the database. Database indexes, like those of a book, allow specific data to be quickly referenced from a table. The most common method for creating indexes is through use of the CREATE INDEX command. There are different types of indexes available among various SQL implementations. Unique indexes, single-column indexes, and composite indexes are among those different types of indexes. There are many factors to consider when deciding on the index type used to best meet the needs of your database. The effective use of indexes often requires some experimentation, a thorough knowledge of table relationships and data, and a little patience—but patience now can save minutes, hours, or even days of work later.

## Q&A

**Q Does an index actually take up space the way a table does?**

A Yes. An index takes up physical space in a database. In fact, an index can become much larger than the table for which the index was created.

**Q If you drop an index in order for a batch job to complete faster, how long does it take to recreate the index?**

A Many factors are involved, such as the size of the index being dropped, CPU usage, and the machine's power.

**Q Should all indexes be unique indexes?**

A No. Unique indexes allow no duplicate values. There may be a need for the allowance of duplicate values in a table.

## Workshop

The following workshop is composed of a series of quiz questions and practical exercises. The quiz questions are designed to test your overall understanding of the current material. The practical exercises are intended to afford you the opportunity to apply the concepts discussed during the current hour, as well as build upon the knowledge acquired in previous hours of study. Please take time to complete the quiz questions and exercises before continuing. You may refer to the answers in Appendix C.

**16**

## Quiz

1. What are some major disadvantages of using indexes?
2. Why is the order of columns in a composite important?
3. Should a column with a large percentage of NULLs be indexed?
4. Is the main purpose of an index to stop duplicate values in a table?
5. True or false: The main reason for a composite index is for aggregate function usage in an index.

## Exercises

1. For the following situations, decide whether an index should be used and if so, what type of index should be used.

    a. Several columns, but a rather small table.

    b. Medium-sized table, no duplicates should be allowed.

    c. Several columns, very large table, several columns used as filters in the WHERE clause.

    d. Large table, many columns, lot of data manipulation.

**16**

# Hour **17**

# Improving Database Performance

During this hour you learn how to tune your SQL statement for maximum performance using some very simple methods.

The highlights of this hour include:

- [ ] What is SQL statement tuning?
- [ ] Database tuning versus SQL statement tuning
- [ ] Formatting your SQL statement
- [ ] Properly joining tables
- [ ] The most restrictive condition
- [ ] Full table scans
- [ ] Invoking the use of indexes
- [ ] Avoiding the use of OR and HAVING
- [ ] Avoiding large sort operations

# What Is SQL Statement Tuning?

*SQL statement tuning* is the process of optimally building SQL statements to achieve results in the most effective and efficient manner. SQL tuning begins with the basic arrangement of the elements in a query. Simple formatting plays a rather large role in the optimization of a statement.

SQL statement tuning mainly involves tweaking a statement's FROM and WHERE clauses. It is in these two clauses that the database server decides how to evaluate a query. To this point you have learned the FROM and WHERE clauses' basics. Now it is time to learn how to fine-tune them for better results and happier users.

# Database Tuning Versus SQL Tuning

Before continuing with your SQL statement tuning lesson, it is important to understand the difference between tuning a database and tuning the SQL statements that access the database.

*Database tuning* is the process of tuning the actual database, which encompasses the allocated memory, disk usage, CPU, I/O, and underlying database processes. Tuning a database also involves the management and manipulation of the database structure itself, such as the design and layout of tables and indexes. There are many other considerations when tuning a database, but these tasks are normally accomplished by the database administrator. The objective of database tuning is to ensure that the database has been designed in a way that best accommodates expected activity within the database.

*SQL tuning* is the process of tuning the SQL statements that access the database. These SQL statements include database queries and transactional operations such as inserts, updates, and deletes. The objective of SQL statement tuning is to formulate statements that most effectively access the database in its current state, taking advantage of database and system resources and indexes.

**NOTE**
> Both database tuning and SQL statement tuning must be performed in order to achieve optimal results when accessing the database. A poorly tuned database may very well render wasted effort in SQL tuning, and vice versa.

# Formatting Your SQL Statement

Formatting your SQL statement sounds like an obvious statement; as obvious as it may sound, it is worth mentioning. There are several things that a newcomer to SQL will probably not take into consideration when building a SQL statement. The following sections discuss the listed considerations; some are common sense, others are not so obvious:

☐ Formatting SQL statements for readability

☐ The order of tables in the FROM clause

☐ The placement of the most restrictive conditions in the WHERE clause

☐ The placement of join conditions in the WHERE clause

**NOTE** Most relational database implementations have what is called a *SQL optimizer*, which evaluates a SQL statement and determines the best method for executing the statement based on the way a SQL statement is written and the availability of indexes in the database. Not all optimizers are the same. Please check your implementation or consult the database administrator on how the optimizer reads SQL code. You should understand how the optimizer works in order to effectively tune a SQL statement.

17

## Formatting a Statement for Readability

Formatting a SQL statement for readability is pretty obvious, but many SQL statements have not been written neatly. Although the neatness of a statement does not affect the actual performance (the database does not care how neat the statement appears), careful formatting is the first step in tuning a statement. When you look at a SQL statement with tuning intentions, making the statement readable is always the first thing to do. How can you determine if the statement is written well if it is difficult to read?

Some basic rules for making a statement readable include:

☐ *Always begin a new line with each clause in the statement.* For example, place the FROM clause on a separate line than the SELECT clause. Place the WHERE clause on a separate line than the FROM clause, and so on.

☐ *Use tabs or spaces for indentation when arguments of a clause in the statement exceed one line.*

☐ *Use tabs and spaces consistently.*

☐ *Use table aliases when multiple tables are used in the statement.* The use of the full table name to qualify each column in the statement quickly clutters the statement and makes reading it difficult.

☐ *Use remarks sparingly in SQL statements if it is available in your specific implementation.* Remarks are great for documentation, but too many of them clutter a statement.

☐ *Begin a new line with each column name in the* SELECT *clause if many columns are being selected.*

☐ *Begin a new line with each table name in the* FROM *clause if many tables are being used.*

☐ *Begin a new line with each condition of the* WHERE *clause.* You can easily see all conditions of the statement and the order in which they are used.

An example of an unreadable statement:

**TYPE**
```
SELECT CUSTOMER_TBL.CUST_ID, CUSTOMER_TBL.CUST_NAME,
CUSTOMER_TBL.CUST_PHONE, ORDERS_TBL.ORD_NUM, ORDERS_TBL.QTY
FROM CUSTOMER_TBL, ORDERS_TBL
WHERE CUSTOMER_TBL.CUST_ID = ORDERS_TBL.CUST_ID
AND ORDERS_TBL.QTY > 1 AND CUSTOMER_TBL.CUST_NAME LIKE 'G%'
ORDER BY CUSTOMER_TBL.CUST_NAME;
```

**OUTPUT**
```
CUST_ID    CUST_NAME                    CUST_PHONE ORD_NUM
QTY
---------- ---------------------------- ---------- ---------- ----------
-
287        GAVINS PLACE                 3172719991 18D778
10

1 row selected.
```

Here's an example of a reformatted statement for improved readability:

**TYPE**
```
SELECT C.CUST_ID,
       C.CUST_NAME,
       C.CUST_PHONE,
       O.ORD_NUM,
       O.QTY
FROM ORDERS_TBL O,
     CUSTOMER_TBL C
WHERE O.CUST_ID = C.CUST_ID
  AND O.QTY > 1
  AND C.CUST_NAME LIKE 'G%'
ORDER BY 2;
```

**OUTPUT**
```
CUST_ID    CUST_NAME                    CUST_PHONE ORD_NUM
QTY
---------- ---------------------------- ---------- ---------- ----------
-
287        GAVINS PLACE                 3172719991 18D778
10

1 row selected.
```

Both statements are exactly the same, but the second statement is much more readable. The second statement has been greatly simplified by using table aliases, which have been defined in the query's FROM clause. Spacing has been used to align the elements of each clause, making each clause stand out.

**17**

Again, making a statement more readable does not directly improve its performance, but it assists you in making modifications and debugging a lengthy and otherwise possibly complex statement. Now you can easily identify the columns being selected, the tables being used, the table joins that are being performed, and the conditions that are placed on the query.

## Proper Arrangement of Tables in the FROM Clause

The arrangement or order of tables in the FROM clause may make a difference depending on how the optimizer reads the SQL statement. For instance, it may be more beneficial to list the smaller tables first and the larger tables last. Some users with lots of experience have found that listing the larger tables last in the FROM clause proves to be more efficient.

An example FROM clause:

```
FROM SMALLEST TABLE,
     LARGEST TABLE
```

**NOTE**

Check your particular implementation for performance tips when listing multiple tables in the FROM clause, if any.

## Proper Order of Join Conditions

As you learned in Hour 13, "Joining Tables in Queries," most joins use a base table to link tables that have one or more common columns on which to join. The base table is the main table that most or all tables are joined to in a query. The column from the base table is normally placed on the right side of a join operation in the WHERE clause. The tables being joined to the base table are normally in order from smallest to largest, similar to those the tables listed in the FROM clause.

Should there not be a BASE TABLE, the tables should be listed from smallest to largest, with the largest tables on the right side of the join operation in the WHERE clause. The join conditions should be in the first position(s) of the WHERE clause followed by the filter clause(s). An example:

```
FROM TABLE1,                    Smallest Table
     TABLE2,                             to
     TABLE3                     Largest Table, also BASE TABLE
WHERE TABLE1.COLUMN = TABLE3.COLUMN       Join condition
  AND TABLE2.COLUMN = TABLE3.COLUMN       Join condition
[ AND CONDITION1 ]                    Filter condition
[ AND CONDITION2 ]                    Filter condition
```

In this example, TABLE3 is used as the base table. TABLE1 and TABLE2 are joined to TABLE3 for both simplicity and proven efficiency.

Because joins typically return a high percentage of rows of data from the table(s), join conditions should be evaluated after more restrictive conditions.

## The Most Restrictive Condition

The most restrictive condition is typically the driving factor in achieving optimal performance for a SQL query. The most restrictive condition? The condition in the WHERE clause of a statement that returns the least number of rows of data. Conversely, the least restrictive condition is the condition in a statement that returns the most rows of data. This chapter is concerned with the most restrictive condition simply because it is this condition that most filters the data that is to be returned by the query.

It should be your goal for the SQL optimizer to evaluate the most restrictive condition first, because a smaller subset of data is returned by the condition, thus reducing the query's overhead. The effective placement of the most restrictive condition in the query requires knowledge of how the optimizer operates. The optimizers worked with in some cases seem to read from the bottom of the WHERE clause up. Therefore, you want to place the most restrictive condition last in the WHERE clause, which is the condition that is first read by the optimizer.

```
FROM TABLE1,                    Smallest Table
     TABLE2,                          to
     TABLE3               Largest Table, also BASE TABLE
WHERE TABLE1.COLUMN = TABLE3.COLUMN   Join condition
  AND TABLE2.COLUMN = TABLE3.COLUMN   Join condition
[ AND CONDITION1 ]              Least restrictive
[ AND CONDITION2 ]              Most restrictive
```

**TIP**

If you do not know how your particular implementation's SQL optimizer works, the DBA does not know, or you do not have sufficient documentation, you can execute a large query that takes a while to run, then rearrange conditions in the WHERE clause. Be sure to record the time it takes the query to complete each time you make changes. You should only have to run a couple of tests in order to figure out whether the optimizer reads the WHERE clause from the top to bottom, or bottom to top.

An example using a phony table:

| | |
|---|---|
| Table: | TEST |
| Row count: | 95,867 |
| Conditions: | `WHERE LAST_NAME = 'SMITH'` |
| | returns 2,000 rows |
| | `WHERE CITY = 'INDIANAPOLIS'` |
| | returns 30,000 rows |
| Most restrictive condition is: | `WHERE LAST_NAME = 'SMITH'` |

QUERY1:

```
SELECT COUNT(*)
FROM TEST
WHERE LAST_NAME = 'SMITH'
  AND CITY = 'INDIANAPOLIS';


  COUNT(*)
----------
     1,024
```

QUERY2:

```
SELECT COUNT(*)
FROM TEST
WHERE CITY = 'INDIANAPOLIS'
  AND LAST_NAME = 'SMITH';


  COUNT(*)
----------
     1,024
```

Suppose that QUERY1 completed in 20 seconds, where as QUERY2 completed in 10 seconds. Because QUERY2 returned faster results and the most restrictive condition was listed last in the WHERE clause, it would be safe to assume that the optimizer reads the WHERE clause from the bottom up.

**NOTE**

It is a good practice to try to use an indexed column as the most restrictive condition in a query. Indexes generally improve a query's performance.

# Full Table Scans

A full table scan occurs when an index is either not used or there is no index on the table(s) being used by the SQL statement. Full table scans are usually much slower in returning data than when an index is used. The larger the table, the slower that data is returned when a full table scan is performed. The query optimizer decides whether to use an index when executing the SQL statement. The index is used—if it exists—in most cases.

Some implementations have sophisticated query optimizers that can decide whether an index should be used. Decisions such as this are based on statistics that are gathered on database objects, such as the size of an object and the estimated number of rows that are returned by a condition with an indexed column. Please refer to your implementation documentation for specifics on the decision-making capabilities of your relational database's optimizer.

## When and How to Avoid Full Table Scans

Full table scans should be avoided when reading large tables. For instance, a full table scan is performed when a table that does not have an index is read, which usually takes a considerably longer time to return the data. An index should be considered for most larger tables. On small tables, as previously mentioned, the optimizer may choose the full table scan over using the index, if the table is indexed. In the case of a small table with an index, consideration should be taken to drop the index and reserve the space that was used for the index for other needy objects in the database.

**TIP**

> The easiest and most obvious way to avoid a full table scan—outside of ensuring that indexes exist on the table—is to use conditions in a query's WHERE clause, in order to filter data to be returned.

A reminder of data that should be indexed:

- ☐ Columns used as primary keys
- ☐ Columns used as foreign keys
- ☐ Columns frequently used to join tables
- ☐ Columns frequently used as conditions in a query
- ☐ Columns that have a high percentage of unique values

**NOTE**

> Sometimes full table scans are good. Full table scans should be performed on queries against small tables, or queries whose conditions return a high percentage of rows. The easiest way to force a full table scan is to avoid creating an index on the table.

**17**

# Other Performance Considerations

There are other performance considerations that should be noted when tuning SQL statements. The following concepts are discussed in the following sections:

- ☐ Using the LIKE operator and wildcards
- ☐ Avoiding the OR operator
- ☐ Avoiding the HAVING clause
- ☐ Avoiding large sort operations
- ☐ Using stored procedures

## Using the LIKE Operator and Wildcards

The LIKE operator is a useful tool that is used to place conditions on a query in a flexible manner. The placement and use of wildcards in a query can eliminate many possibilities of data that should be retrieved. Wildcards are very flexible for queries that search for similar data (data that is not equivalent to an exact value specified).

Suppose you want to write a query using the EMPLOYEE_TBL selecting the EMP_ID, LAST_NAME, FIRST_NAME, and STATE columns. You need to know the employee identification, name, and state for all the employees with the last name Stevens. Three SQL statement examples with different wildcard placements serve as examples.

QUERY1:

```
SELECT EMP_ID, LAST_NAME, FIRST_NAME, STATE
FROM EMPLOYEE_TBL
WHERE LAST_NAME LIKE '%E%'
```

QUERY2:

```
SELECT EMP_ID, LAST_NAME, FIRST_NAME, STATE
FROM EMPLOYEE_TBL
WHERE LAST_NAME LIKE '%EVENS%'
```

QUERY3:

```
SELECT EMP_ID, LAST_NAME, FIRST_NAME, STATE
FROM EMPLOYEE_TBL
WHERE LAST_NAME LIKE 'ST%'
```

The SQL statements do not necessarily return the same results. More than likely, QUERY1 will return more rows than the other two queries. QUERY2 and QUERY3 are more specific as to the data desired for return, thus eliminating more possibilities than QUERY1 and speeding data retrieval time. Additionally, QUERY3 is probably faster than QUERY2, because the first letters of the string for which you are searching are specified (and the column LAST_NAME is likely to be indexed). QUERY3 can take advantage of an index.

## Avoiding the OR Operator

Rewriting the SQL statement using the IN predicate instead of the OR operator consistently and substantially improves data retrieval speed. Your implementation will tell you about tools you can use to time or check the performance between the OR operator and the IN predicate. An example of how to rewrite a SQL statement taking the OR operator out and replacing the OR operator with the IN predicate follows:

**NOTE**

Hour 8, "Using Operators to Catergorize Data," can be referenced for the use of the OR operator and the IN predicate.

A query using the OR operator:

```
SELECT EMP_ID, LAST_NAME, FIRST_NAME
FROM EMPLOYEE_TBL
WHERE CITY = 'INDIANAPOLIS'
    OR CITY = 'BROWNSBURG'
    OR CITY = 'GREENFIELD'
```

The same query using the IN operator:

```
SELECT EMP_ID, LAST_NAME, FIRST_NAME
FROM EMPLOYEE_TBL
WHERE CITY IN ('INDIANAPOLIS', 'BROWNSBURG',
                'GREENFIELD')
```

The SQL statements retrieve the very same data; however, through testing and experience, you find that the data retrieval is measurably faster by replacing OR conditions with the IN, as in the second query.

## Avoiding the HAVING Clause

The HAVING clause is a useful clause; however, you can't use it without cost. Using the HAVING clause causes the SQL optimizer extra work, which results in extra time. If possible, SQL statements should be written without the use of the HAVING clause.

**17**

## Avoid Large Sort Operations

Large sort operations mean the use of the ORDER BY, GROUP BY, and HAVING clauses. Subsets of data must be stored in memory or to disk (if there is not enough space in allotted memory) whenever sort operations are performed. You must often sort data. The main point is that these sort operations affect a SQL statement's response time.

## Use Stored Procedures

Stored procedures should be created for SQL statements executed on a regular basis—particularly large transactions or queries. Stored procedures are simply SQL statements that are compiled and permanently stored in the database in an executable format.

Normally, when a SQL statement is issued in the database, the database must check the syntax and convert the statement into an executable format within the database (called *parsing*). The statement, once parsed, is stored in memory; however, it is not permanent. This means that when memory is needed for other operations, the statement may be ejected from memory. In the case of stored procedures, the SQL statement is always available in an executable format, and remains in the database until it is dropped like any other database object. Stored procedures are discussed in more detail in Hour 22, "Advanced SQL Topics."

# Summary

You have learned the meaning of tuning SQL statements in a relational database. You have learned that there are two basic types of tuning: database tuning and SQL statement tuning—both of which are most vital to the efficient operation of the database and SQL statements within. Each is equally important and cannot be optimally tuned without the other. Tuning the database falls in the hands of the DBA, whereas tuning SQL statements falls into the hands of the individuals writing the statements. This book is more concerned with the latter.

You have read about methods for tuning a SQL statement, starting with a statement's actual readability, which does not directly improve performance, but aids the programmer in the development and management of statements. One of the main issues in SQL statement performance is the use of indexes. There are times to use indexes, and times to avoid using them. A full table scan is performed when a table is read and an index is not used. In a full table scan, each row of data in a table is completely read. Other considerations for statement tuning, such as the arrangement of elements in a query, were discussed. Of foremost importance is the placement of the most restrictive condition in a statement's WHERE clause. For all measures taken to improve SQL statement performance, it is important to understand the data itself, database design and relationships, and the users' needs as far as accessing the database.

Like building indexes on tables, SQL statement tuning often involves extensive testing, which can be qualified as trial and error. There is no one way to tune a database or SQL statements within a database. All databases are different, as the business needs for each company are different. These differences affect the data within the database and the methods in which the data is retrieved. It is your job to crack the riddle on the most efficient SQL statement design for optimal database performance.

## Q&A

**Q By following what I have learned about performance, what realistic performance gains, as far as data retrieval time, can I really expect to see?**

A Realistically, you could see performance gains from fractions of a second to minutes, hours, or even days.

**Q How can I test my SQL statements for performance?**

A Each implementation should have a tool or system to check performance. Oracle7 was used to test the SQL statements in this book. Oracle has several tools for use in checking performance. Some of these tools are called Explain Plan, TKPROF, and Set Timing. Check your particular implementation for tools that are similar to Oracle's.

# Workshop

The following workshop is composed of a series of quiz questions and practical exercises. The quiz questions are designed to test your overall understanding of the current material. The practical exercises are intended to afford you the opportunity to apply the concepts discussed during the current hour, as well as build upon the knowledge acquired in previous hours of study. Please take time to complete the quiz questions and exercises before continuing. You may refer to the answers in Appendix C.

## Quiz

1. Would the use of a unique index on a small table be of any benefit?

2. What happens when the optimizer chooses not to use an index on a table when a query has been executed?

3. Should the most restrictive clause(s) be placed before the join condition(s) or after the join conditions in the WHERE clause?

## Exercises

Rewrite the following SQL statements to improve their performance. Use the EMPLOYEE_TBL and the EMPLOYEE_PAY_TBL as described here:

17

*EMPLOYEE_TBL*

| emp_id | varchar2(9) | not null, |
| last_name | varchar2(15) | not null, |
| first_name | varchar2(15) | not null, |
| middle_name | varchar2(15), | |
| address | varchar2(30) | not null, |
| city | varchar2(15) | not null, |
| state | char(2) | not null, |
| zip | number(5) | not null, |
| phone | char(10), | |
| pager | char(10), | |
| constraint emp_pk primary key (emp_id) | | |

*EMPLOYEE_PAY_TBL*

| emp_id | varchar2(9) | not null, |
| position | varchar2(15) | not null, |
| date_hire | date, | |
| pay_rate | number(4,2) | not null, |
| date_last_raise | date, | |
| salary | number(8,2), | |
| bonus | number(8,2), | |
| constraint emp_fk foreign key (emp_id) | | |
| references employee_tbl (emp_id) | | |

**17**

a.

```
SELECT EMP_ID, LAST_NAME, FIRST_NAME,
          PHONE
   FROM EMPLOYEE_TBL
   WHERE SUBSTR(PHONE, 1, 3) = '317' OR
         SUBSTR(PHONE, 1, 3) = '812' OR
         SUBSTR(PHONE, 1, 3) = '765'
```

b.

```
SELECT LAST_NAME, FIRST_NAME
   FROM EMPLOYEE_TBL
   WHERE LAST_NAME LIKE '%ALL%
```

c.

```
SELECT E.EMP_ID, E.LAST_NAME, E.FIRST_NAME,
          EP.SALARY
   FROM EMPLOYEE_TBL E,
   EMPLOYEE_PAY_TBL EP
   WHERE LAST_NAME LIKE 'S%'
   AND E.EMP_ID = EP.EMP_ID
```

# PART
# VI

## Using SQL to Manage Users and Security

## Hour

# Hour 18

# Managing Database Users

During this hour you learn about one of the most fundamental purposes for any relational database: managing database users. You will learn the concepts behind creating users in SQL, user security, the user versus the schema, user profiles, user attributes, and tools users utilize.

The highlights of this hour include:

- ☐ Types of users
- ☐ User management
- ☐ The user's place in the database
- ☐ The user versus the schema
- ☐ User sessions
- ☐ Altering a user's attributes
- ☐ User profiles
- ☐ Dropping users from the database
- ☐ Tools utilized by users

**NOTE** The SQL standard refers to a database user identification as an *Authorization Identifier* (`authID`). In most major implementations, `authID`s are referred to simply as *users*. This book refers to Authorization Identifiers as users, database users, usernames, or database user accounts. The SQL standard states that the Authorization Identifier is a name by which the system knows the database user.

# Users Are the Reason

Users are the reason for the season—the season of designing, creating, implementing, and maintaining any database. The user's needs are taken into consideration when the database is designed, and the final goal in implementing a database is making the database available to users, who in turn utilize the database that you and possibly many others have had a hand in developing.

A common perception of users is that if there were no users, nothing bad would ever happen to the database. Although this statement reeks with truth, the database was nevertheless created to hold data so that users can function in their day-to-day jobs.

Although user management is often the database administrator's implicit task, other individuals often take a part in the user management process. User management is vital in the life of a relational database and is ultimately managed through the use of SQL concepts and commands, although varied from vendor to vendor.

## Types of Users

There are several types of database users:

☐ Data entry clerks

☐ Programmers

☐ System engineers

☐ Database administrators

☐ Systems analysts

☐ Developers

☐ Testers

☐ Management

☐ End user

Each type of user has its own set of job functions (and problems), all of which are critical to their daily survival and job security. Furthermore, each type of user has different levels of authority and its own place in the database.

**18**

# Who Manages Users?

A company's management staff is responsible for the day-to-day management of users; however, the database administrator or other assigned individuals are ultimately responsible for the management of users within the database.

The *database administrator* usually handles the creation of the database user accounts, roles, privileges, profiles, as well as dropping those user accounts from the database. Because it can become an overwhelming task in a large and active environment, some companies have a security officer who assists the database administrator with the user management process.

The *security officer*, if one is assigned, is usually responsible for the paper work, relaying to the database administrator a user's job requirements, and letting the database administrator know when a user no longer requires access to the database.

The *system analyst*, or system administrator, is usually responsible for the operating system security, which entails creating users and assigning appropriate privileges. The security officer also may assist the system analyst in the same way they do the database administrator.

# The User's Place in the Database

A user should be given the necessary roles and privileges necessary to accomplish his or her job. No user should have database access that extends beyond the scope of his or her job duties. Protecting the data is the whole reason for setting up user accounts and security. Data can be damaged or lost, even if unintentionally, if the wrong user has access to the wrong data. When the user no longer requires database access, that user's account should be either removed from the database or disabled.

All users have their place in the database; some have more responsibilities than others. Database users are like parts of a human body—all work together in unison (at least that is the way it is supposed to be) to accomplish some goal.

# How Does a User Differ from a Schema?

A database's objects are associated with database user accounts, called schemas. A *schema* is a set of database objects that a database user owns. This database user is called the *schema owner*. The difference between a regular database user and a schema owner is that a schema owner owns objects within the database, whereas most users do not own objects. Most users are given database accounts in order to access data that is contained in other schemas.

# The Management Process

A stable user management system is mandatory for data security in any database system. The user management system starts with the new user's immediate supervisor, who should initiate the access request, then go through the company's approval authorities, at which time the request, if accepted by management, is routed to the security officer or database administrator, who takes action. A good notification process is necessary; the supervisor and the user must be notified that the user account has been created and that access to the database has been granted. The user account password should only be given to the user, who should immediately change the password upon initial login to the database.

**NOTE** You must check your particular implementation for the creation of users. Also refer to company policies and procedures when creating and managing users. The following section compares the user creation processes in Oracle, Sybase, and Microsoft SQL Server.

## Creating Users

The creation of database users involves the use of SQL-type commands within the database. There is no one standard command for creating database users in SQL; each implementation has a method for doing so. Some implementations have similar commands, while others vary in syntax. The basic concept is the same, regardless of the implementation.

When the database administrator or assigned security officer receives a user account request, the request should be analyzed for the necessary information. The information should include your particular company's requirements for establishing a user ID.

Some items that should be included are social security number, full name, address, phone number, office or department name, assigned database, and sometimes, a suggested user ID.

There are syntactical examples of creating users compared between two different implementations shown in the following sections.

### Creating Users in Oracle

Steps for creating a user account in an Oracle database:

1. Create the database user account with default settings.

2. Grant appropriate privileges to the user account.

Creating the user:

```
CREATE USER USER_ID
IDENTIFIED BY PASSWORD
[ DEFAULT TABLESPACE TABLESPACE_NAME ]
[ TEMPORARY TABLESPACE TABLESPACE_NAME ]
[ QUOTA (INTEGER (K ¦ M) ¦ UNLIMITED) ON TABLESPACE_NAME ]
[ PROFILE PROFILE_TYPE ]
```

18

**NOTE**

> The previous syntax for creating users can be used to add a user to an Oracle database, as well as a few other, major relational database implementations.

If you are not using Oracle, do not over concern yourself with some of the options in this syntax. A *tablespace* is a logical area that houses database objects, such as tables and indexes. The DEFAULT TABLESPACE is the tablespace in which objects created by the particular user reside. The TEMPORARY TABLESPACE is the tablespace used for sort operations (table joins, ORDER BY, GROUP BY) from queries executed by the user. The QUOTA is space limits placed on a particular tablespace to which the user has access. PROFILE is a particular database profile that has been assigned to the user.

Granting privileges to the user account:

```
GRANT PRIV1 [ , PRIV2, ... ] TO USERNAME ¦ ROLE [ , USERNAME ]
```

The GRANT statement can grant one or more privileges to one or more users in the same statement. The privilege(s) may also be granted to a role, which in turn may be granted to a user(s).

## Creating Users in Sybase and Microsoft SQL Server

The steps for creating a user account in a Sybase and Microsoft SQL Server database follow:

1. Create the database user account for SQL Server and assign a password and a default database for the user.
2. Add the user to the appropriate database(s).
3. Grant appropriate privileges to the user account.

Creating the user account:

```
SP_ADDLOGIN USER_ID ,PASSWORD, DEFAULT_DATABASE ]
```

Adding the user to a database:

```
SP_ADDUSER USER_ID [, NAME_IN_DB [, GRPNAME ] ]
```

Granting privileges to the user account:

```
GRANT PRIV1 [ , PRIV2, ... ] TO USER_ID
```

> NOTE
>
> The discussion of privileges within a relational database are further elaborated upon during Hour 19, "Managing Database Security," of this book.

## CREATE SCHEMA

Schemas are created via the CREATE SCHEMA statement.

 The syntax is:

```
CREATE SCHEMA [ SCHEMA_NAME ] [ USER_ID ]
                [ DEFAULT CHARACTER SET CHARACTER_SET ]
                [ SCHEMA_ELEMENT_LIST ]
```

Here's an example:

```
CREATE SCHEMA USER1
CREATE TABLE TBL1
   (COLUMN1     DATATYPE     [NOT NULL],
    COLUMN2     DATATYPE     [NOT NULL]...)
CREATE TABLE TBL2
   (COLUMN1     DATATYPE     [NOT NULL],
    COLUMN2     DATATYPE     [NOT NULL]...)
GRANT SELECT ON TBL1 TO USER2
GRANT SELECT ON TBL2 TO USER2
[ OTHER DDL COMMANDS ... ]
```

Here's the application of the CREATE SCHEMA command in one implementation:

TYPE
```
CREATE SCHEMA AUTHORIZATION USER1
CREATE TABLE EMP
   (ID          NUMBER            NOT NULL,
    NAME        VARCHAR2(10)      NOT NULL)
CREATE TABLE CUST
   (ID          NUMBER            NOT NULL,
    NAME        VARCHAR2(10)      NOT NULL)
GRANT SELECT ON TBL1 TO USER2
GRANT SELECT ON TBL2 TO USER2
/
```

OUTPUT   Schema created.

The AUTHORIZATION keyword is added to the CREATE SCHEMA command. This example was performed in an Oracle database. This goes to show you, as you have also seen in this book's previous examples, that vendors' syntax for commands often varies in their implementations.

**18**

> NOTE
>
> Some implementations may not support the CREATE SCHEMA command. However, schemas may be implicitly created when a user creates objects. The CREATE SCHEMA command is simply a single-step method of accomplishing this task. Once objects have been created by a user, the user may grant privileges that allows access to the user's objects to other users.

# Dropping a Schema

A schema may be removed from the database using the DROP SCHEMA statement. There are two options that must be considered when dropping a schema. First, the RESTRICT option. If RESTRICT is specified, an error occurs if objects currently exist in the schema. The second option is CASCADE. The CASCADE option must be used if any objects currently exist in the schema. Remember that when you drop a schema, you also drop all database objects associated with that schema.

```
DROP SCHEMA SCHEMA_NAME { RESTRICT ¦ CASCADE }
```

**NOTE**

The absence of objects in a schema is possible because objects such as tables may be dropped using the DROP TABLE command. Some implementations may have a procedure or command that drops a user, which may also be used to drop a schema. If the DROP SCHEMA command is not available in your implementation, you can remove a schema by removing the user that owns the schema objects.

# Altering Users

A very important part of managing users is the ability to alter a user's attributes after user creation. Life for the database administrator would be a lot simpler if personnel with user accounts were never promoted, never left the company, or if the addition of new employees was minimized; in the real world, high personnel turnover, as well as users' duties, is a reality and a significant factor in user management. Nearly everyone changes jobs or job duties, therefore, user privileges in a database must be adjusted to fit a user's needs.

One implementation's example of altering the current state of a user:

For Oracle:

```
ALTER USER USER_ID [ IDENTIFIED BY PASSWORD ¦ EXTERNALLY ]
[ DEFAULT TABLESPACE TABLESPACE_NAME ]
[ TEMPORARY TABLESPACE TABLESPACE_NAME ]
[ QUOTA  INTEGER K¦M ¦UNLIMITED ON TABLESPACE_NAME ]
[ PROFILE PROFILE_NAME ]
[ DEFAULT ROLE ROLE1 [, ROLE2 ] ¦ ALL
[ EXCEPT ROLE1 [, ROLE2 ¦ NONE ] ]
```

Many of the user's attributes may be altered in this syntax. Unfortunately, not all implementations provide a simple command that allows the manipulation of database users. Some implementations also provide GUI tools that allow users to be created, modified, and removed.

18

**NOTE**

> You must check your particular implementation for the correct syntax for altering users. Oracle's ALTER USER syntax is shown here. In most major implementations, there is a tool used to alter or change a user's roles, privileges, attributes, and password.

 **NOTE**

> A user can change an established password. You must check your particular implementation for the exact syntax or tool used to reset a password. The ALTER USER command is typically used in Oracle.

## User Sessions

A user database *session* is the time that begins at database login time and ends when a user logs out. During the time a user is logged into the database (a *user session*), the user may perform various actions, such as queries and transactions.

A SQL session is initiated when a user connects from the client to the server using the CONNECT statement. Upon the establishment of the connection and the initiation of the session, any number of transactions can be started and performed until the connection is disconnected; at that time the database user session terminates.

Users may explicitly connect and disconnect from the database, starting and terminating SQL sessions, using commands such as the following:

 **SYNTAX**

```
CONNECT TO DEFAULT ¦ STRING1 [ AS STRING2 ] [ USER STRING3 ]

DISCONNECT DEFAULT ¦ CURRENT ¦ ALL ¦ STRING

SET CONNECTION DEFAULT ¦ STRING
```

 **NOTE**

> Remember that the syntax varies between implementations. In addition, most database users do not manually issue the commands to connect or disconnect from the database. Most users access the database through a vendor-provided or third-party tool that prompts the user for a username and password, which in turn connects to the database and initiates a database user session.

User sessions may be—and are often—monitored by the database administrator or other personnel having interest in user activities. A user session is associated with a particular user account when a user is monitored. A database user session is ultimately represented as a process on the host operating system.

 **18**

## Removing User Access

Removing a user from the database or disallowing a user's access can easily be accomplished through a couple of simple commands. Once again, however, variations among different implementations are numerous, and therefore you must check your particular implementation for the syntax or tools used to accomplish user removal or access revocation.

Methods for removing user database access:

☐ Change the user's password.

☐ Drop the user account from the database.

☐ Revoke appropriate previously granted privileges from the user.

**SYNTAX**

The DROP command can be used in some implementations to drop a user from the database.

```
DROP USER USER_ID [ CASCADE ]
```

**SYNTAX**

The REVOKE command is the counterpart of the GRANT command in many implementations, allowing privileges that have been granted to a user to be revoked. An example syntax for this command in some implementations follows:

```
REVOKE PRIV1 [ ,PRIV2, ... ] FROM USERNAME
```

18

# Tools Utilized by Database Users

Some people say that you do not need to know SQL to perform database queries. In a sense, they may be correct; however, knowing SQL definitely helps querying a database, even when using Graphical User Interface (GUI) tools. Even though GUI tools are good and should be used when available, it is most beneficial to understand what is happening behind the scenes, so that you can maximize the efficiency of utilizing these user-friendly tools.

There are many GUI tools that aid the database user automatically generate SQL code by navigating through windows, responding to prompts, and selecting options. There are reporting tools that generate reports. Forms can be created for users to query, update, insert, or delete data from a database. There are tools that convert data into graphs and charts. There are database administration tools used to monitor database performance, and some that allow remote connectivity to a database. Database vendors provide some of these tools, while others are provided as third-party tools from other vendors.

# Summary

All databases have users, whether it be one or thousands. The user is the reason for the database. There are three basic steps in the management of users. First, the database user account must be created. Second, privileges must be granted to the user in order to accommodate the tasks the user must perform within the database. Finally, a user account must either be removed from the database or certain privileges within the database must be revoked from a user.

Some of the most common tasks of managing users have been touched on; too much detail is avoided here, because most databases differ in the user management process. However, it is important to discuss user management due to its relationship with SQL. Many of the commands used to manage users have not been defined or discussed in great detail by the ANSI standard, but the concept remains the same.

## Q&A

**Q  Is there a SQL standard for adding users to a database?**

**A**  Some commands and concepts are provided by ANSI, although each implementation and each company has its own commands, tools, and rules for creating or adding users to a database.

**Q  Can user access be temporarily suspended without removing the user ID completely from the database?**

**A**  Yes. User access can temporarily be suspended by simply changing the user's password or by revoking privileges that allow the user to connect to the database. The functionality of the user account can be reinstated by changing and issuing the password to the user, or by granting privileges to the user that may have been revoked.

**Q  Can a user change his or her own password?**

**A**  Yes, in most major implementations. Upon user creation or addition to the database, a generic password is usually given to the user and must be changed as quickly as possible by the user to a password of his or her choice. Once this has been accomplished, even the database administrator does not know the user's password.

# Workshop

The following workshop is composed of a series of quiz questions and practical exercises. The quiz questions are designed to test your overall understanding of the current material. The practical exercises are intended to afford you the opportunity to apply the concepts discussed during the current hour, as well as build upon the knowledge acquired in previous hours of study. Please take time to complete the quiz questions and exercises before continuing. You may refer to the answers in Appendix C.

**18**

## Quiz

1. What command is used to establish a session?
2. Which option must be used to drop a schema that still contains database objects?
3. What statement is used to remove a database privilege?
4. What command creates a grouping or collection of tables, views, and privileges?

## Exercises

Describe or list the steps that allow a new employee database access.

18

# Hour 19

# Managing Database Security

During this hour you learn the basics of implementing and managing security within a relational database using SQL and SQL-related commands. Each major implementation differs on syntax with it security commands, but the overall security for the relational database follows the same basic guidelines discussed in the ANSI standard. You must check your particular implementation for syntax and any special guidelines for security.

The highlights of this hour include:

- ☐ Database security
- ☐ Security versus user management
- ☐ Database system privileges
- ☐ Database object privileges
- ☐ Granting privileges to users
- ☐ Revoking privileges from users
- ☐ Security features in the database

# What Is Database Security?

Database security is the process of simply protecting the data from unauthorized usage. Unauthorized usage includes data access by database users who should have access to part of the database, but not all parts. This protection also includes the act of policing against unauthorized connectivity and distribution of privileges. There are many user levels in a database, from the database creator, individuals responsible for maintaining the database (such as the DBA), database programmers, and end users. End users, although individuals with the most limited access, are the users for which the database exists. Each user has a different level of access to the database and should be limited to the fewest number of privileges needed to perform their particular job.

# How Does Security Differ from User Management?

You may be wondering what the difference between user management and database security is. After all, the last hour discussed user management, which seems to cover security. Although user management and database security are definitely related, each have their own purpose and work together to achieve a secure database.

A well planned and maintained user management program goes hand-in-hand with the overall security of a database. Users are assigned user accounts and passwords, which give them general access to the database. The user accounts within the database should be stored with information such as user's actual name, office and department in which the user works, telephone number or extension, and the database name to which the user has access. An initial password for the database user account is assigned by the DBA or security officer and should be changed immediately by the new user.

Security entails more; for instance, if a user no longer requires certain privileges granted to them, those privileges should be revoked. If a user no longer requires access to the database, then the user account should be dropped from the database.

Generally, *user management* is the process of creating user accounts, removing user accounts, and keeping track of users' actions within the database. Database security is going a step further by granting privileges for specific database access, revoking those privileges from users, and taking measures in order to protect other parts of the database, such as the underlying database files.

**19**

**NOTE**

> Because this is a SQL book, not a database book, it focuses on database privileges. However, you should keep in mind that there are other aspects to database security, such as the protection of underlying database files, which holds equal importance with the distribution of database privileges. High-level database security can become complex and differs immensely between relational database implementations.

# What Are Privileges?

*Privileges* are authority levels used to access the database itself, objects within the database, to manipulate data in the database, and to perform various administrative functions within the database. Privileges are issued via the GRANT command and are taken away via the REVOKE command.

Just because a user can connect to a database does not mean that the user can access data within a database. Access to data within the database is handled through these privileges. There are two types of privileges:

1. System privileges
2. Object privileges

## System Privileges

*System privileges* are those that allow database users to perform administrative actions within the database, such as the following: creating a database, dropping a database, creating user accounts, dropping users, dropping and altering database objects, altering the state of objects, altering the state of the database, and other actions which could result in serious repercussions if not carefully used.

System privileges vary greatly among the different relational database vendors, so you must check your particular implementation for all of the available system privileges and their correct usage.

Some common system privileges in Sybase:

```
CREATE DATABASE
CREATE DEFAULT
CREATE PROCEDURE
CREATE RULE
CREATE VIEW
DUMP DATABASE
DUMP TRANSACTION
EXECUTE
```

19

Some common system privileges in Oracle:

```
CREATE TABLE
CREATE ANY TABLE
ALTER ANY TABLE
DROP TABLE
CREATE USER
DROP USER
ALTER USER
ALTER DATABASE
ALTER SYSTEM
BACKUP ANY TABLE
SELECT ANY TABLE
```

## Object Privileges

*Object privileges* are authority levels on objects, meaning you must have been granted the appropriate privileges in order to perform certain operations on database objects. For instance, in order to select data from another user's table, the user must first grant you access to do so. Object privileges are granted to users in the database by the object's owner. Remember that this owner is also called the *schema owner*.

The ANSI standard for privileges includes the following object privileges:

USAGE    Authorizes usage of a specific domain

SELECT    Allows access to a specific table

INSERT(column_name)    Allows data insertion to a specific column of a specified table

INSERT    Allows insertion of data into all columns of a specific table

UPDATE(column_name)    Allows a specific column of a specified table to be updated

UPDATE    Allows all columns of a specified table to be updated

REFERENCES(column_name)    Allows a reference to a specified column of a specified table in integrity constraints; this privilege is required for all integrity constraints

REFERENCES    Allows references to all columns of a specified table

**NOTE**

> The owner of an object has been automatically granted all privileges that relate to the objects owned. These privileges have also been granted with the GRANT OPTION. The GRANT OPTION is discussed later this hour, which is a nice feature available in some SQL implementations.

**19**

These object-level privileges are those privileges that should be used in order to grant and restrict access to objects in a schema. These privileges can be used to protect objects in one schema from database users that have access to another schema in the same database.

There are a variety of object privileges available among different implementations not listed in this section. The ability to delete data from another user's object is another common object privilege available in many implementations. Be sure to check your implementation documentation for all of the available object-level privileges.

## Who Grants and Revokes Privileges?

The database administrator (DBA) is usually the one who issues the GRANT and REVOKE commands, although a security administrator, if one exists, may have the authority to do so. The authority on what to GRANT or REVOKE would come from management and would hopefully be in writing.

The owner of an object must grant privileges to other users in the database on the object. Even the DBA cannot grant database users privileges on objects that do not belong to the DBA, although there are ways to work around that.

# Controlling User Access

User access is primarily controlled by a user account and password, but that is not enough to access the database in most major implementations. The creation of a user account is only the first step in allowing access to the database as well as controlling that access.

Once the user account has been created, the database administrator, security officer, or designated individual must be able to assign appropriate system-level privileges to a user in order for that user to allowed to perform actual functions within the database, such as creating tables or selecting from tables. What good is it to connect to a database if you cannot do anything? Furthermore, the schema owner usually needs to grant database users access to objects in the schema so that the user can do his or her job.

There are two commands in SQL that allow database access control involving the assignment of privileges and the revocation of privileges.

The two commands used to distribute both system and object privileges in a relational database are:

    GRANT

    REVOKE

19

# The GRANT **Command**

The GRANT command is used to grant both system-level and object-level privileges to an existing database user account.

The syntax is as follows:

```
GRANT PRIVILEGE1 [, PRIVILEGE2 ][ ON OBJECT ]
TO USERNAME [ WITH GRANT OPTION ]
```

Granting one privilege to a user is as follows:

**GRANT SELECT ON EMPLOYEE_TBL TO USER1;**

Grant succeeded.

Granting multiple privileges to a user:

**GRANT SELECT, INSERT ON EMPLOYEE_TBL TO USER1;**

Grant succeeded.

Notice that when granting multiple privileges to a user in a single statement, each privilege is separated by a comma.

Granting privileges to multiple users is as follows:

**GRANT SELECT, INSERT ON EMPLOYEE_TBL TO USER1, USER2;**

Grant succeeded.

**NOTE**

> Notice the phrase Grant succeeded denoting the successful completion of each grant statement. This is the feedback that you receive upon issuing these statements in the implementation used for the book examples (Oracle). Most implementations have some sort of feedback, although the phrase used may vary.

## GRANT OPTION

The GRANT OPTION is a very powerful GRANT command option. When an object's owner grants privileges on an object to another user with the GRANT OPTION, the new user can also grant privileges on that object to other users, even though the user does not actually own the object. An example follows:

**GRANT SELECT ON EMPLOYEE_TBL TO USER1 WITH GRANT OPTION;**

Grant succeeded.

**19**

# The REVOKE **Command**

The REVOKE command removes privileges that have been granted to database users. The REVOKE command has two options, RESTRICT and CASCADE. When the RESTRICT option is used, REVOKE succeeds only if the privileges specified explicitly in the REVOKE statement leave no other users with abandoned privileges. The CASCADE option revokes any privileges that would otherwise be left with other users. In other words, if the owner of an object granted user1 privileges with the GRANT OPTION, user1 granted user2 privileges with the GRANT OPTION, and the owner revokes user1's privileges, the CASCADE also removes the privileges from user2.

 *Abandoned privileges* are privileges that are left with a user who was granted privileges with the GRANT OPTION.

The syntax is as follows:

```
REVOKE PRIVILEGE1 [, PRIVILEGE2 ] [ GRANT OPTION FOR ] ON OBJECT
FROM USER { RESTRICT ¦ CASCADE }
```

An example follows:

```
REVOKE INSERT ON EMPLOYEE_TBL FROM USER1;

Revoke succeeded.
```

# The PUBLIC **Database Account**

The PUBLIC database user account is a database account that represents all users in the database. All users are part of the public account. If a privilege is granted to the PUBLIC account, then all database users have the privilege. Likewise, if a privilege is revoked from the PUBLIC account, then the privilege is revoked from all database users, unless that privilege was explicitly granted to a specific user. An example follows:

```
GRANT SELECT ON EMPLOYEE_TBL TO PUBLIC;

Grant succeeded.
```

**WARNING**

Extreme caution should be taken when granting privileges to PUBLIC; all database users acquire the privileges granted.

# Groups of Privileges

Some implementations have groups of privileges in the database. These groups of permissions are referred to with different names. Having a group of privileges allows simplicity for granting and revoking common privileges to and from users. For instance, if a group consists of ten privileges, then the group can be granted to a user instead of all ten privileges.

19

SQLBase has groups of privileges called *authority levels*, where these groups of privileges in Oracle are called *roles*. SQLBase and Oracle both include the following groups of privileges with their implementations:

```
CONNECT
RESOURCE
DBA
```

The CONNECT group allows a user to connect to the database and perform operations on any database objects to which the user has access.

The RESOURCE group allows a user to create objects, drop objects they own, grant privileges to objects they own, and so on.

The DBA group allows a user to perform any function within the database. The user can access any database object and perform any operation with this group.

Example for granting a group of privileges to a user follows:

```
GRANT DBA TO USER1;

Grant succeeded.
```

 **NOTE**

> Each implementation differs on the use of groups of database privileges. If available, this feature should be used for ease of database security administration.

# Summary

You were shown the basics on implementing security in a SQL database, or a relational database. You learned the basics of managing database users. The first step in implementing security at the database level for users is to create the user; once the user has been created, the user must be assigned certain privileges that allow the user access to specific parts of the database. There are two types of privileges: system privileges and object privileges.

System privileges are those that allow the user to perform various different tasks within the database, such as actually connecting to the database, creating tables, creating users, altering the state of the database, and so on. Object privileges are those that allow a user access to specific objects within the database, such as the ability to select data or manipulate data in a specific tables.

There are two commands in SQL that allow a user to grant and revoke privileges to and from other users in the database: the GRANT command and the REVOKE command. These two commands are used to control the overall administration of privileges in the database. Although there are many other considerations for implementing security in a relational database, the basics that relate to the language of SQL are discussed during this hour.

## Q&A

**Q  If a user forgets his or her password, what should the user do to gain access to the database again?**

**A**  The user should go to their immediate management or an available help desk. A help desk should be able to reset a user's password. If not, the DBA or security officer can reset the password. The user should change the password to a password of their choosing as soon as the password is reset and the user is notified.

**Q  What could I do if I wanted to grant CONNECT to a user, but the user does not need all the privileges that are assigned to the connect role?**

**A**  You would simply not grant CONNECT, but only the privileges required. Should you ever grant CONNECT and the user no longer needs all the privileges that go with it, simply revoke CONNECT from the user and grant the specific privileges required.

**Q  Why is it so important for the new user to change the password when received from whomever created the new user?**

**A**  An initial password is assigned upon creation of the user ID. No one, not even the DBA or management, should know a user's password. The password should be kept a secret at all times in order to prevent another user from logging on to the database under another user's account.

# Workshop

The following workshop is composed of a series of quiz questions and practical exercises. The quiz questions are designed to test your overall understanding of the current material. The practical exercises are intended to afford you the opportunity to apply the concepts discussed during the current hour, as well as build upon the knowledge acquired in previous hours of study. Please take time to complete the quiz questions and exercises before continuing. You may refer to the answers in Appendix C.

## Quiz

1. What option must a user have to grant another user privileges on an object not owned by the user?

2. When privileges are granted to PUBLIC, do all database users acquire the privileges, or just a listing of specified users?

3. What privilege is required to look at data in a specific table?

4. What type of privilege is SELECT?

## Exercises

1. Write a statement to grant select access on a table called employee_tbl, which you own, to a user ID, rplew. It should allow rplew to grant privileges to another user on the same table.

2. Write the statement that revokes the connect role from both of the users in Exercise 1.

3. Write the statement that allows rplew to select, insert, and update the employee_tbl table.

# PART VII

## Summarized Data Structures

## Hour

# Hour 20

# Creating and Using Views and Synonyms

During this hour you learn about performance, as well as how to create and drop views, how to use views for security, and how to provide simplicity in data retrieval for end users and reports. You also read a discussion on synonyms.

The highlights of this hour include the following:

- [ ] What are views?
- [ ] How are views used?
- [ ] Views and security
- [ ] Storage of views
- [ ] Creating views
- [ ] Joining views
- [ ] Data manipulation in a view
- [ ] What are synonyms?
- [ ] Managing synonyms
- [ ] Creation of synonyms
- [ ] Dropping synonyms

# What Is a View?

A *view* is a virtual table. That is, a view looks like a table and acts like a table as far as a user is concerned. A view is actually a composition of a table in the form of a predefined query. For instance, a view can be created, from the EMPLOYEE_TBL table, that contains only the employee's name and address, instead of all columns in the EMPLOYEE_TBL table. A view can contain all rows of a table or select rows from a table. A view can be created from one or many tables.

 **NEW TERM**    A *view* is a predefined query that is stored in the database and has the appearance of an ordinary table and is accessed like a table, but does not require physical storage.

When a view is created, a SELECT statement is actually run against the database, which defines the view. The SELECT statement used to define the view may simply contain column names from the table, or may be more explicitly written using various functions and calculations to manipulate or summarize the data that the user sees. Study the illustration of a view in Figure 20.1.

**Figure 20.1.**
*The view.*

A view is considered a database object, although the view takes up no storage space on its own. The main difference between a view and a table is that data in a table consumes physical storage, whereas a view does not require physical storage because it is actually referring to data from a table.

A view is used in the same manner a table is used in the database, meaning that data can be selected from a view as it is from a table. Data can also be manipulated in a view, although there are some restrictions. The following sections discuss some common uses for views and how views are stored in the database.

> If a table that was used to create a view is dropped, the view becomes inaccessible. You receive an error when trying to query against the view.

**WARNING**

## Views Can Be Utilized as a Form of Security

Views can be utilized as a form of security in the database. Say you have a table called EMPLOYEE_TBL. The EMPLOYEE_TBL includes employee names, addresses, phone numbers, emergency contacts, department, position, and salary or hourly pay. You have some temporary help come in to write some reports; you need a report of employees' names, addresses, and phone numbers. If you give access to the EMPLOYEE_TBL to the temporary help, they can see how much each of your employees receive in compensation—you do not want this to happen. To prevent that, you have created a view containing only the required information: employee name, address, phone numbers, and emergency contacts. The temporary help can then be given access to the view to write the report without having access to the compensation columns in the table.

 **TIP**

> Views can be used to restrict user access to particular columns in a table, or to rows in a table that meet specific conditions as defined in the WHERE clause of the view definition.

## Views Can Be Utilized to Maintain Summarized Data

Views may be utilized to maintain summarized data. If you have a summarized data report in which the data in the table or tables is updated often and the report is created often, then a view with summarized data may be an excellent choice.

For example, suppose that you have a table containing information about individuals, such as their city of residence, their sex, their salary, and their age. You could create a view based on the table that shows summarized figures for individuals for each city, such as the average age, average salary, total number of males, and total number of females. Once the view is created to retrieve this information from the base table(s), you can simply query the view instead of composing a SELECT statement that may, in some cases, turn out to be complex.

The only difference between the syntax for creating a view with summarized data and creating a view from a single or multiple tables is the use of aggregate functions. Review Hour 9, "Summarizing Data Results from a Query," for the use of aggregate functions.

**20**

## How Is a View Stored?

A view is stored in memory only. A view takes up no storage space—as do other database objects—other than the space required to store the view definition itself. A view is owned by the view's creator or the schema owner. The view owner automatically has all applicable privileges on that view and can grant privileges on the view to other users, as with tables. The GRANT command's GRANT OPTION privilege works the same as on a table. See Hour 19, "Managing Database Security," for more information.

# Creating Views

Views are created using the CREATE VIEW statement. Views can be created from a single table, multiple tables, or another view. To create a view, a user must have the appropriate system privilege according to the specific implementation.

The basic CREATE VIEW syntax is as follows:

```
CREATE VIEW VIEW_NAME AS
{SELECT STATEMENT}
```

The following subsections explore different methods for creating views using the CREATE VIEW statement.

**NOTE**

There is no provision for an ALTER VIEW statement in ANSI SQL.

## Creating a View from a Single Table

A view can be created from a single table. The WITH CHECK OPTION is discussed later this hour.

The syntax is as follows:

```
CREATE VIEW VIEW_NAME AS
SELECT * ¦ COLUMN1 [, COLUMN2 ]
FROM TABLE_NAME
[ WHERE EXPRESSION1 [, EXPRESSION2 ]]
[ WITH CHECK OPTION ]
[ GROUP BY ]
```

The simplest form for creating a view is one based on the entire contents of a single table, as in the following example:

```
create view customers as
select *
from customer_tbl;
```

  View created.

The next example narrows down the contents for a view by selecting only specified columns from the base table:

```
create view emp_view as
select last_name, first_name, mid_init
from employee_tbl;
```

  View Created.

**20**

Following is an example of how columns from the base table can be combined or manipulated in order to form a column in a view. The view column is titled NAME by using an alias in the SELECT clause.

**TYPE**
```
create view names as
select last_name || ', ' || first_name || ' ' || mid_init name
from employee_tbl;
```

**OUTPUT**  View created.

Now you select all data from the view that you created, called NAMES.

**TYPE**
```
select *
from names;
NAME
```

**OUTPUT**
```
------------------
STEPHENS, TINA D
PLEW, LINDA C
GLASS, BRANDON S
GLASS, JACOB
WALLACE, MARIAH
SPURGEON, TIFFANY
6 rows selected.
```

The following example shows how to create a view with summarized data from one or more underlying tables:

**TYPE**
```
create view city_pay as
select e.city, avg(p.pay_rate) avg_pay
from employee_tbl e,
     employee_pay_tbl p
where e.emp_id = p.emp_id
group by e.city;
```

**OUTPUT**  View created.

Now, if you select from your summarized view:

**TYPE**
```
select *
from city_pay;
```

**OUTPUT**
```
CITY            AVG_PAY
------------    ----------
GREENWOOD          17.5
INDIANAPOLIS    13.3875
WHITELAND         18.25
3 rows selected.
```

By summarizing a view, selects that may occur in the future are simplified against the underlying table of the view.

**20**

## Creating a View from Multiple Tables

A view can be created from multiple tables by using a JOIN in the SELECT statement. The WITH CHECK OPTION is discussed later this hour. The syntax is as follows:

**SYNTAX**

```
CREATE VIEW VIEW_NAME AS
SELECT * ¦ COLUMN1 [, COLUMN2 ]
FROM TABLE_NAME1, TABLE_NAME2 [, TABLE_NAME3 ]
WHERE TABLE_NAME1 = TABLE_NAME2
[ AND TABLE_NAME1 = TABLE_NAME 3 ]
[ EXPRESSION1 ][, EXPRESSION2 ]
[ WITH CHECK OPTION ]
[ GROUP BY ]
```

An example of creating a view from multiple tables:

**TYPE**

```
create view employee_summary as
select e.emp_id, e.last_name, p.position, p.date_hire, p.pay_rate
from employee_tbl e,
        employee_pay_tbl p
where e.emp_id = p.emp_id;
```

**OUTPUT**

```
View created.
```

Remember that when selecting data from multiple tables, the tables must be joined by common keys in the WHERE clause. A view is nothing more than a SELECT statement itself; therefore, tables are joined in a view definition the same as they are in a regular SELECT statement. Recall the use of table aliases in order to simplify the readability of a multiple-table query.

## Creating a View from a View

A view can be created from another view using the following format:

```
CREATE VIEW2 AS
SELECT * FROM VIEW1
```

### Do Not Create Views too Deep

A view may be created from a view many layers deep (a view of a view of a view and so on). How deep you may go is implementation-specific. The only problem with creating views based on other views is their manageability. For example, suppose that you create view2 based on view1 and then create view3 based on view2. If view1 is dropped, view2 and view3 are no good. The underlying information that supports these views no longer exists. Therefore, always maintain a good understanding of the views in the database, and upon which other objects those views rely. See Figure 20.2 on view dependency.

**NOTE**

If a view is as easy and efficient to create from the base table as from another view, then preference should go to the view being created from the base table.

**20**

**Figure 20.2.**

*View dependencies.*

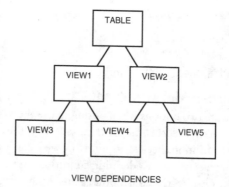

VIEW DEPENDENCIES

Figure 20.2 shows the relationship of views that are dependent not only on tables, but on other views. VIEW1 and VIEW2 are dependent on the TABLE. VIEW3 is dependent on VIEW1. VIEW4 is dependent on both VIEW1 and VIEW2. VIEW5 is dependent on VIEW2. Based on these relationships, the following can be concluded:

- ☐ If VIEW1 is dropped, then VIEW3 and VIEW4 are invalid.
- ☐ If VIEW2 is dropped, then VIEW4 and VIEW5 are invalid.
- ☐ If the TABLE is dropped, then none of the views are valid.

## The WITH CHECK OPTION

The WITH CHECK OPTION is a CREATE VIEW statement option. The purpose of the WITH CHECK OPTION is to ensure that all UPDATE and INSERTs satisfy the condition(s) in the view definition. If they do not satisfy the condition(s), the UPDATE or INSERT returns an error. The WITH CHECK OPTION has two options of its own, CASCADED and LOCAL. The WITH CHECK OPTION actually enforces referential integrity by checking the view's definition to see that it is not violated.

The following is an example of creating a view with the WITH CHECK OPTION:

```
create view employee_pagers as
select last_name, first_name, pager
from employee_tbl
where pager is not null
with check option;
```

  View created.

The WITH CHECK OPTION in this case should deny the entry of any NULL values in the view's PAGER column, because the view is defined by data that does not have a NULL value in the PAGER column.

Try to insert a NULL value in the PAGER column:

**TYPE**
```
insert into employee_pagers
values ('SMITH','JOHN',NULL);
```

```
insert into employee_pagers
              *
ERROR at line 1:
ORA-01400: mandatory (NOT NULL) column is missing or NULL during insert
```

The WITH CHECK OPTION worked.

### CASCADED Versus LOCAL

There are two options when opting to use the WITH CHECK OPTION during creation of a view from a view: CASCADED and LOCAL. CASCADED is the default, assumed if neither is specified. The CASCADED option checks all underlying views, all integrity constraints during an update for the base table, and against defining conditions in the second view. The LOCAL option is used to check only integrity constraints against both views and the defining conditions in the second view, not the underlying base table. Therefore, it is safer to create views with the CASCADED option because the base table's referential integrity is preserved.

## Updating a View

A view may be updated under certain conditions:

- ☐ The view must not involve joins.
- ☐ The view must not contain a GROUP BY clause.
- ☐ The view cannot contain any reference to the pseudocolumn ROWNUM.
- ☐ The view cannot contain any group functions.
- ☐ The DISTINCT clause cannot be used.
- ☐ The WHERE clause cannot include a nested table expression that includes a reference to the same table as referenced in the FROM clause.

Review Hour 14, "Using Subqueries to Define Unknown Data," for the UPDATE command's syntax.

## Inserting Rows into a View

Rows of data may be inserted into a view. The same rules that apply to the UPDATE command also apply to the INSERT command. Review Hour 14 for the syntax of the INSERT command.

## Deleting Rows from a View

Rows of data may be deleted from a view. The same rules that apply to the UPDATE and INSERT commands apply to the DELETE command. Review Hour 14 for the syntax of the DELETE command.

## Joining Views with Tables and Other Views

A view can be joined with tables and with other views. The same principals apply to joining views with tables and other views that apply to joining tables to other tables. Review Hour 13, "Joining Tables in Queries," on the joining of tables.

# Creating a Table from a View

A table may be created from a view, just as a table can be created from another table (or a view from another view).

The syntax is as follows:

```
CREATE TABLE TABLE_NAME AS
SELECT {* ¦ COLUMN1 [, COLUMN2 ]
FROM VIEW_NAME
[ WHERE CONDITION1 [, CONDITION2 ]
[ ORDER BY ]
```

First, create a view based on two tables:

**TYPE**
```
create view active_customers as
select c.*
from customer_tbl c,
     orders_tbl o
where c.cust_id = o.cust_id;
```

**OUTPUT**    View created.

Next, create a table based on the previously created view:

**TYPE**
```
create table customer_roster_tbl as
select cust_id, cust_name
from active_customers;
```

**OUTPUT**    Table created.

Finally, select data from the table, the same as any other table:

**TYPE**
```
select *
from customer_roster_tbl;
```

**OUTPUT**
```
CUST_ID    CUST_NAME
---------- ----------------------------
232        LESLIE GLEASON
12         MARYS GIFT SHOP
43         SCHYLERS NOVELTIES
090        WENDY WOLF
287        GAVINS PLACE
432        SCOTTYS MARKET
6 rows selected.
```

20

**NOTE**    Remember that the main difference between a table and a view is that a table contains actual data and consumes physical storage, whereas a view contains no data and requires no storage other than to store the view definition (the query).

## Views and the ORDER BY **Clause**

The ORDER BY clause cannot be used in the CREATE VIEW statement; however, the GROUP BY clause when used in the CREATE VIEW statement has the same effect as an ORDER BY clause.

> **NOTE**
> Using the ORDER BY clause in the SELECT statement that is querying the view is better and simpler than using the GROUP BY in the CREATE VIEW statement.

Here's an example of a GROUP BY clause in a CREATE VIEW statement:

**TYPE**
```
create view names2 as
select last_name || ', ' || first_name || ' ' || mid_init name
from employee_tbl
group by last_name || ', ' || first_name || ' ' || mid_init;
```

**OUTPUT**    View created.

If you select all data from the view, the data is in alphabetical order (because you grouped by NAME).

**TYPE**
```
select *
from names2;
NAME
```

**OUTPUT**
```
--------------------
GLASS, BRANDON S
GLASS, JACOB
PLEW, LINDA C
SPURGEON, TIFFANY
STEPHENS, TINA D
WALLACE, MARIAH
6 rows selected.
```

# Dropping a View

The DROP VIEW command is used to drop a view from the database. There are two options to the DROP VIEW command, RESTRICT and CASCADE. If a view is dropped with the RESTRICT option when any other views are referenced in a constraint, the DROP VIEW errors. If the CASCADE option is used and another view or constraint is referenced, the DROP VIEW succeeds and the underlying view or constraint is also dropped. An example follows:

**TYPE**    DROP VIEW NAMES2;

**OUTPUT**    View dropped.

**20**

# What Is a Synonym?

A *synonym* is merely another name for a table or a view. Synonyms are usually created so that a user can avoid having to qualify another user's table or view to access the table or view. Synonyms can be created as PUBLIC or PRIVATE. A PUBLIC synonym can be used by any user of the database; a PRIVATE synonym can be used only by the owner and any users that have been granted privileges.

**NOTE**

Synonyms are used by several major implementations. Synonyms are not ANSI SQL standard; however, because synonyms are used by major implementations, it is best to discuss them briefly. You must check your particular implementation for the exact use of synonyms, if available.

## Managing Synonyms

Synonyms are either managed by the database administrator (or another designated individual) or by individual users. Because there are two types of synonyms, PUBLIC and PRIVATE, different system-level privileges may be required in order to create one or the other. All users can generally create a private synonym. Typically, only a DBA or privileged database user can create a PUBLIC synonym. Refer to your specific implementation for required privileges when creating synonyms.

### Creating Synonyms

The general syntax to create a synonym is as follows:

```
CREATE [PUBLIC¦PRIVATE] SYNONYM SYNONYM_NAME FOR TABLE¦VIEW
```

You create a synonym called CUST, short for CUSTOMER_TBL, in the following example. This alleviates you from having to spell out the full table name.

**TYPE**
```
create synonym cust for customer_tbl;
```

**OUTPUT**
```
Synonym created.
```

**TYPE**
```
select cust_name
from cust;
```

**OUTPUT**
```
CUST_NAME
-----------------------------
LESLIE GLEASON
NANCY BUNKER
ANGELA DOBKO
WENDY WOLF
MARYS GIFT SHOP
```

```
SCOTTYS MARKET
JASONS AND DALLAS GOODIES
MORGANS CANDIES AND TREATS
SCHYLERS NOVELTIES
GAVINS PLACE
HOLLYS GAMEARAMA
HEATHERS FEATHERS AND THINGS
RAGANS HOBBIES INC
ANDYS CANDIES
RYANS STUFF
15 rows selected.
```

It is also a common practice for a table owner to create a synonym for the table to which you have been granted access so that you do not have to qualify the table name by the name of the owner.

**TYPE**    `CREATE SYNONYM PRODUCTS_TBL FOR USER1.PRODUCTS_TBL;`

**OUTPUT**    `Synonym created.`

### Dropping Synonyms

Dropping synonyms is like dropping most any database object. The general syntax to drop a synonym is as follows:

`DROP [PUBLIC¦PRIVATE] SYNONYM SYNONYM_NAME`

An example follows:

**TYPE**    `DROP SYNONYM CUST;`

**OUTPUT**    `Synonym dropped.`

# Summary

Views and synonyms, two important features in SQL, are discussed this hour. In many cases, these things are not used when they could aid in the overall functionality of relational database users. Views were defined as virtual tables—objects that look and act like tables, but do not take physical space like tables. Views are actually defined by queries against tables and possible other views in the database. Views are typically used to restrict data that a user sees and to simplify and summarize data. Views can be created from views, but care must be taken not to embed views too deeply, so as to not lose control over their management. There are various options when creating views, some implementation-specific.

Synonyms, objects in the database that represent other objects, are also discussed. Synonyms are used to simplify the name of another object in the database, either by creating a synonym

**20**

with a short name for an object with a long name or by creating a synonym on an object owned by another user to which you have access. There are two types of synonyms: PUBLIC and PRIVATE. A PUBLIC synonym is one that is accessible to all database users, whereas a PRIVATE synonym is accessible to a single user. A DBA typically creates a public synonym in which each individual user normally creates his or her own private synonyms.

## Q&A

**Q  How can a view contain data but take no storage space?**

**A**  A view does not contain data. A view is a virtual table or a stored query. The only space required for a view is for the actual view creation statement, called the *view definition*.

**Q  What happens to the view if a table from which a view was created is dropped?**

**A**  The view is invalid because the underlying data for the view no longer exists.

**Q  What are limits on naming the synonym when creating synonyms?**

**A.**  This is implementation-specific. However, the naming convention for synonyms in most major implementations follows the same rules that apply to the tables and other objects in the database.

# Workshop

The following workshop is composed of a series of quiz questions and practical exercises. The quiz questions are designed to test your overall understanding of the current material. The practical exercises are intended to afford you the opportunity to apply the concepts discussed during the current hour, as well as build upon the knowledge acquired in previous hours of study. Please take time to complete the quiz questions and exercises before continuing. You may refer to the answers in Appendix C, "Answers to Quizzes and Exercises."

## Quiz

1. Can a row of data be deleted from a view that was created from multiple tables?
2. When creating a table, the owner is automatically granted the appropriate privileges on that table. Is this true when creating a view?
3. What clause is used to order data when creating a view?
4. What option can be used, when creating a view from a view, to check integrity constraints?
5. You try to drop a view and receive an error because there are one or more underlying views. What must you do to drop the view?

**20**

## Exercises

1. Write a statement to create a view based on the total contents of the EMPLOYEE_TBL table.

2. Write a statement that creates a summarized view containing the average pay rate and average salary for each city in the EMPLOYEE_TBL table.

3. Write statements that drop the two views that you created in exercises 1 and 2.

# Hour 21

# Working with the System Catalog

During this hour you learn about the system catalog, commonly referred to as the data dictionary in some relational database implementations. By the end of this hour you will understand the purpose and contents of the system catalog, and will be able to query the system catalog to find information about the database based on commands that you have learned in previous hours. Each major implementation has some form of a system catalog that stores information about the database itself. This chapter shows examples of the elements contained in a few different system catalogs.

The highlights of this hour include:

- ☐ What is the system catalog?
- ☐ How is the system catalog created?
- ☐ What data is contained in the system catalog?
- ☐ Examples of system catalog tables
- ☐ Querying the system catalog
- ☐ Updating the system catalog

# What Is the System Catalog?

The *system catalog* is a collection of tables and views that contain important information about a database. A system catalog is available for each database. Information in the system catalog defines the structure of the database. For example, the DDL (data dictionary language) for all tables in the database are stored in the system catalog. See Figure 21.1 for an illustration of the system catalog within the database.

**Figure 21.1.**

*The system catalog.*

As you can see in Figure 21.1, the system catalog for a database is actually part of the database. Within the database are objects such as tables, indexes, and views. The system catalog is basically a group of objects that contain information that defines other objects in the database, the structure of the database itself, and various other significant information.

The system catalog for your implementation may be divided into logical groups of objects, so as to provide tables that are accessible by not only the database administrator, but any other database user as well. For instance, a user may need to view the particular database privileges that he or she has been granted, but has no need to know about the internal structure or processes of the database. A user typically queries the system catalog to acquire information on the user's own objects and privileges, whereas the DBA needs to be able to inquire about any structure or event within the database. In some implementations, there are system catalog objects that are accessible only to the database administrator.

The system catalog is crucial to the database administrator or any other database user that needs to know about the database's structure and nature. The system catalog allows order to be kept, not only by the database administrator and users, but by the database server itself.

**NOTE**

Each implementation has its own naming conventions for the system catalog's tables and views. The naming is not of importance; learning what the system catalog does is important, as is what it contains and how and where to retrieve the information.

# How Is the System Catalog Created?

The system catalog is either created automatically with the creation of the database, or by the database administrator immediately following the creation of the database. For instance, a set of predefined vendor-provided SQL scripts in Oracle is executed, which builds all the database tables and views in the system catalog that are accessible to a database user. The system catalog tables and views are system-owned and not specific to any one schema. In Oracle, for example, the system catalog owner is a user account called SYS, which has full authority in the database. In Sybase, the system catalog for the SQL server is located in the master database.

# What Is Contained in the System Catalog?

The system catalog contains a variety of information accessible to many users and is sometimes used for different specific purposes among each of those users.

The system catalog contains information such as the following:

- [ ] User accounts and default settings
- [ ] Privileges and other security information
- [ ] Performance statistics
- [ ] Object sizing
- [ ] Object growth
- [ ] Table structure and storage
- [ ] Index structure and storage
- [ ] Information on other database objects such as views, synonyms, triggers, and stored procedures
- [ ] Table constraints and referential integrity information
- [ ] User sessions
- [ ] Auditing information
- [ ] Internal database settings
- [ ] Locations of database files

The system catalog is maintained by the database server. For example, when a table is created, the database server inserts the data into the appropriate system catalog table or view. When a table's structure is modified, appropriate objects in the data dictionary are also updated. The following sections describe, by category, the types of data that are contained in the system catalog.

**21**

### User Data

All information about individual users is stored in the system catalog: the system and object privileges a user has been granted, the objects a user owns, and the objects not owned by the user to which the user has access. The user tables or views are accessible to the individual to query for information. See your implementation documentation on the system catalog objects.

### Security Information

The system catalog also stores security information such as user identifications, encrypted passwords, and various privileges and groups of privileges database users utilize to access the data. Audit tables exist in some implementations for tracking actions that occur within the database, as well as by whom, when, and so on. Database user sessions can also be closely monitored through the use of the system catalog in many implementations.

### Database Design Information

The system catalog contains information regarding the actual database. That information includes the database's creation date, name, objects sizing, size and location of data files, referential integrity information, indexes that exist in the database, and specific column information and column attributes for each table in the database.

### Performance Statistics

Performance statistics are typically maintained in the system catalog as well. Performance statistics include information concerning the performance of SQL statements, both elapsed time and the execution method of a SQL statement taken by the optimizer. Other information for performance concerns memory allocation and usage, free space in the database, and information that allows table and index fragmentation to be controlled within the database. This performance information can be used to properly tune the database, rearrange SQL queries, or redesign methods of access to data in order to achieve better overall performance and SQL query response time.

## Examples of System Catalog Tables by Implementation

Each implementation has several tables and views that compose the system catalog, some of which are categorized by user level, system level, and DBA level. For your particular implementation, you should query these tables and read your implementation's documentation for more information on system catalog tables. See Table 21.1 for a few examples of five major implementations.

## Table 21.1. Major implementations' system catalog objects.

### Microsoft SQL Server

| Table Name | Description |
| --- | --- |
| SYSUSERS | Information on database users |
| SYSSEGMENTS | Information on all database segments |
| SYSINDEXES | Information on all indexes |
| SYSCONSTRAINTS | Information on all constraints |

### dBase

| Table Name | Description |
| --- | --- |
| SYSVIEWS | Information on all views |
| SYSTABLS | Information on all tables |
| SYSIDXS | Information on all indexes |
| SYSCOLS | Information on columns of tables |

### Microsoft Access

| Table Name | Description |
| --- | --- |
| MSysColumns | Information about columns in tables |
| MSysIndexes | Information about indexes on tables |
| MSysMacros | Information about macros created |
| MSysObjects | Information about all database objects |
| MSysQueries | Information about queries created |
| MSysRelationships | Information about table relationships |

### Sybase

| Table Name | Description |
| --- | --- |
| SYSMESSAGES | Lists all server error messages |
| SYSKEYS | Primary and foreign key information |
| SYSTABLES | Information on all tables and views |
| SYSVIEWS | Text of all views |
| SYSCOLUMNS | Information on table columns |

21

**Table 21.1. continued**

### Sybase

| Table Name | Description |
| --- | --- |
| SYSINDEXES | Information on indexes |
| SYSOBJECTS | Information on tables, triggers, views, and the like |
| SYSDATABASES | Information on all databases on server |
| SYSPROCEDURES | Information on views, triggers, and stored procedures |

### Oracle

| Table Name | Description |
| --- | --- |
| ALL_TABLES | Information on tables accessible by a user |
| USER_TABLES | Information on tables owned by a user |
| DBA_TABLES | Information on all tables in the database |
| DBA_SEGMENTS | Information about segment storage |
| DBA_INDEXES | Information on all indexes |
| DBA_USERS | Information on all users of the database |
| DBA_ROLE_PRIVS | Information about roles granted |
| DBA_ROLES | Information about roles in the database |
| DBA_SYS_PRIVS | Information about system privileges granted |
| DBA_FREE_SPACE | Information about database free space |
| V$DATABASE | Information about the creation of the database |
| V$SESSION | Information on current sessions |

**NOTE**

These are just a few of the system catalog objects from a few various relational database implementations. Many of the system catalog objects that are similar between implementations are shown here, but the chapter strives to provide some variety. Overall, each implementation is very specific to the organization of the system catalog's contents.

# Querying the System Catalog

The system catalog tables or views are queried as any other table or view in the database using SQL. A user can usually query the user-related tables, but may be denied access to various system tables that can be accessed only by privileged database user accounts, such as the database administrator.

You create a SQL query, just as you create a query to access any other table in the database, in order to retrieve data from the system catalog.

For example, the following query returns all rows of data from the Sybase table SYSTABLES:

```
SELECT * FROM SYSTABLES
```

The following section displays a few examples of querying system catalog tables and some of the information that you may stumble across.

# Examples of System Catalog Queries

The following examples use Oracle's system catalog. Oracle is chosen for no particular reason other than that is the implementation in which this book's authors are most familiar.

The following query lists all user accounts in the database:

**TYPE**
```
SELECT USERNAME
FROM ALL_USERS;
```

**OUTPUT**
```
USERNAME
- - - - - - - - - - - - - - - - - - - - - - - - - - - - - -
SYS
SYSTEM
RYAN
SCOTT
DEMO
RON
USER1
USER2
8 rows selected.
```

The following query lists all tables owned by a user:

**TYPE**
```
SELECT TABLE_NAME
FROM USER_TABLES;
```

**OUTPUT**
```
TABLE_NAME
- - - - - - - - - - - - - - - - - - - - - - - - - - - - - -
CANDY_TBL
CUSTOMER_TBL
EMPLOYEE_PAY_TBL
EMPLOYEE_TBL
PRODUCTS_TBL
ORDERS_TBL
6 rows selected.
```

This query returns all the system privileges that have been granted to the database user BRANDON.

**21**

**TYPE**
```
SELECT GRANTEE, PRIVILEGE
FROM SYS.DBA_SYS_PRIVS
WHERE GRANTEE = 'BRANDON';
```

**OUTPUT**
```
GRANTEE                          PRIVILEGE
-------------------------------  -------------------------------
BRANDON                          ALTER ANY TABLE
BRANDON                          ALTER USER
BRANDON                          CREATE USER
BRANDON                          DROP ANY TABLE
BRANDON                          SELECT ANY TABLE
BRANDON                          UNLIMITED TABLESPACE
6 rows selected.
```

An example from MS Access:

**TYPE**
```
SELECT NAME
FROM MSYSOBJECTS
WHERE NAME = 'MSYSOBJECTS'
```

**OUTPUT**
```
NAME
------------------
MSYSOBJECTS
```

**NOTE**

The examples shown in this section are a drop in the bucket compared to the information that you can retrieve from any system catalog. Please refer to your implementation documentation for specific system catalog tables and columns within those available tables.

# Updating System Catalog Objects

The system catalog is used only for query operations—even when being used by the database administrator. Updates to the system catalog are accomplished automatically by the database server. For example, a table is created in the database when a CREATE TABLE statement is issued by a database user. The database server then places the DDL that was used to create the table in the system catalog, under the appropriate system catalog table. There is never a need to manually update any table in the system catalog. The database server for each implementation performs these updates according to actions that occur within the database, as shown in Figure 21.2.

**WARNING**

Never directly manipulate tables in the system catalog in any way. Doing so may compromise the database's integrity. Remember that information concerning the structure of the database, as well as all objects in the database, are maintained in the system catalog. The system catalog is typically isolated from all other data in the database.

**Figure 21.2.**

*Updates to the system catalog.*

## Summary

You have learned about the system catalog for a relational database. The system catalog is, in a sense, a database within a database. The system catalog is essentially a database that contains all information about the database in which it resides. It is a way of maintaining the database's overall structure, tracking events and changes that occur within the database, and providing a vast pool of information necessary for overall database management. The system catalog is only used for query operations. No database user should ever make changes directly to system tables. However, changes are implicitly made each time a change is made to the database structure itself, such as the creation of a table. These entries in the system catalog are made automatically by the database server.

## Q&A

**Q As a database user, I realize I can find information about my objects. How can I find information about other users' objects?**

**A** There are sets of tables and/or views that users can use to query in most system catalogs. One set of these tables and views include information on what objects to which you have access.

**Q If a user forgets his or her password, is there a table that the database administrator can query to get the password?**

**A** Yes and no. The password is maintained in a system table, but is typically encrypted, so that even the database administrator cannot read the password. The password would have to be reset if the user forgot it, which the database administrator could easily accomplish.

**Q How can I tell what columns are in a system catalog table?**

**A** The system catalog tables can be queried as any other table. Simply query the table that holds that particular information.

21

# Workshop

The following workshop is composed of a series of quiz questions and practical exercises. The quiz questions are designed to test your overall understanding of the current material. The practical exercises are intended to afford you the opportunity to apply the concepts discussed during the current hour, as well as build upon the knowledge acquired in previous hours of study. Please take time to complete the quiz questions and exercises before continuing. You may refer to the answers in Appendix C.

## Quiz

1. The system catalog is also known as what in some implementations?
2. Can a regular user update the system catalog?
3. What Sybase system table is used to retrieve information about views that exist in the database?
4. Who owns the system catalog?
5. What is the difference between the Oracle system objects ALL_TABLES and DBA_TABLES?
6. Who makes modifications to the system tables?

## Exercises

1. Try querying the system catalog tables for your implementation. You can start with the tables that hold information about your user database user account.
2. Query the system catalog in order to list all tables to which you have access.
3. Query the tables that contain system and object privileges that you have been granted.
4. If you have the DBA or SELECT privilege on the database administrator tables, then query these tables. If you do not have these privileges, take a look at a hard copy of the tables, which should be located in your implementation documentation set.

21

# PART

# VIII

## Applying SQL Fundamentals in Today's World

## Hour

# Hour 22

# Advanced SQL Topics

During this hour you are introduced to some advanced SQL topics. By the end of the hour you understand the concepts behind cursors, stored procedures, triggers, dynamic SQL, direct versus embedded SQL, and SQL generated from SQL.

The highlights of this hour include:

- ☐ What are cursors?
- ☐ Using stored procedures
- ☐ What are triggers?
- ☐ Basics of dynamic SQL
- ☐ Using SQL to generate SQL
- ☐ Direct SQL versus embedded SQL
- ☐ Call-level interface

## Advanced Topics

The advanced SQL topics discussed this hour are those that extend beyond the basic operations that you have learned so far, such as querying data from the database, building database structures, and manipulating data within the database. These advanced topics are features available in many implementations, all of which provide enhancements to the parts of SQL discussed as of yet.

> **NOTE**
>
> Not all topics are ANSI SQL, so you must check your particular implementation for variations in syntax and rules. A few major vendors' syntax is shown here for comparison.

# Cursors

To most people, a cursor is commonly known as a blinking dot or square that appears on the monitor and indicates where you are in a file or application; however, that is not the same type of cursor discussed here. A SQL *cursor* is an area in database memory where the last SQL statement is stored. If the current SQL statement is a database query, then a row from the query is also stored in memory. This row is the cursor's *current value* or *current row*. The area in memory is named and is available to programs.

A cursor is typically used to retrieve a subset of data from the database. Thereby, each row in the cursor can be evaluated by a program, one row at a time. Cursors are normally used in SQL that is embedded in procedural-type programs. Some cursors are created implicitly by the database server, whereas others are defined by the SQL programmer. Each SQL implementation may define the use of cursors differently.

This section shows syntax examples from two popular implementations: Microsoft SQL Server and Oracle.

The syntax to declare a cursor for Microsoft SQL Server is as follows:

```
DECLARE CURSOR_NAME CURSOR
FOR SELECT_STATEMENT
[ FOR [READ ONLY ¦ UPDATE [ COLUMN_LIST ]}]
```

The syntax for Oracle is as follows:

```
DECLARE CURSOR CURSOR_NAME
IS {SELECT_STATEMENT}
```

The following cursor contains the result subset of all records from the EMPLOYEE_TBL table:

```
DECLARE CURSOR EMP_CURSOR IS
SELECT * FROM EMPLOYEE_TBL
{ OTHER PROGRAM STATEMENTS }
```

According to the ANSI standard, the following operations are used to access a cursor once it has been defined:

22

22

OPEN     Opens a defined cursor
FETCH    Fetches rows from a cursor into a program variable
CLOSE    Closes the cursor when operations against the cursor are complete

# Opening a Cursor

When a cursor is opened, the specified cursor's SELECT statement is executed and the results of the query are stored in a staging area in memory.

**SYNTAX**

The syntax to open a cursor in dBase is as follows:

```
OPEN CURSOR_NAME
```

The syntax in Oracle is as follows:

```
OPEN CURSOR [ PARAMETER1 [, PARAMETER2 ]]
```

To open the EMP_CURSOR:

```
OPEN EMP_CURSOR
```

# Fetching Data from a Cursor

The contents of the cursor (results from the query) may be retrieved through the use of the FETCH statement once a cursor has been opened.

**SYNTAX**

The syntax for the FETCH statement in Microsoft SQL Server is as follows:

```
FETCH CURSOR_NAME [ INTO FETCH_LIST ]
```

The syntax for Oracle is as follows:

```
FETCH CURSOR_NAME {INTO : HOST_VARIABLE
[[ INDICATOR ] : INDICATOR_VARIABLE ]
[, : HOST_VARIABLE
[[ INDICATOR ] : INDICATOR_VARIABLE ]]
¦ USING DESCRIPTOR DESCRIPTOR }
```

The syntax for dBase is as follows:

```
FETCH CURSOR_NAME into MEMORY_VARIABLES
```

To fetch the contents of EMP_CURSOR into a variable called EMP_RECORD, your fetch statement may appear as follows:

```
FETCH EMP_CURSOR INTO EMP_RECORD
```

# Closing a Cursor

You can obviously close a cursor if you can open a cursor. Closing a cursor is quite simple. Once it's closed, it is no longer available to user programs.

**NOTE**

Closing a cursor does not necessarily free the memory associated with the cursor. In some implementations, the memory used by a cursor must be deallocated by using the `deallocate` statement. When the cursor is deallocated, the memory associated is freed and the name of the cursor can then be reused. In other implementations, memory is implicitly deallocated when the cursor is closed. Memory is available for other operations, such as opening another cursor, once space used by a cursor is reclaimed.

**SYNTAX**

The Microsoft SQL Server syntax for the closing of a cursor and the deallocation of a cursor is as follows:

```
CLOSE CURSOR_NAME

DEALLOCATE CURSOR CURSOR_NAME
```

When the cursor is closed in Oracle, the resources and name are released without the `deallocate` statement. The syntax for Oracle is as follows:

```
CLOSE CURSOR_NAME
```

To release the resources in dBase, the table must be closed and reopened before the resources are released and the name can be reused. The syntax for dBase is as follows:

```
CLOSE CURSOR_NAME
```

**NOTE**

As you can see from the previous examples, variations among the implementations are extensive, especially with advanced features of and extensions to SQL, which are covered during Hour 24, "Extensions to Standard SQL." You must check your particular implementation for the exact usage of a cursor.

# Stored Procedures

*Stored procedures* are groupings of related SQL statements—commonly referred to as *functions* and *subprograms*—that allow ease and flexibility for a programmer. This ease and flexibility is derived from the fact that a stored procedure is often easier to execute than a number of individual SQL statements. Stored procedures may be nested within other stored procedures. That is, a stored procedure may call another stored procedure, which may call another stored procedure, and so on.

**22**

**NEW TERM**   A *stored procedure* is a group of one or more SQL statements or functions that is stored in the database and compiled and is ready to be executed by a database user.

When a stored procedure is created, the various subprograms and functions (that use SQL) that compose the stored procedure are actually stored in the database. These stored procedures are pre-parsed, and are immediately ready to execute upon their invocation by the user.

**SYNTAX**

The Microsoft SQL Server syntax for creating a stored procedures is as follows:

```
CREATE PROCEDURE PROCEDURE_NAME
[ [(] @PARAMETER_NAME
DATATYPE [(LENGTH) ¦ (PRECISION [, SCALE ])
[ = DEFAULT ][ OUTPUT ]
[, @PARAMETER_NAME
DATATYPE [(LENGTH) ¦ (PRECISION [, SCALE ])
[ = DEFAULT ][ OUTPUT ]] [)]]
[ WITH RECOMPLIE ]
AS SQL_STATEMENTS
```

The syntax for Oracle is as follows:

```
CREATE [ OR REPLACE ] PROCEDURE PROCEDURE_NAME
[ (ARGUMENT [{IN ¦ OUT ¦ IN OUT} ] TYPE,
ARGUMENT [{IN ¦ OUT ¦ IN OUT} ] TYPE) ] {IS ¦ AS}
PROCEDURE_BODY
```

An example of very simple stored procedure is as follows:

**TYPE**
```
CREATE PROCEDURE NEW_PRODUCT
(PROD_ID IN VARCHAR2, PROD_DESC IN VARCHAR2, COST IN NUMBER)
AS
BEGIN
  INSERT INTO PRODUCTS_TBL
  VALUES (PROD_ID, PROD_DESC, COST);
  COMMIT;
END;
```

**OUTPUT**   Procedure created.

This procedure is used to insert new rows into the PRODUCTS_TBL table.

**SYNTAX**

The syntax for executing a stored procedure in Microsoft SQL Server is as follows:

```
EXECUTE [ @RETURN_STATUS = ]
PROCEDURE_NAME
[[@PAREMETER_NAME = ] VALUE ¦
[@PARAMETER_NAME = ] @VARIABLE [ OUTPUT ]]
[WITH RECOMPLIE]
```

The syntax for Oracle is as follows:

```
EXECUTE [ @RETURN STATUS =] PROCEDURE NAME
[[ @PARAMETER NAME = ] VALUE ¦ [ @PARAMETER NAME = ] @VARIABLE [ OUTPUT ]]]
[ WITH RECOMPLIE ]
```

Now execute the procedure you have created:

**TYPE**    `EXECUTE NEW_PRODUCT ('9999','INDIAN CORN',1.99);`

**OUTPUT**    `PL/SQL procedure successfully completed.`

## Advantages of Stored Procedures

Stored procedures pose several distinct advantages over individual SQL statements executed in the database. Some of these advantages include the following:

- ☐ The statements are already stored in the database.
- ☐ The statements are already parsed and in an executable format.
- ☐ Stored procedures support modular programming.
- ☐ Stored procedures may call other procedures and functions.
- ☐ Stored procedures can be called by other types of programs.
- ☐ Overall response time is typically better with stored procedures.
- ☐ Overall ease of use.

# Triggers

A *trigger* is a form of a stored procedure that is executed when a specified (Data Manipulation Language) action is performed on a table. The trigger may be executed before or after an INSERT, DELETE, or UPDATE. Triggers may also be used to check data integrity before and INSERT, DELETE, or UPDATE. Triggers can roll back transactions; they can modify data in one table and read from another table in another database.

**NEW TERM**    A *trigger* is a compiled SQL procedure in the database used to perform actions based on other actions that occur within the database.

Triggers, for the most part, are very good functions to use; they can, however, cause more I/O overhead. Triggers should not be used when a stored procedure or a program can accomplish the same results with less overhead. The Microsoft SQL Server syntax to create a trigger is as follows:

**SYNTAX**
```
CREATE TRIGGER TRIGGER_NAME
ON TABLE_NAME
FOR { INSERT ¦ UPDATE ¦ DELETE [, ..]}
AS
SQL_STATEMENTS
[ RETURN ]
```

**22**

The syntax for Oracle is as follows:

```
CREATE [ OR REPLACE ] TRIGGER TRIGGER_NAME
[ BEFORE ¦ AFTER ]
[ DELETE ¦ INSERT ¦ UPDATE [ OF COLUMN_NAME ]
ON [ USER.TABLE_NAME ]
[ FOR EACH ROW ] [ WHEN CONDITION ]
[ PL/SQL BLOCK ]
```

An example trigger follows:

**TYPE**

```
CREATE TRIGGER EMP_PAY_TRIG
AFTER UPDATE ON EMPLOYEE_PAY_TBL
FOR EACH ROW
BEGIN
  INSERT INTO EMPLOYEE_PAY_HISTORY
  (EMP_ID, PREV_PAY_RATE, PAY_RATE, DATE_LAST_RAISE,
   TRANSACTION_TYPE)
  VALUES
  (:NEW.EMP_ID, :OLD.PAY_RATE, :NEW.PAY_RATE,
   :NEW.DATE_LAST_RAISE, 'PAY CHANGE');
END;
/
```

**OUTPUT**    Trigger created.

This example shows the creation of a trigger called EMP_PAY_TRIG. This trigger inserts a row into the EMPLOYEE_PAY_HISTORY table, reflecting the changes made every time a row of data is updated in the EMPLOYEE_PAY_TBL table.

**NOTE**

> The body of a trigger may not be altered. You must either replace or recreate the trigger. Some implementations allow a trigger to be replaced (if the trigger with the same name already exists) as part of the CREATE TRIGGER statement.

The syntax for dropping a trigger is as follows:

```
DROP TRIGGER TRIGGER_NAME
```

# Dynamic SQL

Dynamic SQL allows a programmer or end user to create a SQL statement's specifics at runtime and pass the statement to the database. The database then returns data into the program variables, which are bound at SQL runtime.

In order to comprehend dynamic SQL, review static SQL. Static SQL is what this book has discussed thus far. A *static SQL statement* is written and not meant to be changed. Although static SQL statements may be stored as files ready to be executed later, or as stored procedures in the database, static SQL does not quite offer the flexibility that is allowed with dynamic SQL.

The problem with static SQL is that even though numerous queries may be available to the end user, there is a good chance that none of these "canned queries" will satisfy the users' needs on every occasion. Dynamic SQL is often used by ad hoc query tools, which allow a SQL statement to be created on-the-fly by a user in order to satisfy the particular query requirements for that particular situation. Once the statement is customized according to the user's needs, the statement is sent to the database, checked for syntax errors and privileges required to execute the statement, and is compiled in the database where the statement is carried out by the database server. Dynamic SQL can be created by using call-level interface, which is explained in the next section.

**NOTE**

> Although dynamic SQL provides more flexibility for the end user's query needs, the performance may not compare to that of a stored procedure, whose code has already been analyzed by the SQL optimizer.

## Call-Level Interface

Application programmers should be very familiar with the concept of call-level interface. It is one of the methods that allows a programmer to embed SQL in different procedural programming languages. When using call-level interface (CLI), you simply pass the text of a SQL statement into a variable using the rules of the host programming language. You can execute the SQL statement in the host program through the use of the variable into which you passed the SQL text.

**NEW TERM**    *Call-level interface* is used to embed SQL code in a host program, such as ANSI C.

EXEC SQL is a common host programming language command that allows you to call a SQL statement (CLI) from within the program.

### EXEC SQL

Examples of programming languages that support CLI are:

☐  COBOL
☐  ANSI C

**22**

☐ Pascal

☐ Fortran

☐ Ada

**NOTE** Refer to the syntax of the host programming language with which you are using call-level interface options.

# Using SQL to Generate SQL

Using SQL to generate SQL is very valuable time-budgeting when writing SQL statements. Assume you have 100 users in the database already. A new role, ENABLE (a user-defined object that is granted privileges), has been created and must be granted to those 100 users. Instead of manually creating 100 GRANT statements, the following SQL statement generates each of those statements for you:

```
SELECT 'GRANT ENABLE TO '|| USERNAME||';'
FROM SYS.DBA_USERS
```

This example uses Oracle's system catalog view (which contains information for users).

Notice the use of single quotation marks around the GRANT ENABLE TO. The use of single quotation marks allows whatever is between the marks to be literal. Remember that literal values may be selected from tables, the same as columns from a table. USERNAME is the column in the system catalog table SYS.DBA_USERS. The double pipe signs (||) are used to concatenate the columns. The use of double pipes followed by ';' concatenates the semicolon to the end of the username, thus completing the statement.

The results of the SQL statement look like this:

```
GRANT ENABLE TO RRPLEW;
GRANT ENABLE TO RKSTEP;
```

These results should be spooled to a file, which can be sent to the database. The database, in turn, executes each SQL statement in the file, saving you many keystrokes and much time. The GRANT ENABLE TO *USERNAME*; statement is repeated once for every user in the database.

Next time you are writing SQL statements and have repeated the same statement several times, allow your imagination to take hold and let SQL do the work for you.

# Direct Versus Embedded SQL

Direct SQL is where a SQL statement is executed from some form of an interactive terminal. The SQL results are returned directly to that terminal that issued the statement. Most of this book has focused on direct SQL. Direct SQL is also referred to as *interactive invocation* or *direct invocation*.

*Embedded SQL* is SQL code used within other programs such as Pascal, Fortran, COBOL, and C. SQL code is actually embedded in a host programming language, as discussed previously, with call-level interface. Embedded SQL statements in host programming language code are commonly preceded by EXEC SQL and terminated by a semicolon in many cases. Other termination characters include END-EXEC and the right parenthesis.

This is an example of embedded SQL in a host program, such as the ANSI C language:

```
{host programming commands}
EXEC SQL {SQL statement};
{more host programming commands}
```

# Summary

Some advanced SQL concepts are discussed this hour. Although this chapter does not go into a lot of detail, it does provide you a basic understanding of how you may soon apply the basic concepts that you have no doubt learned up to this point. You start with cursors, which are used to pass a data set selected by a query into a location in memory. Once a cursor is declared in a program, it must first be opened for accessibility, then the contents of the cursor are fetched into a variable, at which time the data can be used for program processing. The result set for the cursor is contained in memory until the cursor is closed and the memory deallocated.

Stored procedures and triggers are covered next. Stored procedures are basically SQL statements that are stored together in the database. These statements, along with other implementation-specific commands, are compiled in the database and are ready to be executed by a database user at any given time. A trigger is also a type of stored procedure—one that allows actions to be automatically performed based on other actions that occur within the database. Stored procedures typically provide better performance benefits than individual SQL statements.

Dynamic SQL, using SQL to generate other SQL statements, and the differences between direct SQL and embedded SQL are the last subjects discussed. Dynamic SQL is SQL code dynamically created during runtime by a user, unlike static SQL. Using SQL code to generate other SQL statements is a great time-saver. It is a way of automating the creation of numerous, tedious SQL statements using features available with your implementation, such as concatenation and the selection of literal values. Finally, the main difference between direct SQL and embedded SQL is that the user directly issues direct SQL statements from some terminal, whereas embedded SQL is actually embedded within a host program in order to help process data.

22

The concepts of some of the advanced topics discussed during this hour are used to illustrate the application of SQL in an enterprise, covered in Hour 23, "Extending SQL to the Enterprise, the Internet, and the Intranet."

## Q&A

**Q Can a stored procedure call another stored procedure?**

**A** Yes. The stored procedure being called is referred to as being nested.

**Q How do I execute a cursor do?**

**A** Simply use the OPEN CURSOR statement. This sends the results of the cursor to a staging area.

# Workshop

The following workshop is composed of a series of quiz questions and practical exercises. The quiz questions are designed to test your overall understanding of the current material. The practical exercises are intended to afford you the opportunity to apply the concepts discussed during the current hour, as well as build upon the knowledge acquired in previous hours of study. Please take time to complete the quiz questions and exercises before continuing. You may refer to the answers in Appendix C.

## Quiz

1. Can a trigger be altered?
2. When a cursor is closed, can you reuse the name?
3. What command is used to retrieve the results after a cursor has been opened?
4. Are triggers executed before or after an INSERT, DELETE, or UPDATE?

## Exercises

1. Using your implementation's system catalog tables, write the SQL that creates the following SQL statements. Substitute the name of an actual object for the object names.

   a.

   ```
   GRANT SELECT ON TABLE_NAME TO USERNAME;
   ```

   b.

   ```
   GRANT, CONNECT, RESOURCE TO USERNAME;
   ```

   c.

   ```
   SELECT COUNT(*) FROM TABLE_NAME;
   ```

2. Write a statement to create a stored procedure that deletes an entry from the PRODUCTS_TBL table; it should be similar to the example used in this hour to insert a new product.

3. Write the statement that executes the stored procedure that you created in Exercise 2 to delete the row for PROD_ID '9999'.

# Hour 23

# Extending SQL to the Enterprise, the Internet, and the Intranet

During this hour you learn how SQL is actually used in an enterprise and a company's intranet and how it has been extended to the Internet.

The highlights of this hour include the following:

- ☐ SQL and the enterprise
- ☐ Front-end and back-end applications
- ☐ Accessing a remote database
- ☐ SQL and the Internet
- ☐ SQL and the intranet

## SQL and the Enterprise

The previous hour covered some advanced SQL topics. These topics built upon earlier hours in the book and began to show you practical applications for the SQL you have learned. During this hour you focus on the concepts behind extending SQL to the enterprise, which involve SQL applications and making data available to all appropriate members of a company for daily use.

**NEW TERM**  An *enterprise* is a business organization or company.

Many commercial enterprises have specific data available to other enterprises, customers, and vendors. For example, the enterprise may have detailed information on its products available for customers' access in hopes of acquiring more purchases. Enterprise employee needs are included as well. For example, employee-specific data can also be made available, such as for timesheet logs, vacation schedules, training schedules, company policies, and so on. A database may be created, and customers and employees can be allowed easy access to an enterprise's important data via SQL and an Internet language.

## The Back End

The heart of any application is the back-end application. This is where things happen behind the scenes, transparent to the database end user. The *back-end application* includes the actual database server, data sources, and the appropriate middleware used to connect an application to the Web or a remote database on the local network.

As a review, some of the major database servers include Oracle, Informix, Sybase, Microsoft SQL Server, and Borland InterBase. This is typically the first step in porting any application, either to the enterprise through a local area network (LAN), to the enterprise's own intranet, or to the Internet. The database server should be established by an onsite database administrator who understands the company's needs and the application's requirements.

**NEW TERM**  *Porting* describes the process of implementing an application in an environment that is available to users.

The middleware for the application includes a Web server and a tool capable of connecting the Web server to the database server. The main objective is to have an application on the Web that can communicate with a corporate database.

## The Front-End Application

The *front-end application* is the part of an application with which an end user interacts. The front-end application is either a commercial, off-the-shelf software product that a company purchases, or an application that is developed in-house using other third-party tools. Third-party tools are those described in the following paragraphs.

Before the rise of many of the new front-end tools available today, users had to know how to program in languages such as C++, HTML, or one of many other procedural programming languages that develop Web-based applications. Other languages, such as ANSI C, COBOL, FORTRAN, and Pascal, have been used to develop front-end, onsite corporate applications, which were mainly character-based. Today, most newly developed front-end applications are GUI—they have a graphical user interface.

**23**

The tools available today are user-friendly and object-oriented, by way of icons, wizards, and dragging and dropping with the mouse. Some of the popular tools to port applications to the Web include C++Builder and IntraBuilder by Borland and Microsoft's Visual J++ and C++. Other popular applications used to develop corporate-based applications on a LAN include PowerBuilder by Powersoft, Developer/2000 by Oracle Corporation, Visual Basic by Microsoft, and Delphi by Borland.

**NOTE**

The front-end application promotes simplicity for the database end user. The underlying database, code, and events that occur within the database are transparent to the user. The front-end application is developed to relieve the end user from guesswork and confusion, which may otherwise be caused by having to be too intuitive to the system itself. The new technologies allow the applications to be more intuitive, enabling the end users to focus on the true aspects of their particular jobs, thereby increasing overall productivity.

Figure 23.1 illustrates the back-end and front-end components of a database application. The back end resides on the host server, where the database resides. Back-end users include developers, programmers, database administrators, system administrators, and system analysts. The front-end application resides on the client machine, which is typically each end user's PC. End users are the vast audience for the front-end component of an application, which may include users such as data entry clerks and accountants. The end user is able to access the back-end database through a network connection—either a local area network (LAN) or a wide area network (WAN). Some type of middleware (such as an ODBC driver) is used to provide a connection between the front and back ends through the network.

**Figure 23.1.**

*A database application.*

# Accessing a Remote Database

Sometimes the database you are accessing is a local database, one you are connected to directly. For the most part, you will probably access some form of a remote database. A *remote database* is one that is nonlocal, meaning that you must utilize the network and some network protocol in order to interface with the database.

> **NEW TERM**    A *remote database* is a database that is located on a server other than the server to which you are currently connected.

There are several ways to access a remote database. From a broad perspective, a remote database is accessed via the network or Internet connection using a middleware product (ODBC, a standard middleware, is discussed in the next section). Figure 23.2 shows three scenarios for accessing a remote database.

**Figure 23.2.**

*Accessing a remote database.*

This figure shows access to a remote server from another local database server, a local front-end application, and a local host server. The local database server and local host server are often the same because the database normally resides on a local host server. However, you can usually connect to a remote database from a local server without a current local database connection. For the end user, the front-end application is the most typical method of remote database access. All methods must route their database requests through the network.

## ODBC

Open Database Connectivity (ODBC) allows connections to remote databases through a library driver. A network driver may also be required for a connection to a remote database. An application calls the ODBC functions, and a *driver manager* loads the ODBC driver. The ODBC driver processes the call, submits the SQL request, and returns the results from the database. ODBC is now a standard and is used by several products, such as Sybase's PowerBuilder, FoxPro, Visual C++, Visual Basic, Borland's Delphi, Microsoft Access, and many more.

**23**

**NEW TERM**  An *ODBC driver* is used by a front-end application to interface with a back-end database.

As a part of ODBC, all the RDBMS vendors have an Application Programmatic Interface (API) with their database. Oracle's Open Call Interface (OCI) and Centura's SQLGateway and SQLRouter are some of the available products.

## Vendor Connectivity Products

In addition to an ODBC driver, many vendors have their own products that allow a user to connect to a remote database. Each of these vendor products is specific to the particular vendor implementation and may not be portable to other types of database servers.

Oracle Corporation has a product called SQL*Net, which allows for remote database connectivity. SQL*Net can be used with almost all the major network products such as TCP/IP, OSI, SPX/IPX, and more. In addition, SQL*Net runs on most of the major operating systems.

Sybase, Inc. has a product called Open Client/C Developers Kit, which supports other vendor products such as Oracle's SQL*Net.

# Accessing a Remote Database Through a Web Interface

Accessing a remote database through a Web interface is very similar to accessing one through a local network. The main difference is that all requests to the database from the user are routed through the Web server (see Figure 23.3).

**Figure 23.3.**

*A Web interface to a remote database.*

You can see in Figure 23.3 that an end user accesses a database through a Web interface by first invoking a Web browser. The Web browser is used to connect to a particular URL or Internet IP address, determined by the location of the Web server. The Web server authenticates user access and sends the user request, perhaps a query, to the remote database, which may also verify user authenticity. The database server then returns the results to the Web server, which displays the results on the user's Web browser. Unauthorized access to a particular server can be controlled by using a firewall.

 A *firewall* is a security mechanism that ensures against unauthorized connections to a server. One or multiple firewalls can be enabled to patrol access to a database or server.

**WARNING**

> Be careful what information you make available on the Web. Always ensure that precautions are taken to properly implement security at all appropriate levels; that may include the Web server, the host server, and the remote database. Privacy act data, such as individuals' social security numbers, should always be protected and should not be broadcast over the Web.

# SQL and the Internet

SQL can be embedded or used in conjunction with programming languages such as C or COBOL. For example, SQL can also be embedded in Internet programming languages such as Java. Text from HTML, another Internet language, can be translated into SQL in order to send a query to a remote database from a Web front-end. Once the database resolves the query, the output is translated back into HTML and displayed on the Web browser of the individual executing the query. The following sections discuss the use of SQL on the Internet.

## Making Data Available to Customers Worldwide

With the advent of the Internet, data became available to customers and vendors worldwide. The data is normally available for read-only access through a front-end tool.

The data that is available to customers may concern general customer information, product information, invoice information, current orders, back orders, and other pertinent information. Private information, such as corporate strategies and employee information, should not be available.

Home Web pages on the Internet have become nearly a necessity for companies that want to keep pace with their competition. A Web page is a very powerful tool than can tell surfers all about a company—its services, products, and other information—with very little overhead.

## Making Data Available to Employees and Privileged Customers

A database may be made accessible through the Internet or a company's intranet, to employees or its customers. Using Internet technologies is a valuable communication asset to keeping employees informed about company policies, benefits, training, and so on.

### Front-End Web Tools Using SQL

There are several tools that can access databases. Many have a graphical user interface, where a user does not necessarily have to understand SQL in order to query a database. These front-end tools allow users to point and click with the mouse, to select objects that represent tables, manipulate data within objects, specify criteria on data to be returned, and so on. These tools are often developed and customized in order to meet a company's database needs.

# SQL and the Intranet

IBM originally created SQL for use between databases located on mainframe computers and between the users on client machines. The users were connected to the mainframes via a local area network. SQL was adopted as the standard language of communi-cation between databases and users. An intranet is basically a small Internet. The main difference is that an *intranet* is for a single organization's use, whereas the Internet is accessible to the general public. The user (client) interface in an intranet remains the same as that in a client/server environment. SQL requests are routed through the Web server and languages (such as HTML) before being directed to the database for evaluation.

**NOTE**  Database security is much more stable than security on the Internet. Always be sure to use the security features available to you through your database server.

# Summary

Some concepts behind deploying SQL and database applications to the Internet are discussed as you near your last hour of study in this book. It is very important, in this day and age, for companies to remain competitive. In order to conform to the rest of the world, it has proven beneficial—almost mandatory—to obtain a presence on the World Wide Web. In accomplishing this presence, applications must be developed and even migrated from client/server systems to the Internet on a Web server. One of the greatest concerns when publishing any kind or any amount of corporate data on the Web is security. Security must be considered, adhered to, and strictly enforced.

Accessing remote databases across local networks as well as over the Internet is discussed. Each major method for accessing any type of a remote database requires the use of the network and protocol adapters used to translate requests to the database. This has been a broad overview of the application of SQL over local networks, company intranets, and the Internet. After the digestion of a few quiz and exercise questions, you should be ready to venture into the last hour of your journey through SQL.

## Q&A

**Q What is the difference between the Internet and an intranet?**

**A** The Internet provides connections, for the public, to information reservoirs by using a Web interface. An intranet also uses a Web interface, but only internal access is allowed, such as to company employees and privileged customers.

**Q Is a back-end database for a Web application any different than a back-end database for a client/server system?**

**A** The back-end database itself for a Web application is not necessarily any different than that of a client/server system. However, there are other requirements that must be met in order to implement a Web-based application. For example, a Web server is used to access the database with a Web application. With a Web application, end users do not typically connect directly to the database.

# Workshop

The following workshop is composed of a series of quiz questions and practical exercises. The quiz questions are designed to test your overall understanding of the current material. The practical exercises are intended to afford you the opportunity to apply the concepts discussed during the current hour, as well as build upon the knowledge acquired in previous hours of study. Please take time to complete the quiz questions and exercises before continuing. You may refer to the answers in Appendix C, "Answers to Quizzes and Exercises."

## Quiz

1. Can a database on a server be accessed from another server?
2. What can a company use to disseminate information to its own employees?
3. Products that allow connections to databases are called what?
4. Can SQL be embedded into Internet programming languages?
5. How is a remote database accessed through a Web application?

**23**

# Exercises

1. Connect to the Internet and take a look at various companies' home pages. If your own company has a home page, compare it to the competition's home pages. Ask yourself these questions about the pages:

   a. Does the page come up quickly or is it bogged down with too many graphics?

   b. Is the page interesting to read?

   c. Do you know anything about the company, services, or products after reading the available information?

   d. If applicable, has access to the database been easy?

   e. Do there appear to be any security mechanisms on the Web page?

2. If your company has an intranet, sign on and take a look at what information is available about the company. Is there a database available? If so, who is the vendor? What type of front-end tools are available?

23

# Hour **24**

# Extensions to Standard SQL

This hour covers extensions to ANSI-standard SQL. Although most implementations conform to the standard for the most part, many vendors have provided extensions to standard SQL through various enhancements.

The highlights of this hour include:

- [ ] Various implementations
- [ ] Differences between implementations
- [ ] Compliance with ANSI SQL
- [ ] Interactive SQL statements
- [ ] Using variables
- [ ] Using parameters

## Various Implementations

There are numerous SQL implementations that are released by various vendors. All of the relational database vendors could not possibly be mentioned; a few of the leading implementations, however, are discussed. The implementations discussed here are Sybase, dBase, Microsoft SQL Server, and Oracle. Other popular vendors providing database products other than those mentioned previously include Borland, IBM, Informix, Progress, CA-Ingres, and many more.

## Differences Between Implementations

Although the implementations listed here are relational database products, there are specific differences between each. These differences stem from the design of the product and the way data is handled by the database engine; however, this book concentrates on the SQL aspect of the differences. All implementations use SQL as the language for communicating with the database, as directed by ANSI. Many have some sort of extension to SQL that is unique to that particular implementation.

> **NOTE**
>
> Differences in SQL have been adopted by various vendors in order to enhance ANSI SQL for performance considerations and ease of use. Vendors also strive to make enhancements that provide them with advantages over other vendors, making their implementation more attractive to the customer.

Now that you know SQL, you should have little problem adjusting to the differences in SQL among the various vendors. In other words, if you can write SQL in a Sybase implementation, you should be able to write SQL in Oracle. Besides, knowing SQL for various vendors accomplishes nothing less than improving your résumé.

The following sections compare the SELECT statement's syntax from a few major vendors to the ANSI standard.

This is the ANSI standard:

```
SELECT [DISTINCT ] {* ¦ COLUMN1 [, COLUMN2 ]
[ INTO HOST_VARIABLE ]
FROM TABLE1 [, TABLE2 ]
[ WHERE SEARCH_ CONDITION ]
GROUP BY [ TABLE_ALIAS ¦ COLUMN1 [, COLUMN2 ]
[ HAVING SEARCH_CONDITION ]]
[{UNION ¦ INTERSECT ¦ EXCEPT}[ ALL ]
[ CORRESPONDING [ BY (COLUMN1 [, COLUMN2 ]) ]
QUERY_SPEC ¦ SELECT * FROM TABLE ¦ TABLE_CONSTRUCTOR ]
[ORDER BY SORT_LIST ]
```

This is the syntax for SQLBase:

```
SELECT  [ ALL ¦ DISTINCT ] COLUMN1 [, COLUMN2 ]
FROM TABLE1 [, TABLE2 ]
[ WHERE SEARCH_CONDITION ]
[ GROUP BY COLUMN1 [, COLUMN2 ]
[ HAVING SEARCH_CONDITION ]]
[ UNION [ ALL ]]
```

24

```
[ ORDER BY SORT_LIST ]
[ FOR UPDATE OF COLUMN1 [, COLUMN2 ]
```

This is the syntax for Oracle:

```
SELECT [ ALL ¦ DISTINCT ] COLUMN1 [, COLUMN2 ]
FROM TABLE1 [, TABLE2 ]
[ WHERE SEARCH_CONDITION ]
[[ START WITH SEARCH_CONDITION ]
CONNECT BY SEARCH_CONDITION ]
[ GROUP BY COLUMN1 [, COLUMN2 ]
[ HAVING SEARCH_CONDITION ]]
[{UNION [ ALL ] ¦ INTERSECT ¦ MINUS} QUERY_SPEC ]
[ ORDER BY COLUMN1 [, COLUMN2 ]
[ NOWAIT ]
```

This is the syntax for Informix:

```
SELECT [ ALL ] ¦ DISTINCT ¦ UNIQUE ] COLUMN1 [, COLUMN2 ]
FROM TABLE1 [, TABLE2 ]
[ WHERE SEARCH_CONDITION ]
[ GROUP BY {COLUMN1 [, COLUMN2 ] ¦ INTEGER}
[ HAVING SEARCH_CONDITION ]]
[ UNION QUERY_SPEC ]
[ ORDER BY COLUMN1 [, COLUMN2 ]
[ INTO TEMP TABLE [ WITH NO LOG ]]
```

As you can see by comparing the syntax examples, the basics are there. All have the SELECT, FROM, WHERE, GROUP BY, HAVING, UNION, and ORDER BY clauses. Each of these clauses work conceptually the same, but some have additional options that may not be found in other implementations. These options are called *enhancements*.

## Compliance with ANSI SQL

Vendors do strive to comply with ANSI SQL; however, none are 100 percent ANSI SQL standard. Some vendors have added commands or functions to ANSI SQL, and many of these new commands or functions have been adopted by ANSI SQL. It is beneficial for a vendor to comply with the standard for many reasons. One obvious benefit to standard compliance is that the vendor's implementation will be easy to learn, and the SQL code used is portable to other implementations. Portability is definitely a factor when a database is being migrated from one implementation to another. Why would a company spend uncountable dollars on a conversion to another implementation that was not compliant to the standard? They probably wouldn't if too many changes would have to be made to the application and the new implementation were difficult to learn. Therefore, ANSI SQL compliance is not a problem in most cases.

## Extensions to SQL

Practically all the major vendors have an extension to SQL. A SQL extension is unique to a particular implementation and is generally not portable between implementations. However, popular standard extensions are reviewed by ANSI and are sometimes implemented as a part of the new standard.

PL/SQL, which is a product of Oracle Corporation, and Transact-SQL, which is used by both Sybase and Microsoft SQL Server, are two examples of standard SQL extensions. Both extensions are discussed in relative detail for the examples during this hour.

# Examples of Extensions from Some Implementations

Both PL/SQL and Transact-SQL are considered fourth-generation programming languages. Both are procedural languages versus SQL, which is a non-procedural language.

The non-procedural language SQL includes statements such as the following:

- ☐ INSERT
- ☐ UPDATE
- ☐ DELETE
- ☐ SELECT
- ☐ COMMIT
- ☐ ROLLBACK

A SQL extension considered a procedural language includes all of the preceding statements, commands, and functions of standard SQL. In addition, extensions include statements such as:

- ☐ Variable declarations
- ☐ Cursor declarations
- ☐ Conditional statements
- ☐ Loops
- ☐ Error handling

- ☐ Variable incrementing
- ☐ Date conversions
- ☐ Wildcard operators
- ☐ Triggers
- ☐ Stored procedures

These statements allow the programmer to have more control over the way data is handled in a procedural language.

 **NOTE**

Standard SQL is primarily a *non-procedural language*, which means that you issue statements to the database server. The database server decides how to optimally execute the statement. *Procedural languages* allow the programmer not only to request the data to be retrieved or manipulated, but to tell the database server exactly how to carry out the request.

# Transact-SQL

Transact-SQL is a procedural language, which means you tell the database the how's and where's of finding and manipulating data; SQL is non-procedural, and the database decides the how's and where's of selecting and manipulating data. Some highlights of Transact-SQL's capabilities include declaring local and global variables, cursors, error handling, triggers, stored procedures, loops, wildcard operators, date conversions, and summarized reports.

An example Transact-SQL statement follows:

```
IF (SELECT AVG(COST) FROM PRODUCTS_TBL) > 50
BEGIN
   PRINT "LOWER ALL COSTS BY 10 PERCENT."
END
ELSE
   PRINT "COSTS ARE REASONABLE."
END
```

**ANALYSIS**  This is a very simple Transact-SQL statement. It states that if the average cost in the PRODUCTS_TBL table is greater than 50, then the text "LOWER ALL COSTS BY 10 PERCENT" will be printed. If the average cost is less-than or equal to 50, then the text "COSTS ARE REASONABLE" will be printed.

Notice the use of the IF...ELSE statement to evaluate conditions of data values. The PRINT command is also a new command. These additional options are not even a drop in the bucket of Transact-SQL capabilities.

# PL/SQL

PL/SQL is Oracle's extension to SQL. Like Transact-SQL, PL/SQL is a procedural language. PL/SQL is structured in logical blocks of code. There are three sections to a PL/SQL block, two of which are optional. The first section is the DECLARE section and is optional. The DECLARE section contains variables, cursors, and constants. The second section is called the PROCEDURE section. The PROCEDURE section contains the conditional commands and SQL statements. This section is where the block is controlled. The PROCEDURE section is mandatory. The third section is called the EXCEPTION section. The EXCEPTION section defines how the program should handle errors and user-defined exceptions. The EXCEPTION section is optional. Highlights of PL/SQL include the use of variables, constants, cursors, attributes, loops, handling exceptions, displaying output to the programmer, transactional control, stored procedures, triggers, and packages.

An example PL/SQL statement follows:

```
DECLARE
   CURSOR EMP_CURSOR IS SELECT EMP_ID, LAST_NAME, FIRST_NAME, MID_INIT
                          FROM EMPLOYEE_TBL;
   EMP_REC EMP_CURSOR%ROWTYPE;
BEGIN
```

```
OPEN EMP_CURSOR;
LOOP
  FETCH EMP_CURSOR INTO EMP_REC;
  EXIT WHEN EMP_CURSOR%NOTFOUND;
  IF (EMP_REC.MID_INIT IS NULL) THEN
    UPDATE EMPLOYEE_TBL
    SET MID_INIT = 'X'
    WHERE EMP_ID = EMP_REC.EMP_ID;
    COMMIT;
  END IF;
END LOOP;
CLOSE EMP_CURSOR;
END;
```

**ANALYSIS**     There are two out of three sections being used in this example: the DECLARE section and the PROCEDURE section. First, a cursor called EMP_CURSOR is defined by a query. Second, a variable called EMP_REC is declared, whose values have the same datatype (%ROWTYPE) as each column in the defined cursor. The first step in the PROCEDURE section (after BEGIN) is to open the cursor. Once the cursor is opened, you use the LOOP command to scroll through each record of the cursor, which is eventually terminated by END LOOP. The EMPLOYEE_TBL table should be updated for all rows in the cursor—if the middle initial of an employee is NULL. The update sets the middle initial to 'X'. Changes are committed and the cursor is eventually closed.

# Interactive SQL Statements

Interactive SQL statements are SQL statements that ask you for a variable, parameter, or some form of data before fully executing. Say you have a SQL statement that is interactive. The statement is used to create users into a database. The SQL statement could prompt you for information such as user ID, name of user, and phone number. The statement could be for one or many users, and would be executed only once. Otherwise, each user would have to be entered individually with the CREATE USER statement. The SQL statement could also prompt you for privileges. Not all vendors have interactive SQL statements; you must check your particular implementation. The following sections show some examples of interactive SQL using Oracle.

## Using Parameters

*Parameters* are variables that are written in SQL and reside within an application. Parameters can be passed into a SQL statement during runtime, allowing more flexibility for the user executing the statement. Many of the major implementations allow use of these parameters. The following sections show examples of passing parameters for Oracle and Sybase.

### Oracle

Parameters in Oracle can be passed into an otherwise static SQL statement.

```
SELECT EMP_ID, LAST_NAME, FIRST_NAME
FROM EMPLOYEE_TBL
WHERE EMP_ID = '&EMP_ID'
```

The preceding SQL statement returns the EMP_ID, LAST_NAME, and FIRST_NAME for whatever emp_id you enter at the prompt.

```
SELECT *
FROM EMPLOYEE_TBL
WHERE CITY = '&CITY'
AND STATE = '&STATE'
```

The preceding statement prompts you for the city and the state. The query returns all data for those employees living in the city and state that you entered.

### Sybase

Parameters in Sybase can be passed into a stored procedure.

```
CREATE PROC EMP_SEARCH
(@EMP_ID)
AS
SELECT LAST_NAME, FIRST_NAME
FROM EMPLOYEE_TBL
WHERE EMP_ID = @EMP_ID
```

Type the following to execute the stored procedure and pass a parameter:

```
SP_EMP_SEARCH "443679012"
```

24

# Summary

This hour discusses extensions to standard SQL among vendors' implementations and their compliance with the ANSI standard. Once you learn SQL, you can easily apply your knowledge—and your code—to other implementations of SQL. SQL is portable between vendors, being that most SQL code can be utilized among most implementations with a few minor modifications.

The last part of this hour was spent showing two specific extensions used by three implementations. Transact-SQL is used by Microsoft SQL Server and Sybase, and PL/SQL is used by Oracle. You should have seen some similarities between Transact-SQL and PL/SQL. One thing to note is that these two implementations have first sought their compliance with the standard, then added enhancements to their implementations for better overall functionality and efficiency. This hour intends to make you aware that many SQL extensions do exist and to teach the importance of a vendor's compliance to the ANSI SQL standard.

If you take what you have learned in this book and apply it—build your code, test it, and build upon your knowledge—then you are well on your way to mastering SQL. Companies have data and cannot function without databases. Relational databases are everywhere—and since SQL is the standard language with which to communicate and administer a relational database, you have made an excellent decision by learning SQL. Good luck!

## Q&A

**Q Why do variations in SQL exist?**

**A** Variations in SQL exist between the various implementations because of the way data is stored, the various vendors' ambition at trying to get an advantage over competition, and new ideas that surface.

**Q After learning basic SQL, will I be able to use SQL in different implementations?**

**A** Yes. However, remember that there are differences and variations between the implementations. The basic framework for SQL is the same among most implementations.

# Workshop

The following workshop is composed of a series of quiz questions and practical exercises. The quiz questions are designed to test your overall understanding of the current material. The practical exercises are intended to afford you the opportunity to apply the concepts discussed during the current hour, as well as build upon the knowledge acquired in previous hours of study. Please take time to complete the quiz questions and exercises before continuing. You may refer to the answers in Appendix C.

## Quiz

1. Is SQL a procedural or non-procedural language?

2. What are some of the reasons differences in SQL exist?

3. What are the three basic operations of a cursor, outside of declaring the cursor?

4. Procedural or non-procedural: With which does the database engine decide how to evaluate and execute SQL statements?

## Exercises

1. Try some research about the SQL variations among the various vendors. Go to a library or book store and look for vendor-specific books on SQL. Compare various SQL statements, such as Data Manipulation Language (DML). Compare the inserts, deletes, and updates for the differences. You might also look for an ANSI SQL book in which to make comparisons.

2. Using the EMPLOYEE_TBL (see Appendix D), write the interactive SQL statement that returns the name of all employees who have a zip code of 46234.

3. Touch up your résumé.

# PART

# IX

## Appendixes

## Hour

# Appendix A

# Common SQL Commands

## SQL Statements

### ALTER TABLE

```
alter table table_name
[modify ¦ add ¦ drop]
  [column column_name][datatype¦null not null] [restrict¦cascade]
[add ¦ drop]  [constraint constraint_name]
```

Description: Alters a table's columns.

### COMMIT

```
COMMIT [ TRANSACTION ]
```

Description: Saves a transaction to the database.

### CREATE INDEX

```
CREATE INDEX INDEX_NAME
ON TABLE_NAME (COLUMN_NAME)
```

Description: Creates an index on a table.

### CREATE TABLE

```
CREATE TABLE TABLE_NAME
( COLUMN1    DATA_TYPE    [NULL|NOT NULL],
  COLUMN2    DATA_TYPE    [NULL|NOT NULL]…)
```

Description: Creates a database table.

### CREATE TABLE AS

```
CREATE TABLE TABLE_NAME AS
SELECT COLUMN1, COLUMN2,...
FROM TABLE_NAME
[ WHERE CONDITIONS ]
[ GROUP BY COLUMN1, COLUMN2,...]
[ HAVING CONDITIONS ]
```

Description: Creates a database table based on another table.

### CREATE VIEW

```
CREATE VIEW AS
SELECT COLUMN1, COLUMN2,...
FROM TABLE_NAME
[ WHERE CONDITIONS ]
[ GROUP BY COLUMN1, COLUMN2,... ]
[ HAVING CONDITIONS ]
```

Description: Creates a view of a table.

### DELETE

```
DELETE
FROM TABLE_NAME
[ WHERE CONDITIONS ]
```

Description: Deletes rows of data from a table.

### DROP INDEX

```
DROP INDEX INDEX_NAME
```

Description: Drops an index on a table.

### DROP TABLE

```
DROP TABLE TABLE_NAME
```

Description: Drops a table from the database.

### DROP VIEW

```
DROP VIEW VIEW_NAME
```

Description: Drops a view of a table.

A

## GRANT

```
GRANT PRIVILEGE1, PRIVILEGE2, ... TO USER_NAME
```

Description: Grants privileges to a user.

## INSERT

```
INSERT INTO TABLE_NAME [ (COLUMN1, COLUMN2,...]
VALUES ('VALUE1','VALUE2',...)
```

Description: Inserts new rows of data into a table.

## INSERT...SELECT

```
INSERT INTO TABLE_NAME
SELECT COLUMN1, COLUMN2
FROM TABLE_NAME
[ WHERE CONDITIONS ]
```

Description: Inserts new rows of data into a table based on data in another table.

## REVOKE

```
REVOKE PRIVILEGE1, PRIVILEGE2, ... FROM USER_NAME
```

Description: Revokes privileges from a user.

## ROLLBACK

```
ROLLBACK [ TO SAVEPOINT_NAME ]
```

Description: Undoes a database transaction.

## SAVEPOINT

```
SAVEPOINT SAVEPOINT_NAME
```

Description: Creates transaction SAVEPOINTs in which to ROLLBACK if necessary.

## SELECT

```
SELECT [ DISTINCT ] COLUMN1, COLUMN2,...
FROM TABLE1, TABLE2,...
[ WHERE CONDITIONS ]
[ GROUP BY COLUMN1, COLUMN2,...]
[ HAVING CONDITIONS ]
[ ORDER BY COLUMN1, COLUMN2,...]
```

Description: Returns data from one or more database tables; used to create queries.

## UPDATE

```
UPDATE TABLE_NAME
SET COLUMN1 = 'VALUE1',
    COLUMN2 = 'VALUE2',...
[ WHERE CONDITIONS ]
```

Description: Updates existing data in a table.

# SQL Clauses

## SELECT

```
SELECT *

SELECT COLUMN1, COLUMN2,...

SELECT DISTINCT (COLUMN1)

SELECT COUNT(*)
```

Description: Defines columns to display as part of query output.

## FROM

```
FROM TABLE1, TABLE2, TABLE3,...
```

Description: Defines tables from which to retrieve data.

## WHERE

```
WHERE COLUMN1 = 'VALUE1'
  AND COLUMN2 = 'VALUE2'
...

WHERE COLUMN1 = 'VALUE1'
  OR COLUMN2 = 'VALUE2'
...
```

Description: Defines conditions, *criteria*, placed on a query in order for data to be returned.

## GROUP BY

```
GROUP BY GROUP_COLUMN1, GROUP_COLUMN2,...
```

Description: A form of a sorting operation; used to divide output into logical groups.

## HAVING

```
HAVING GROUP_COLUMN1 = 'VALUE1'
  AND GROUP_COLUMN2 = 'VALUE2'
...
```

Description: Similar to the WHERE clause; used to place conditions on the GROUP BY clause.

A

## ORDER BY

```
ORDER BY COLUMN1, COLUMN2,...
```

```
ORDER BY 1,2,...
```

Description: Used to sort a query's results.

A

# Appendix B

## ASCII Table

| Dec $X_{10}$ | Hex $X_{16}$ | Binary $X_2$ | ASCII | Dec $X_{10}$ | Hex $X_{16}$ | Binary $X_2$ | ASCII |
|---|---|---|---|---|---|---|---|
| 000 | 00 | 0000 0000 | null | 026 | 1A | 0001 1010 | → |
| 001 | 01 | 0000 0001 | ☺ | 027 | 1B | 0001 1011 | ← |
| 002 | 02 | 0000 0010 | ☻ | 028 | 1C | 0001 1100 | ∟ |
| 003 | 03 | 0000 0011 | ♥ | 029 | 1D | 0001 1101 | ↔ |
| 004 | 04 | 0000 0100 | ♦ | 030 | 1E | 0001 1110 | ▲ |
| 005 | 05 | 0000 0101 | ♣ | 031 | 1F | 0001 1111 | ▼ |
| 006 | 06 | 0000 0110 | ♠ | 032 | 20 | 0010 0000 | space |
| 007 | 07 | 0000 0111 | • | 033 | 21 | 0010 0001 | ! |
| 008 | 08 | 0000 1000 | ◘ | 034 | 22 | 0010 0010 | " |
| 009 | 09 | 0000 1001 | ○ | 035 | 23 | 0010 0011 | # |
| 010 | 0A | 0000 1010 | ◙ | 036 | 24 | 0010 0100 | $ |
| 011 | 0B | 0000 1011 | ♂ | 037 | 25 | 0010 0101 | % |
| 012 | 0C | 0000 1100 | ♀ | 038 | 26 | 0010 0110 | & |
| 013 | 0D | 0000 1101 | ♪ | 039 | 27 | 0010 0111 | ' |
| 014 | 0E | 0000 1110 | ♫ | 040 | 28 | 0010 1000 | ( |
| 015 | 0F | 0000 1111 | ☼ | 041 | 29 | 0010 1001 | ) |
| 016 | 10 | 0001 0000 | ► | 042 | 2A | 0010 1010 | * |
| 017 | 11 | 0001 0001 | ◄ | 043 | 2B | 0010 1011 | + |
| 018 | 12 | 0001 0010 | ↕ | 044 | 2C | 0010 1100 | , |
| 019 | 13 | 0001 0011 | ‼ | 045 | 2D | 0010 1101 | - |
| 020 | 14 | 0001 0100 | ¶ | 046 | 2E | 0010 1110 | . |
| 021 | 15 | 0001 0101 | § | 047 | 2F | 0010 1111 | / |
| 022 | 16 | 0001 0110 | ▬ | 048 | 30 | 0011 0000 | 0 |
| 023 | 17 | 0001 0111 | ↨ | 049 | 31 | 0011 0001 | 1 |
| 024 | 18 | 0001 1000 | ↑ | 050 | 32 | 0011 0010 | 2 |
| 025 | 19 | 0001 1001 | ↓ | 051 | 33 | 0011 0011 | 3 |

| Dec $X_{10}$ | Hex $X_{16}$ | Binary $X_2$ | ASCII | Dec $X_{10}$ | Hex $X_{16}$ | Binary $X_2$ | ASCII |
|---|---|---|---|---|---|---|---|
| 052 | 34 | 0011 0100 | 4 | 078 | 4E | 0100 1110 | N |
| 053 | 35 | 0011 0101 | 5 | 079 | 4F | 0100 1111 | O |
| 054 | 36 | 0011 0110 | 6 | 080 | 50 | 0101 0000 | P |
| 055 | 37 | 0011 0111 | 7 | 081 | 51 | 0101 0001 | Q |
| 056 | 38 | 0011 1000 | 8 | 082 | 52 | 0101 0010 | R |
| 057 | 39 | 0011 1001 | 9 | 083 | 53 | 0101 0011 | S |
| 058 | 3A | 0011 1010 | : | 084 | 54 | 0101 0100 | T |
| 059 | 3B | 0011 1011 | ; | 085 | 55 | 0101 0101 | U |
| 060 | 3C | 0011 1100 | < | 086 | 56 | 0101 0110 | V |
| 061 | 3D | 0011 1101 | = | 087 | 57 | 0101 0111 | W |
| 062 | 3E | 0011 1110 | > | 088 | 58 | 0101 1000 | X |
| 063 | 3F | 0011 1111 | ? | 089 | 59 | 0101 1001 | Y |
| 064 | 40 | 0100 0000 | @ | 090 | 5A | 0101 1010 | Z |
| 065 | 41 | 0100 0001 | A | 091 | 5B | 0101 1011 | [ |
| 066 | 42 | 0100 0010 | B | 092 | 5C | 0101 1100 | \ |
| 067 | 43 | 0100 0011 | C | 093 | 5D | 0101 1101 | ] |
| 068 | 44 | 0100 0100 | D | 094 | 5E | 0101 1110 | ^ |
| 069 | 45 | 0100 0101 | E | 095 | 5F | 0101 1111 | _ |
| 070 | 46 | 0100 0110 | F | 096 | 60 | 0110 0000 | ` |
| 071 | 47 | 0100 0111 | G | 097 | 61 | 0110 0001 | a |
| 072 | 48 | 0100 1000 | H | 098 | 62 | 0110 0010 | b |
| 073 | 49 | 0100 1001 | I | 099 | 63 | 0110 0011 | c |
| 074 | 4A | 0100 1010 | J | 100 | 64 | 0110 0100 | d |
| 075 | 4B | 0100 1011 | K | 101 | 65 | 0110 0101 | e |
| 076 | 4C | 0100 1100 | L | 102 | 66 | 0110 0110 | f |
| 077 | 4D | 0100 1101 | M | 103 | 67 | 0110 0111 | g |

B

| Dec $X_{10}$ | Hex $X_{16}$ | Binary $X_2$ | ASCII | Dec $X_{10}$ | Hex $X_{16}$ | Binary $X_2$ | ASCII |
|---|---|---|---|---|---|---|---|
| 104 | 68 | 0110 1000 | h | 130 | 82 | 1000 0010 | é |
| 105 | 69 | 0110 1001 | i | 131 | 83 | 1000 0011 | â |
| 106 | 6A | 0110 1010 | j | 132 | 84 | 1000 0100 | ä |
| 107 | 6B | 0110 1011 | k | 133 | 85 | 1000 0101 | à |
| 108 | 6C | 0110 1100 | l | 134 | 86 | 1000 0110 | å |
| 109 | 6D | 0110 1101 | m | 135 | 87 | 1000 0111 | ç |
| 110 | 6E | 0110 1110 | n | 136 | 88 | 1000 1000 | ê |
| 111 | 6F | 0110 1111 | o | 137 | 89 | 1000 1001 | ë |
| 112 | 70 | 0111 0000 | p | 138 | 8A | 1000 1010 | è |
| 113 | 71 | 0111 0001 | q | 139 | 8B | 1000 1011 | ï |
| 114 | 72 | 0111 0010 | r | 140 | 8C | 1000 1100 | î |
| 115 | 73 | 0111 0011 | s | 141 | 8D | 1000 1101 | ì |
| 116 | 74 | 0111 0100 | t | 142 | 8E | 1000 1110 | Ä |
| 117 | 75 | 0111 0101 | u | 143 | 8F | 1000 1111 | Å |
| 118 | 76 | 0111 0110 | v | 144 | 90 | 1001 0000 | É |
| 119 | 77 | 0111 0111 | w | 145 | 91 | 1001 0001 | æ |
| 120 | 78 | 0111 1000 | x | 146 | 92 | 1001 0010 | Æ |
| 121 | 79 | 0111 1001 | y | 147 | 93 | 1001 0011 | ô |
| 122 | 7A | 0111 1010 | z | 148 | 94 | 1001 0100 | ö |
| 123 | 7B | 0111 1011 | { | 149 | 95 | 1001 0101 | ò |
| 124 | 7C | 0111 1100 | ¦ | 150 | 96 | 1001 0110 | û |
| 125 | 7D | 0111 1101 | } | 151 | 97 | 1001 0111 | ù |
| 126 | 7E | 0111 1110 | ~ | 152 | 98 | 1001 1000 | ÿ |
| 127 | 7F | 0111 1111 | Δ | 153 | 99 | 1001 1001 | Ö |
| 128 | 80 | 1000 0000 | Ç | 154 | 9A | 1001 1010 | Ü |
| 129 | 81 | 1000 0001 | ü | 155 | 9B | 1001 1011 | ¢ |

**B**

| Dec $X_{10}$ | Hex $X_{16}$ | Binary $X_2$ | ASCII | Dec $X_{10}$ | Hex $X_{16}$ | Binary $X_2$ | ASCII |
|---|---|---|---|---|---|---|---|
| 156 | 9C | 1001 1100 | £ | 182 | B6 | 1011 0110 | ╢ |
| 157 | 9D | 1001 1101 | ¥ | 183 | B7 | 1011 0111 | ╖ |
| 158 | 9E | 1001 1110 | ₧ | 184 | B8 | 1011 1000 | ╕ |
| 159 | 9F | 1001 1111 | ƒ | 185 | B9 | 1011 1001 | ╣ |
| 160 | A0 | 1010 0000 | á | 186 | BA | 1011 1010 | ║ |
| 161 | A1 | 1010 0001 | í | 187 | BB | 1011 1011 | ╗ |
| 162 | A2 | 1010 0010 | ó | 188 | BC | 1011 1100 | ╝ |
| 163 | A3 | 1010 0011 | ú | 189 | BD | 1011 1101 | ╜ |
| 164 | A4 | 1010 0100 | ñ | 190 | BE | 1011 1110 | ╛ |
| 165 | A5 | 1010 0101 | Ñ | 191 | BF | 1011 1111 | ┐ |
| 166 | A6 | 1010 0110 | ª | 192 | C0 | 1100 0000 | └ |
| 167 | A7 | 1010 0111 | º | 193 | C1 | 1100 0001 | ┴ |
| 168 | A8 | 1010 1000 | ¿ | 194 | C2 | 1100 0010 | ┬ |
| 169 | A9 | 1010 1001 | ⌐ | 195 | C3 | 1100 0011 | ├ |
| 170 | AA | 1010 1010 | ¬ | 196 | C4 | 1100 0100 | ─ |
| 171 | AB | 1010 1011 | ½ | 197 | C5 | 1100 0101 | ┼ |
| 172 | AC | 1010 1100 | ¼ | 198 | C6 | 1100 0110 | ╞ |
| 173 | AD | 1010 1101 | ¡ | 199 | C7 | 1100 0111 | ╟ |
| 174 | AE | 1010 1110 | « | 200 | C8 | 1100 1000 | ╚ |
| 175 | AF | 1010 1111 | » | 201 | C9 | 1100 1001 | ╔ |
| 176 | B0 | 1011 0000 | ░ | 202 | CA | 1100 1010 | ╩ |
| 177 | B1 | 1011 0001 | ▒ | 203 | CB | 1100 1011 | ╦ |
| 178 | B2 | 1011 0010 | ▓ | 204 | CC | 1100 1100 | ╠ |
| 179 | B3 | 1011 0011 | │ | 205 | CD | 1100 1101 | ═ |
| 180 | B4 | 1011 0100 | ┤ | 206 | CE | 1100 1110 | ╬ |
| 181 | B5 | 1011 0101 | ╡ | 207 | CF | 1100 1111 | ╧ |

B

| Dec $X_{10}$ | Hex $X_{16}$ | Binary $X_2$ | ASCII | Dec $X_{10}$ | Hex $X_{16}$ | Binary $X_2$ | ASCII |
|---|---|---|---|---|---|---|---|
| 208 | D0 | 1101 0000 | ⊥ | 234 | EA | 1110 1010 | Ω |
| 209 | D1 | 1101 0001 | ⊤ | 235 | EB | 1110 1011 | δ |
| 210 | D2 | 1101 0010 | π | 236 | EC | 1110 1100 | ∞ |
| 211 | D3 | 1101 0011 | ⊥ | 237 | ED | 1110 1101 | ø |
| 212 | D4 | 1101 0100 | ⊦ | 238 | EE | 1110 1110 | ∈ |
| 213 | D5 | 1101 0101 | ⊨ | 239 | EF | 1110 1111 | ∩ |
| 214 | D6 | 1101 0110 | π | 240 | F0 | 1110 0000 | ≡ |
| 215 | D7 | 1101 0111 | ╫ | 241 | F1 | 1111 0001 | ± |
| 216 | D8 | 1101 1000 | ╪ | 242 | F2 | 1111 0010 | ≥ |
| 217 | D9 | 1101 1001 | ⌐ | 243 | F3 | 1111 0011 | ≤ |
| 218 | DA | 1101 1010 | Γ | 244 | F4 | 1111 0100 | ⌠ |
| 219 | DB | 1101 1011 | ■ | 245 | F5 | 1111 0101 | ⌡ |
| 220 | DC | 1101 1100 | ■ | 246 | F6 | 1111 0110 | ÷ |
| 221 | DD | 1101 1101 | ▌ | 247 | F7 | 1111 0111 | ≈ |
| 222 | DE | 1101 1110 | ▐ | 248 | F8 | 1111 1000 | ° |
| 223 | DF | 1101 1111 | ▀ | 249 | F9 | 1111 1001 | • |
| 224 | E0 | 1110 0000 | α | 250 | FA | 1111 1010 | · |
| 225 | E1 | 1110 0001 | β | 251 | FB | 1111 1011 | √ |
| 226 | E2 | 1110 0010 | Γ | 252 | FC | 1111 1100 | $^n$ |
| 227 | E3 | 1110 0011 | π | 253 | FD | 1111 1101 | $^2$ |
| 228 | E4 | 1110 0100 | Σ | 254 | FE | 1111 1110 | ■ |
| 229 | E5 | 1110 0101 | σ | 255 | FF | 1111 1111 | |
| 230 | E6 | 1110 0110 | μ | | | | |
| 231 | E7 | 1110 0111 | γ | | | | |
| 232 | E8 | 1110 1000 | Φ | | | | |
| 233 | E9 | 1110 1001 | θ | | | | |

B

# Appendix C

# Answers to Quizzes and Exercises

## Hour 1, "Welcome to the World of SQL"

### Quiz Answers

1. What does the acronym SQL stand for?

    a. SQL stands for Structured Query Language.

2. What are the six main categories of SQL commands?

    a. Data Definition Language (DDL)

      Data Manipulation Language (DML)

      Data Query Language (DQL)

      Data Control Language (DCL)

      Data Administration Commands (DAC)

      Transactional Control Commands (TCC)

3. What are the four transactional control commands?

a.

```
Commit

Rollback

Savepoint

Set Transactions
```

4. What is the main difference between client/server technologies and the mainframe?

a. The mainframe is a centralized computer linked to the user through a dumb terminal. In the client/server environment, the user is linked to the server via a network and the user typically has a personal computer versus a dumb terminal.

5. If a field is defined as null, does that mean that something has to be entered into that field?

a. No. If a column is defined as NULL, nothing has to be in the column. If a column is defined as not null, then something has to be entered.

## Exercise Answers

1. Identify in what categories the following SQL commands fall.

```
create table
delete
select
insert
alter table
update
```

a.

CREATE TABLE—DDL, Data Definition Language

DELETE—DML, Data Manipulation Language

SELECT—DQL, Data Query Language

INSERT—DML, Data Manipulation Language

ALTER TABLE—DDL, Data Definition Language

UPDATE—DML, Data Manipulation Language

# Hour 2, "Defining Data Structures"

## Quiz Answers

1. True or false: An individual's social security number can be any of the following datatypes: constant length character, varying length character, numeric.

    a. True, as long as the precision is the correct length.

2. True or false: The scale of a numeric value is the total length allowed for values.

    a. False. The precision is the total length, where the scale represents the number of places reserved to the right of a decimal point.

3. Do all implementations use the same datatypes?

    a. No. Most implementations differ in their use of datatypes. The datatypes prescribed by ANSI are adhered to, but may differ between implementations according to storage precautions taken by each vendor.

4. What is the precision and scale of the following:

    a. `DECIMAL(4,2)`

        a. precision = 4, scale = 2

    b. `DECIMAL(10,2)`

        b. precision = 10, scale = 2

    c. `DECIMAL(14,1)`

        c. precision = 14, scale = 1

5. Which numbers could be inserted into a `DECIMAL(4,1)`?

    a. `16.2`

    b. `116.2`

    c. `16.21`

    d. `1116.2`

    e. `1116.21`

The first three fit, although `16.21` is rounded off. The numbers `1116.2` and `1116.21` exceed the maximum precision, which was set at `4`.

# Exercise Answers

1. Take the following column titles, assign them to a datatype, and decide on the proper length.

    a. `ssn` constant-length character

    b. `city` constant-length character

    c. `state` varying-length character

    d. `zip` constant-length character

    e. `phone_number` constant-length character

    f. `last_name` varying-length character

    g. `first_name` varying-length character

C

    h. `middle_name`   varying-length character

    i. `salary`   numeric datatype

    j. `hourly_pay_rate`   decimal

    k. `date_hired`   date

2. Take the same column titles and decide if they should be NULL or NOT NULL.

    a. `ssn`   NOT NULL

    b. `state`   NOT NULL

    c. `city`   NOT NULL

    d. `phone_number`   NULL

    e. `zip`   NOT NULL

    f. `last_name`   NOT NULL

    g. `first_name`   NOT NULL

    h. `middle_name`   NULL

    i. `salary`   NULL

    j. `hourly_pay_rate`   NULL

    k. `date_hired`   NOT NULL

Every individual may not have a phone (however rare that may be) and not everyone has a middle name, so these columns should allow NULL values. In addition, not all employees are paid an hourly rate.

# Hour 3, "Managing Database Objects"

## Quiz Answers

1. Will the following `create table` statement work? If not, what needs to be done to correct the problem(s)?

```
a.   create table employee_table as
        ( SSN          NUMBER(9)      NOT NULL,
LAST_NAME    VARCHAR2(20)     NOT NULL
    FIRST_NAME    VARCHAR2(20)      NOT NULL,
    MIDDLE_NAME    VARCHAR2(20)      NOT NULL,
    ST ADDRESS    VARCHAR2(30)      NOT NULL,
    CITY         CHAR(20)      NOT NULL,
    STATE         CHAR2)          NOT NULL,
    ZIP          NUMBER(4)      NOT NULL,
    DATE HIRED    DATE)
    STORAGE
        (INITIAL       3K,
         next                 1k);
```

C

a. The create table statement will not work, as there are several errors in the syntax. The corrected statement follows. A listing of what was incorrect follows a corrected statement.

```
create table employee_table
   ( ssn          number(9)     not null,
   last_name      varchar2(20)  not null,
   first_name     varchar2(20)   not null,
   middle_name    varchar2(20),
   st_address     varchar2(30)   not null,
   city         varchar2(20)   not null,
   state          char(2)       not null,
   zip          number(5)    not null,
   date_hired     date )
   storage
      (initial       3k
      next              1k);
```

The following needs to be done:

1. The as should not be in this CREATE TABLE statement.

2. Missing a comma after the NOT NULL for the LAST_NAME column.

3. The MIDDLE_NAME column should be NULL, because not everyone has a middle name.

4. The column ST ADDRESS should be ST_ADDRESS. Being two words, the database looked at ST as being the column name, which would make the database look for a valid datatype, where it would find the word ADDRESS.

5. The city column works, although it would be better to use the varchar2 datatype. If all city names were constant length, CHAR would be okay.

6. The STATE column is missing a left parenthesis.

7. The ZIP column length should be (5), not (4).

8. The DATE HIRED column should be DATE_HIRED with an underscore, in order to make the column name one continuous string.

9. The comma after 3k in the STORAGE clause should not be there.

2. Can I drop a column from a table?

a. Yes. However, even though it is an ANSI standard, you must check your particular implementation to see if it has been accepted.

3. What happens if I do not include the STORAGE clause in the CREATE TABLE statement?

a. The CREATE TABLE statement should process, barring any syntax errors of course; however, most implementations have a default sizing. Check your particular implementation for the sizing.

C

# Hour 4, "The Normalization Process"

## Quiz Answers

1. True or false: Normalization is the process of grouping data into logical related groups.

   a. True.

2. True or false: Having no duplicate or redundant data in a database and having everything in the database normalized is always the best way to go.

   a. False. Not always; normalization can and does slow performance because more tables must be joined which results in more I/O and CPU time.

3. True or false: If data is in the third normal form, it is automatically in the first and second normal forms.

   a. True.

4. What is a major advantage of a denormalized database versus a normalized database?

   a. Improved performance.

5. What are some major disadvantages of denormalization?

   a. Having redundant and duplicate data takes up valuable space; it is harder to code, and much more data maintenance is required.

## Exercise Answers

1. Employees:

   Angela Smith, secretary, 317-545-6789, RR 1 Box 73, Greensburg, Indiana, 47890, $9.50 hour, date started January 22, 1996, SSN is 323149669.

   Jack Lee Nelson, salesman, 3334 N Main St, Brownsburg, IN, 45687, 317-852-9901, salary of $35,000.00 year, SSN is 312567342, date started 10/28/95.

   Customers:

   Robert's Games and Things, 5612 Lafayette Rd, Indianapolis, IN, 46224, 317-291-7888, customer ID is 432A.

   Reed's Dairy Bar, 4556 W 10th St, Indianapolis, IN, 46245, 317-271-9823, customer ID is 117A.

   Customer Orders:

   Customer ID is 117A, date of last order is February 20, 1997, product ordered was napkins and the product ID is 661.

a.

| Employees | Customers | Orders |
|---|---|---|
| ssn | customer ID | customer ID |
| name | name | product ID |
| street address | street address | product |
| city | city | date ordered |
| state | state | |
| zip | zip | |
| phone number | phone number | |
| salary | | |
| hourly pay | | |
| start date | | |
| position | | |

# Hour 5, "Manipulating Data"

## Quiz Answers

1. Using the `employee_tbl` with the structure:

| COLUMN | DATATYPE | (NOT)NULL |
|---|---|---|
| LAST_NAME | VARCHAR2(20) | NOT NULL |
| FIRST_NAME | VARCHAR2(20) | NOT NULL |
| SSN | CHAR(9) | NOT NULL |
| PHONE | NUMBER(10) | NULL |

| LAST_NAME | FIRST_NAME | SSN | PHONE |
|---|---|---|---|
| SMITH | JOHN | 312456788 | 3174549923 |
| ROBERTS | LISA | 232118857 | 3175452321 |
| SMITH | SUE | 443221989 | 3178398712 |
| PIERCE | BILLY | 310239856 | 3176763990 |

What would happen if the following statements were run?

a. `insert into employee_tbl`
`('JACKSON', 'STEVE', '313546078', '3178523443');`

  a. The `insert` statement would not run because the key word `values` is missing in the syntax.

b. `insert into employee_tbl values`
`('JACKSON', 'STEVE', '313546078', '3178523443');`

   a.  One row would be inserted into the `employee_tbl`.

c. `insert into employee_tbl values`
`('MILLER', 'DANIEL', '230980012', NULL);`

   a.  One row would be inserted into the `employee_tbl`, with a NULL value in the
      phone column.

d. `insert into employee_tbl values`
`('TAYLOR', NULL, 445761212, '3179221331');`

   a.  The insert statement would not process because the `first_name` column is NOT
      NULL.

e. `delete from employee_tbl;`

   a.  All rows in the `employee_tbl` would be deleted.

f. `delete from employee_tbl`
`where last_name = 'SMITH';`

   a.  All employees with the last name of SMITH would be deleted from the
      `employee_tbl`.

g. `delete from employee_tbl`
`where last_name = 'SMITH'`
`and first_name = 'JOHN';`

   a.  Only JOHN SMITH would be deleted from the `employee_tbl`.

h. `update employee_tbl`
`set last_name = 'CONRAD';`

   a.  All last names would be changed to CONRAD.

i. `update employee_tbl`
`set last_name = 'CONRAD'`
`where last_name = 'SMITH';`

   a.  Both JOHN and SUE SMITH would now be JOHN and SUE CONRAD.

j. `update employee_tbl`
`set last_name = 'CONRAD',`
`first_name = 'LARRY';`

   a.  All employees are now LARRY CONRAD.

k. `update employee_tbl`
`set last_name = 'CONRAD',`
`first_name = 'LARRY'`
`where ssn = '312456788';`

   a.  JOHN SMITH is now LARRY CONRAD.

## Exercise Answers

2. Using the `employee_tbl` with the following structure:

| COLUMN | DATATYPE | (NOT)NULL |
| --- | --- | --- |
| LAST_NAME | VARCHAR2(20) | NOT NULL |
| FIRST_NAME | VARCHAR2(20) | NOT NULL |
| SSN | CHAR(9) | NOT NULL |
| PHONE | NUMBER(10) | NULL |

| LAST_NAME | FIRST_NAME | SSN | PHONE |
| --- | --- | --- | --- |
| SMITH | JOHN | 312456788 | 3174549923 |
| ROBERTS | LISA | 232118857 | 3175452321 |
| SMITH | SUE | 443221989 | 3178398712 |
| PIERCE | BILLY | 310239856 | 3176763990 |

Write DML to accomplish the following:

a. Change Billy Pierce's ssn to 310239857.

```
a. update employee_tbl
   set ssn = '310239857'
   where ssn = '310239856';
```

b. Add Ben Moore to the `employee_tbl`, phone number is 317-564-9880, ssn = 313456789.

```
a. insert into employee_tbl values
   ('MOORE', 'BEN', '313456789', '3175649880');
```

c. John Smith quit; remove his record.

```
a. delete from employee_tbl
   where ssn = '312456788';
```

# Hour 6, "Managing Database Transactions"

## Quiz Answers

1. True or false: If you have committed several transactions and have several more transactions that have not been committed and you issue a rollback command, all your transactions for the same session will be undone.

a. False. When a transaction is committed, the transaction cannot be rolled back.

2. True or false: A SAVEPOINT actually saves transactions after a specified amount of transactions have executed.

   a. False. A SAVEPOINT is only used as a point for a rollback to return to.

3. Briefly describe the purpose of each one of the following commands: COMMIT, ROLLBACK, and SAVEPOINT.

   a. The COMMIT saves changes made by a transaction. The ROLLBACK undoes changes made by a transaction. The SAVEPOINT creates logical points in transaction in which to roll back.

## Exercise answers

1. Take the following transactions and create savepoints after every three transactions; then commit the transactions.

```
savepoint savepoint1
transaction1;
transaction2;
transaction3;
savepoint savepoint2
transaction4;
transaction5;
transaction6;
savepoint savepoint3
transaction7;
transaction8;
transaction9;
savepoint savepoint4
transaction10;
transaction11;
transaction12;
commit;
```

# Hour 7, "Introduction to the Database Query"

## Quiz Answers

1. Name the required parts for any SELECT statement.

   a. The SELECT and FROM keywords, also called clauses, are required for all SELECT statements.

2. In the WHERE clause, are single quotation marks required for all the data?

   a. No. Single quotation marks are required when selecting alphanumeric datatypes. Number datatypes do not require single quotation marks.

C

3. Under what part of the SQL language does the SELECT statement (database query) fall?

   a. The SELECT statement is considered Data Query Language.

4. Can multiple conditions be used in the WHERE clause?

   a. Yes. Multiple conditions can be specified in the WHERE clause of both SELECT statements and INSERT, UPDATE, and DELETE statements. Multiple conditions are used with the operators AND and OR, which are thoroughly discussed next hour.

# Exercise Answers

1. Look over the following SELECT statements. Determine whether the syntax is correct. If the syntax is not correct, what would correct the syntax? A table called EMPLOYEE_TBL is used.

   a.
   ```
   SELECT employee_id, last_name, first_name,
   FROM EMPLOYEE_TBL;
   ```

   b.
   ```
   SELECT EMPLOYEE_ID, LAST_NAME
   ORDER BY EMPLOYEE_ID
   FROM EMPLOYEE_TBL;
   ```

   c.
   ```
   SELECT EMPLOYEE_ID, LAST_NAME, FIRST_NAME
   FROM EMPLOYEE_TBL
   WHERE EMPLOYEE_ID = '333333333'
   ORDER BY EMPLOYEE_ID;
   ```

   d.
   ```
   SELECT EMPLOYEE_ID SSN, LAST_NAME
   FROM EMPLOYEE_TBL
   WHERE EMPLOYEE_ID = '333333333'
   ORDER BY 1;
   ```

   e.
   ```
   SELECT EMPLOYEE_ID, LAST_NAME, FIRST_NAME
   FROM EMPLOYEE_TBL
   WHERE EMPLOYEE_ID = '333333333'
   ORDER BY 3, 1, 2;
   ```

   a. This SELECT statement does not work because there is a comma after the first_name column that does not belong there. The correct syntax follows:
   ```
   SELECT employee_id, last_name, first_name
      FROM EMPLOYEE_TBL;
   ```

b. This SELECT statement does not work because the FROM and ORDER BY clauses are in the incorrect order. The correct syntax follows:

```
SELECT EMPLOYEE_ID, LAST_NAME
FROM EMPLOYEE_TBL
ORDER BY EMPLOYEE_ID;
```

c. The syntax for this SELECT statement is correct.

d. The syntax for this SELECT statement is correct. Notice that the employee_id column is renamed SSN.

e. Yes. The syntax is correct for this SELECT statement. Notice the order of the columns in the ORDER BY. This SELECT statement returns the first_name, employee_id, and then the last_name.

# Hour 8, "Using Operators to Categorize Data"

## Quiz Answers

1. True or false: Both conditions when using the OR operator must be TRUE.

   a. False. Only one of the conditions must be TRUE.

2. True or false: All specified values must match when using the IN operator.

   a. False. Only one of the values must match.

3. True or false: The AND operator can be used in the SELECT and the WHERE clauses.

   a. False. The AND can only be used in the WHERE clause.

4. What, if anything, is wrong with the following SELECT statements?

   a.
```
SELECT SALARY
FROM EMPLOYEE_PAY_TBL
WHERE SALARY BETWEEN 20000, 30000
```

   a. The AND is missing between 20000, 30000. The correct syntax is:
```
SELECT SALARY
FROM EMPLOYEE_PAY_TBL
WHERE SALARY BETWEEN 20000 AND 30000
```

   b.
```
SELECT SALARY + DATE_HIRE
FROM EMPLOYEE_PAY_TBL
```

   b. The date_hire column is a date datatype and is in the incorrect format for arithmetic functions.

c.

```
SELECT SALARY, BONUS
FROM EMPLOYEE_PAY_TBL
WHERE DATE_HIRE BETWEEN 22-SEP-97
AND 23-NOV-97
AND POSITION = 'SALES'
OR POSITION = 'MARKETING'
AND EMPLOYEE_ID LIKE '%55%'
```

    c. The syntax is correct.

# Exercise Answers

1. Using the CUSTOMER_TBL as described here:

   ```
   describe customer_tbl
   ```

   | Name | Null? | Type |
   | --- | --- | --- |
   | CUST_ID | NOT NULL | VARCHAR2(10) |
   | CUST_NAME | NOT NULL | VARCHAR2(30) |
   | CUST_ADDRESS | NOT NULL | VARCHAR2(20) |
   | CUST_CITY | NOT NULL | VARCHAR2(12) |
   | CUST_STATE | NOT NULL | CHAR(2) |
   | CUST_ZIP | NOT NULL | CHAR(5) |
   | CUST_PHONE | | NUMBER(10) |
   | CUST_FAX | | NUMBER(10) |

   Write a SELECT statement that returns customer IDs and customer names (alpha order) for customers who live in Indiana, Ohio, Michigan, and Illinois, with names that begin with the letters A or B.

       a.

   ```
   SELECT CUST_ID, CUST_NAME, CUST_STATE
   FROM CUSTOMER_TBL
   WHERE CUST_STATE IN ('IN', 'OH', 'MI', 'IL')
   AND CUST_NAME LIKE 'A%'
   OR CUST_NAME LIKE 'B%'
   ORDER BY CUST_NAME
   ```

2. Using the PRODUCTS_TBL as described:

   ```
   describe products_tbl
   ```

   | Name | Null? | Type |
   | --- | --- | --- |
   | PROD_ID | NOT NULL | VARCHAR2(10) |
   | PROD_DESC | NOT NULL | VARCHAR2(25) |
   | COST | NOT NULL | NUMBER(6,2) |

   Write a SELECT statement that returns the product ID, prod_desc, and the product cost. Limit the product cost to range from $1.00 to $12.50.

a.

```
SELECT *
FROM PRODUCTS_TBL
WHERE COST BETWEEN 1.00 AND 12.50
```

# Hour 9, "Summarizing Data Results from a Query"

## Quiz Answers

1. The AVG function returns an average of all rows from a select column including any NULL values.

   a. False. The NULLs are not considered.

2. The SUM function is used to add column totals.

   a. False. The SUM function is used to return a total for a group of rows.

3. The COUNT(*) function counts all rows in a table.

   a. True.

4. Will the following SELECT statements work? If not, what will fix the statements?

   a.
   ```
   SELECT COUNT *
   FROM EMPLOYEE_PAY_TBL;
   ```

   a. This statement will not work because the left and right parentheses are missing around the asterisk. The correct syntax is:
   ```
   SELECT COUNT(*)
   FROM EMPLOYEE_PAY_TBL;
   ```

   b.
   ```
   SELECT COUNT(EMPLOYEE_ID), SALARY
   FROM EMPLOYEE_PAY_TBL;
   ```

   a. Yes, this statement will work.

   c.
   ```
   SELECT MIN(BONUS), MAX(SALARY)
   FROM EMPLOYEE_PAY_TBL
   WHERE SALARY > 20000;
   ```

   a. Yes, this statement will work.

C

# Exercise Answers

1. Using the EMPLOYEE_PAY_TBL:

| EMP_ID | POSITION | DATE_HIRE | PAY_RATE | DATE_LAST | SALARY | BONUS |
|--------|----------|-----------|----------|-----------|--------|-------|
| 311549902 | MARKETING | 23-MAY-89 | | 01-MAY-97 | 30000 | 2000 |
| 442346889 | TEAM LEADER | 17-JUN-90 | 14.75 | 01-JUN-97 | | |
| 213764555 | SALES MANAGER | 14-AUG-94 | | 01-AUG-97 | 40000 | 3000 |
| 313782439 | SALESMAN | 28-JUN-97 | | | 20000 | 1000 |
| 220984332 | SHIPPER | 22-JUL-96 | 11 | 01-JUL-97 | | |
| 443679012 | SHIPPER | 14-JAN-91 | 15 | 01-JAN-97 | | |

6 rows selected.

Construct SQL statements to find:

a. The average salary.

   a. The average salary is $30,000.00. The SQL statement to return the data is:

```
SELECT AVG(SALARY)
FROM EMPLOYEE_PAY_TBL;
```

b. The maximum bonus.

   a. The maximum bonus is $3000.00. The SQL statement to return the data is:

```
SELECT MAX(BONUS)
FROM EMPLOYEE_PAY_TBL;
```

c. The total salaries.

   a. The sum of all the salaries is $60,000.00. The SQL statement to return the data is:

```
SELECT SUM(SALARY)
FROM EMPLOYEE_PAY_TBL;
```

d. The minimum pay rate.

   a. The minimum pay rate is $11.00 an hour. The SQL statement to return the data is:

```
SELECT MIN(PAY_RATE)
FROM EMPLOYEE_PAY_TBL;
```

e. The total rows in the table.

   a. The total row count of the table is six. The SQL statement to return the data is:

```
SELECT COUNT(*)
FROM EMPLOYEE_PAY_TBL;
```

C

# Hour 10, "Sorting and Grouping Data"

## Quiz Answers

1. Will the following SQL statements work?

   a.
   ```
   SELECT SUM(SALARY), EMP_ID
   FROM EMPLOYEE_PAY_TBL
   GROUP BY 1 and 2;
   ```

   a. No, this statement does not work. The and in the GROUP BY clause does not belong there, and you cannot use an integer in the GROUP BY clause. The correct syntax is:
   ```
   SELECT SUM(SALARY), EMP_ID
   FROM EMPLOYEE_PAY_TBL
   GROUP BY SALARY, EMP_ID;
   ```

   b.
   ```
   SELECT EMP_ID, MAX(SALARY)
   FROM EMPLOYEE_PAY_TBL
   GROUP BY SALARY, EMP_ID;
   ```

   a. Yes, this statement will work.

   c.
   ```
   SELECT EMP_ID, COUNT(SALARY)
   FROM EMPLOYEE_PAY_TBL
   ORDER BY EMP_ID
   GROUP BY SALARY;
   ```

   a. No, this statement will not work. The ORDER BY clause and the GROUP BY clause are not in the correct sequence. The correct syntax is:
   ```
   SELECT EMP_ID, COUNT(SALARY)
   FROM EMPLOYEE_PAY_TBL
   GROUP BY SALARY
   ORDER BY EMP_ID;
   ```

2. True or false: You must also use the GROUP BY clause whenever using the HAVING clause.

   a. False. The HAVING clause can be used without a GROUP BY clause.

3. True or false: This SQL statement returns a total of the salaries by groups.
   ```
   SELECT SUM(SALARY)
   FROM EMPLOYEE_PAY_TBL;
   ```

   a. False. The statement cannot return a total of the salaries by groups, because there is no GROUP BY clause.

4. True or false: The columns selected must appear in the GROUP BY clause in the same order.

    a. False. The order of the columns in the SELECT clause can be in a different order in the GROUP BY clause.

5. The HAVING clause tells the GROUP BY which groups to include.

    a. True.

## Exercise Answers

1. Write a SQL statement that returns the employee ID, employee name, and city from the EMPLOYEE_TBL. Group by the city column first.

    a.

```
select emp_id, last_name, first_name, city
from employee_tbl
group by city, emp_id, last_name, first_name
```

2. Write a SQL statement that returns the city and a count of all employees per city from EMPLOYEE_TBL. Add a HAVING clause to display only those cities that have a count of more than two employees.

    a.

```
select city, count(emp_id)
from employee_tbl
group by city
having count(emp_id) > 2
```

# Hour 11, "Restructuring the Appearance of Data"

## Quiz Answers

Match the Descriptions with the possible Functions.

| | DESCRIPTIONS | ANSWERS |
|---|---|---|
| a. | Used to select a portion of a character string. | SUBSTR |
| b. | Used to trim characters from either the right or left of a string. | LTRIM/RTRIM |
| c. | Used to change all letters to lower case. | LOWER |
| d. | Used to find the length of a string. | LENGTH |
| e. | Used to combine strings. | CONCATENATION (CONCATENATION is the same as ¦¦.) |

2. True or false: The SOUNDEX function is used to compare strings that may sound alike.

   a. True.

3. The outermost function is always resolved first when functions are embedded within other functions in a query.

   a. False. The innermost function is always resolved first when embedding functions within one another.

## Exercise Answers

1. Use the appropriate function to convert the string hello to all uppercase letters.

   a.

```
SELECT UPPER('hello') FROM TABLE_NAME
```

2. Use the appropriate function to print only the first four characters of the string JOHNSON.

   a.

```
SELECT SUBSTR('JOHNSON',1,4) FROM TABLE_NAME
```

3. Use an appropriate function to concatenate the strings JOHN and SON.

   a. Oracle

```
SELECT 'JOHN' ¦¦ 'SON' FROM TABLE_NAME
```

or

   a. SQL Server

```
SELECT 'JOHN' + 'SON' FROM TABLE_NAME
```

# Hour 12, "Understanding Dates and Time"

## Quiz Answers

1. From where is the system date and time normally derived?

   a. The system date is derived from the current date and time of the operating system on the host machine.

2. List the standard internal elements of a DATETIME value.

   a. YEAR, MONTH, DAY, HOUR, MINUTE, and SECOND.

3. What could be a major factor concerning the representation and comparison of date and time values if your company is an international organization?

   a. The awareness of time zones may be a concern.

C

4. Can a character string date value be compared to a date value defined as a valid DATETIME datatype?

    a. A DATETIME datatype cannot be accurately compared to a date value defined as a character string. The character string must first be converted to the DATETIME datatype.

## Exercise Answers

1. Provide SQL code for the exercises given the following information:

Use SYSDATE to represent the current date and time.

Use the table called DATES.

Use the TO_CHAR function to convert dates to character strings, with syntax:

```
TO_CHAR('EXPRESSION','DATE_PICTURE')
```

Use the TO_DATE function to convert character strings to dates, with syntax:

```
TO_DATE('EXPRESSION','DATE_PICTURE')
```

Date picture information:

| DATE PICTURE | MEANING |
| --- | --- |
| MONTH | Month spelled out |
| DAY | Day spelled out |
| DD | Day of month, number |
| MM | Month of year, number |
| YY | Two-digit year |
| YYYY | Four-digit year |
| MI | Minutes of the hour |
| SS | Seconds of the minute |

1. Assuming today is 1997-12-31, convert the current date to the format December 31 1997.

    a.

```
SELECT TO_CHAR(SYSDATE,'MONTH DD YYYY')
FROM DATES;
```

2. Convert the following string to DATE format:

```
'DECEMBER 31 1997'
```

    a.

```
SELECT TO_DATE('DECEMBER 31 1997','MONTH DD YYYY')
FROM DATES;
```

3. Write the code to return the day of the week that New Year's Eve of 1998 falls upon. Assume that the date is stored in the format 31-DEC-97, which is a valid DATETIME datatype.

   a.

```
SELECT TO_CHAR('31-DEC-97','DAY')
FROM DATES;
```

# Hour 13, "Joining Tables in Queries"

## Quiz Answers

1. What type of join would you use to return records from one table, regardless of the existence of associated records in the related table?

   a. You would use an OUTER JOIN.

2. The JOIN conditions are located in what part of the SQL statement?

   a. The JOIN conditions are located in the WHERE clause.

3. What type of JOIN do you use to evaluate equality among rows of related tables?

   a. You would use an EQUIJOIN.

4. What happens if you select from two different tables but fail to join the tables?

   a. You receive a Cartesian Product by not joining the tables (this is also called a cross join).

5. Use the following tables:

ORDERS_TBL

| ord_num | varchar2(10) | not null | primary key |
|---|---|---|---|
| cust_id | varchar2(10) | not null | |
| prod_id | varchar2(10) | not null | |
| qty | number(6) | not null | |
| ord_date | date | | |

PRODUCTS_TBL

| prod_id | varchar2(10) | not null | primary key |
|---|---|---|---|
| prod_desc | varchar2(40) | not null | |
| cost | number(6,2) | not null | |

Is the following syntax correct for using an OUTER JOIN?

```
SELECT C.CUST_ID, C.CUST_NAME, O.ORD_NUM
FROM CUSTOMER_TBL C, ORDERS_TBL O
WHERE C.CUST_ID(+) = O.CUST_ID(+)
```

a. No, the syntax is not correct. The (+) operator should only follow the
O.CUST_ID column in the WHERE clause. The correct syntax is:

```
SELECT C.CUST_ID, C.CUST_NAME, O.ORD_NUM
FROM CUSTOMER_TBL C, ORDERS_TBL O
WHERE C.CUST_ID = O.CUST_ID(+);
```

# Exercise Answers

1. Perform the exercises using the following tables:

EMPLOYEE_TBL

| | | | |
|---|---|---|---|
| emp_id | varchar2(9) | not null | PRIMARY KEY |
| last_name | varchar2(15) | not null | |
| first_name | varchar2(15) | not null | |
| middle_name | varchar2(15) | | |
| address | varchar2(30) | not null | |
| city | varchar2(15) | not null | |
| state | char(2) | not null | |
| zip | number(5) | not null | |
| phone | char(10) | | |
| pager | char(10) | | |

EMPLOYEE_PAY_TBL

| | | | |
|---|---|---|---|
| emp_id | varchar2(9) | not null | primary key |
| position | varchar2(15) | not null | |
| date_hire | date | | |
| pay_rate | number(4,2) | not null | |
| date_last_raise | date | | |
| salary | number(6,2) | | |
| bonus | number(4,2) | | |
| constraint emp_fk foreign key | (emp_id) references | | |
|   employee_tbl (emp_id) | | | |

| CUSTOMER_TBL | | | |
|---|---|---|---|
| cust_id | varchar2(10) | not null | primary key |
| cust_name | varchar2(30) | not null | |
| cust_address | varchar2(20) | not null | |
| cust_city | varchar2(15) | not null | |
| cust_state | char(2) | not null | |
| cust_zip | number(5) | not null | |
| cust_phone | number(10) | | |
| cust_fax | number(10) | | |

| ORDERS_TBL | | | |
|---|---|---|---|
| ord_num | varchar2(10) | not null | primary key |
| cust_id | varchar2(10) | not null | |
| prod_id | varchar2(10) | not null | |
| qty | number(6) | not null | |
| ord_date | date | | |

| PRODUCTS_TBL | | | |
|---|---|---|---|
| prod_id | varchar2(10) | not null | primary key |
| prod_desc | varchar2(40) | not null | |
| cost | number(6,2) | not null | |

1. Write a SQL statement to return the EMP_ID, LAST_NAME, and FIRST_NAME from the EMPLOYEE_TBL and salary, bonus from the EMPLOYEE_PAY_TBL.

   a.
   ```
   SELECT E.EMP_ID, E.LAST_NAME, E.FIRST_NAME
           EP.SALARY, EP.BONUS
      FROM EMPLOYEE_TBL E,
           EMPLOYE_PAY_TBL EP
     WHERE E.EMP_ID = EP.EMP_ID
   ```

2. Select from the CUSTOMERS_TBL the columns: CUST_ID, CUST_NAME. Select from the PRODUCTS_TBL the columns: PROD_ID, COST. Select from the ORDERS_TBL the columns: ORD_NUM, QTY. Join all three of the tables into one SQL statement.

   a.
   ```
   SELECT C.CUST_ID, C.CUST_NAME, P.PROD_ID, P.COST,
      O.ORD_NUM, O.QTY
      FROM CUSTOMER_TBL C,
           PRODUCT_TBL P,
   ```

```
       ORDERS_TBL O
WHERE C.CUST_ID = O.CUST_ID
AND P.PROD_ID = O.PROD_ID
```

# Hour 14, "Using Subqueries to Define Unknown Data"

## Quiz Answers

1. What is the function of a subquery when used with a SELECT statement?

   a. The main function of a subquery when used with a SELECT statement is to return data that the main query can use to resolve the query.

2. Can you update more than one column when using the UPDATE statement in conjunction with a subquery?

   a. Yes, you can update more than one column using the same UPDATE and subquery statement.

3. Are the following syntaxes correct? If not, what is the correct syntax?

   a.
```
SELECT CUST_ID, CUST_NAME
       FROM CUSTOMER_TBL
       WHERE CUST_ID =
                       (SELECT CUST_ID
                        FROM ORDERS_TBL
                        WHERE ORD_NUM = '16C17')
```

   a. Yes, this syntax is correct.

   b.
```
SELECT EMP_ID, SALARY
       FROM EMPLOYEE_PAY_TBL
       WHERE SALARY BETWEEN '20000'
                     AND (SELECT SALARY
                          FROM EMPLOYEE_ID
                          WHERE SALARY = '40000')
```

   a. No. The BETWEEN operator cannot be used in this format.

   c.
```
UPDATE PRODUCTS_TBL
   SET COST = 1.15
   WHERE CUST_ID =
                   (SELECT CUST_ID
                    FROM ORDERS_TBL
                    WHERE ORD_NUM = '32A132')
```

   a. Yes, this syntax is correct.

C

4. What would happen if the following statement were run?

```
DELETE FROM EMPLOYEE_TBL
WHERE EMP_ID IN
            (SELECT EMP_ID
             FROM EMPLOYEE_PAY_TBL)
```

    a. All rows that were retrieved from the EMPLOYEE_PAY_TBL would be used by the DELETE to remove them from the EMPLOYEE_TBL. A WHERE clause in the subquery is highly advised.

## Exercise Answers

1. Use the following tables:

EMPLOYEE_TBL

| | | | |
|---|---|---|---|
| emp_id | varchar2(9) | not null | primary key |
| last_name | varchar2(15) | not null | |
| first_name | varchar2(15) | not null | |
| middle_name | varchar2(15) | | |
| address | varchar2(30) | not null | |
| city | varchar2(15) | not null | |
| state | char(2) | not null | |
| zip | number(5) | not null | |
| phone | char(10) | | |
| pager | char(10) | | |

EMPLOYEE_PAY_TBL

| | | | |
|---|---|---|---|
| emp_id | varchar2(9) | not null | primary key |
| position | varchar2(15) | not null | |
| date_hire | date | | |
| pay_rate | number(4,2) | not null | |
| date_last_raise | date | | |

constraint emp_fk foreign key (emp_id) references

employee_tbl (emp_id)

CUSTOMER_TBL

| | | | |
|---|---|---|---|
| cust_id | varchar2(10) | not null | primary key |
| cust_name | varchar2(30) | not null | |
| cust_address | varchar2(20) | not null | |

| | | | |
|---|---|---|---|
| cust_city | varchar2(15) | not null | |
| cust_state | char(2) | not null | |
| cust_zip | number(5) | not null | |
| cust_phone | number(10) | | |
| cust_fax | number(10) | | |

**ORDERS_TBL**

| | | | |
|---|---|---|---|
| ord_num | varchar2(10) | not null | primary key |
| cust_id | varchar2(10) | not null | |
| prod_id | varchar2(10) | not null | |
| qty | number(6) | not null | |
| ord_date | date | | |

**PRODUCTS_TBL**

| | | | |
|---|---|---|---|
| prod_id | varchar2(10) | not null | primary key |
| prod_desc | varchar2(40) | not null | |
| cost | number(6,2) | not null | |

2. Using a subquery, write a SQL statement to update the CUSTOMER_TBL table, changing the customer name to DAVIDS MARKET, with order number 23E934.

   a.

```
UPDATE CUSTOMER_TBL
   SET CUST_NAME = 'DAVIDS MARKET'
   WHERE CUST_ID =
                 (SELECT CUST_ID
                  FROM ORDERS_TBL
                  WHERE ORD_NUM = '23E934'
```

3. Using a subquery, write a query that returns the names of all employees who have a pay rate greater than JOHN DOE, whose employee identification number is 343559876.

   a.

```
SELECT E.LAST_NAME, E.FIRST_NAME, E.MIDDLE_NAME
   FROM EMPLOYEE_TBL E,
        EMPLOYEE_PAY_TBL P
   WHERE P.PAY_RATE > (SELECT PAY_RATE
                       FROM EMPLOYEE_PAY_TBL
                       WHERE EMP_ID = '343559876');
```

4. Using a subquery, write a query that lists all products that cost more than the average cost of all products.

a.

```
SELECT PROD_DESC
    FROM PRODUCTS_TBL
    WHERE COST > (SELECT AVG(COST)
                    FROM PRODUCTS_TBL);
```

# Hour 15, "Combining Multiple Queries into One"

## Quiz Answers

1. Is the syntax correct for the following compound queries? If not, what would correct the syntax? Use the EMPLOYEE_TBL and the EMPLOYEE_PAY_TBL shown as follows:

EMPLOYEE_TBL

| | | |
|---|---|---|
| emp_id | varchar2(9) | not null, |
| last_name | varchar2(15) | not null, |
| first_name | varchar2(15) | not null, |
| middle_name | varchar2(15), | |
| address | varchar2(30) | not null, |
| city | varchar2(15) | not null, |
| state | char(2) | not null, |
| zip | number(5) | not null, |
| phone | char(10), | |
| pager | char(10), | |
| constraint emp_pk primary key (emp_id) | | |

EMPLOYEE_PAY_TBL

| | | | |
|---|---|---|---|
| emp_id | varchar2(9) | not null | primary key, |
| position | varchar2(15) | not null, | |
| date_hire | date, | | |
| pay_rate | number(4,2) | not null, | |
| date_last_raise | date, | | |
| salary | number(8,2), | | |
| bonus | number(8,2), | | |
| constraint emp_fk foreign key (emp_id) | | | |
|   references employee_tbl (emp_id) | | | |

C

a.

```
SELECT EMP_ID, LAST_NAME, FIRST_NAME
FROM EMPLOYEE_TBL
UNION
SELECT EMP_ID, POSITION, DATE_HIRE
FROM EMPLOYEE_PAY_TBL
```

a. This compound query does not work because the datatypes do not match. The EMP_ID columns match, but the LAST_NAME and FIRST_NAME datatypes do not match the POSITION and DATE_HIRE datatypes.

b.

```
SELECT EMP_ID FROM EMPLOYEE_TBL
UNION ALL
SELECT EMP_ID FROM EMPLOYEE_PAY_TBL
ORDER BY EMP_ID
```

a. Yes, the statement is correct.

c.

```
SELECT EMP_ID FROM EMPLOYEE_PAY_TBL
INTERSECT
SELECT EMP_ID FROM EMPLOYEE_TBL
ORDER BY 1
```

a. Yes, this compound query works.

2. Match the correct operator to the following statements:

| STATEMENT | |
|---|---|
| a. | Show duplicates<br>a. UNION ALL |
| b. | Return only rows from the first query that match those in the second query.<br>a. INTERSECT |
| c. | Return no duplicates.<br>a. UNION |
| d. | Return only rows from the first query not returned by the second.<br>a. EXCEPT |

C

## Exercise Answers

1. Using the CUSTOMER_TBL and the ORDERS_TBL as listed:

CUSTOMER_TBL

| | | | |
|---|---|---|---|
| cust_id | varchar2(10) | not null | primary key, |
| cust_name | varchar2(30) | not null, | |
| cust_address | varchar2(20) | not null, | |
| cust_city | varchar2(15) | not null, | |
| cust_state | char(2) | not null, | |
| cust_zip | number(5) | not null, | |
| cust_phone | number(10), | | |
| cust_fax | number(10) | | |

ORDERS_TBL

| | | | |
|---|---|---|---|
| ord_num | varchar2(10) | not null | primary key, |
| cust_id | varchar2(10) | not null, | |
| prod_id | varchar2(10) | not null, | |
| qty | number(6) | not null, | |
| ord_date | date | | |

a. Write a compound query to find the customers who have placed an order.

   a.

```
SELECT CUST_ID FROM CUSTOMER_TBL
INTERSECT
SELECT CUST_ID FROM ORDERS_TBL
```

b. Write a compound query to find the customers who have not placed an order.

   a.

```
SELECT CUST_ID FROM CUSTOMER_TBL
EXCEPT
SELECT CUST_ID FROM ORDERS_TBL
```

# Hour 16, "Using Indexes to Improve Performance"

## Quiz Answers

1. What are some major disadvantages of using indexes?

   a. Major disadvantages of an index include slowing batch jobs, storage space on the disk, and maintenance upkeep on the index.

2. Why is the order of columns in a composite important?

    a. Because query performance is improved by putting the column with the most restrictive values first.

3. Should a column with a large percentage of NULLs be indexed?

    a. No. A column with a large percentage of NULLs should not be indexed, because the speed of accessing these rows degrades when the value of a large percentage of rows is the same.

4. Is the main purpose of an index to stop duplicate values in a table?

    a. No. The main purpose of an index is to enhance data retrieval speed, although a unique index stops duplicate values in a table.

5. True or false: The main reason for a composite index is for aggregate function usage in an index.

    a. False. The main reason for composite indexes is for two or more columns in the same table to be indexed.

# Exercise Answers

1. Decide whether an index should be used in the following situations, and if so, what type of index should be used.

    a. Several columns, but a rather small table.

        a. Being a very small table, no index needed.

    b. Medium-sized table, no duplicates should be allowed.

        a. A unique index could be used.

    c. Several columns, very large table, several columns are used as filters in the WHERE clause.

        a. A composite index on the columns used as filter in the WHERE clause should be the choice.

    d. Large table, many columns, lots of data manipulation.

        a. A choice of a single-column or composite index should be considered, depending on filtering, ordering, and grouping. For the large amount of data manipulation, the index could be dropped and recreated once the insert, update, or delete jobs were done.

# Hour 17, "Improving Database Performance"

## Quiz Answers

1. Would the use of a unique index on a small table be of any benefit?

    a. The index may not be of any use for performance issues; but, the unique index would keep referential integrity intact. Referential integrity is discussed in Hour 3.

2. What happens when the optimizer chooses not to use an index on a table when a query has been executed?

    a. A full table scan occurs.

3. Should the most restrictive clause(s) be evaluated before or after the join condition(s) in the WHERE clause?

    a. The most restrictive clause(s) should be evaluated before the join condition(s), since join conditions normally return a large number of rows.

## Exercise Answers

1. Rewrite the following SQL statements to improve their performance. Use the EMPLOYEE_TBL and the EMPLOYEE_PAY_TBL as described here:

EMPLOYEE_TBL

```
emp_id          varchar2(9)      not null,
last_name       varchar2(15)     not null,
first_name      varchar2(15)     not null,
middle_name     varchar2(15),
address         varchar2(30)     not null,
city            varchar2(15)     not null,
state           char(2)          not null,
zip             number(5)        not null,
phone           char(10),
pager           char(10),
constraint emp_pk primary key (emp_id)
```

C

```
EMPLOYEE_PAY_TBL
```

| | | |
|---|---|---|
| emp_id | varchar2(9) | not null, |
| position | varchar2(15) | not null, |
| date_hire | date, | |
| pay_rate | number(4,2) | not null, |
| date_last_raise | date, | |
| salary | number(8,2), | |
| bonus | number(8,2), | |

```
constraint emp_fk foreign key (emp_id)
       references employee_tbl (emp_id)
```

a.

```
SELECT EMP_ID, LAST_NAME, FIRST_NAME,
           PHONE
   FROM EMPLOYEE_TBL
   WHERE SUBSTR(PHONE, 1, 3) = '317' OR
         SUBSTR(PHONE, 1, 3) = '812' OR
         SUBSTR(PHONE, 1, 3) = '765'
```

a.

```
SELECT EMP_ID, LAST_NAME, FIRST_NAME, PHONE
   FROM EMPLOYEE_TBL
   WHERE SUBSTR(PHONE, 1, 3) IN ('317', '812', '765')
```

b.

```
SELECT LAST_NAME, FIRST_NAME
   FROM EMPLOYEE_TBL
   WHERE LAST_NAME LIKE '%ALL%
```

a.

```
SELECT LAST_NAME, FIRST_NAME
 FROM EMPLOYEE_TBL
 WHERE LAST_NAME LIKE 'WAL%
```

c.

```
SELECT E.EMP_ID, E.LAST_NAME, E.FIRST_NAME,
         EP.SALARY
   FROM EMPLOYEE_TBL E,
   EMPLOYEE_PAY_TBL EP
   WHERE LAST_NAME LIKE 'S%'
   AND E.EMP_ID = EP.EMP_ID
```

a.

```
SELECT E.EMP_ID, E.LAST_NAME, E.FIRST_NAME,
         EP.SALARY
   FROM EMPLOYEE_PAY_TBL EP,
       EMPLOYEE_TBL E
   WHERE E.EMP_ID = EP.EMP_ID
   AND LAST_NAME LIKE 'S'
```

C

# Hour 18, "Managing Database Users"

## Quiz Answers

1. What command is used to establish a session?

    a. The CONNECT TO statement.

2. Which option must be used to drop a schema that still contains database objects?

    a. The CASCADE option allows the schema to be dropped if there are still objects under that schema.

3. What statement is used to remove a database privilege?

    a. The REVOKE statement is used to remove database privileges.

4. What command creates a grouping or collection of tables, views, and privileges?

    a. The CREATE SCHEMA statement.

## Exercise Answers

1. Describe or list the steps that allow a new employee database access.

    a. The immediate supervisor should instigate the request process by completing a user ID request form, which contains all the information necessary to add the user to the database. The form should then be forwarded to the security officer. The user request is then routed to either the database administrator or the individual designated to assist the database administrator with security, so that the user may be added to the database. This is a general process that should be followed and modified accordingly for each company.

# Hour 19, "Managing Database Security"

## Quiz Answers

1. What option must a user have to grant another user privileges to an object not owned by the user?

    a. The GRANT OPTION.

2. When privileges are granted to PUBLIC, do all users of the database acquire the privileges, or just a listing of chosen users?

    a. All users of the database will be granted the privileges.

3. What privilege is required to look at data in a specific table?

    a. The SELECT privilege.

4. What type of privilege is the SELECT privilege?

    a. An object-level privilege.

C

## Exercise Answers

1. Write a statement to grant select access on a table called EMPLOYEE_TBL, which you own, to a user ID, RPLEW. It should allow RPLEW to grant privileges to another user on the same table.

    a.

```
GRANT SELECT ON EMPLOYEE_TBL TO RPLEW WITH GRANT OPTION
```

2. Write the statement that revokes the connect role from both of the users in Exercise 1.

    a.

```
REVOKE CONNECT ON EMPLOYEE_TBL FROM RPLEW
```

3. Write the statement that allows RPLEW to select, insert, and update the EMPLOYEE_TBL table.

    a.

```
GRANT SELECT, INSERT, UPDATE ON EMPLOYEE_TBL TO RPLEW
```

# Hour 20, "Creating and Using Views and Synonyms"

## Quiz Answers

1. Can a row of data be deleted from a view that was created from multiple tables?

    a. No. The DELETE, INSERT, and UPDATE commands can only be used on views created from a single table.

2. When creating a table, the owner is automatically granted the appropriate privileges on that table. Is this true when creating a view?

    a. Yes. The owner of a view is automatically granted the appropriate privileges on the view.

3. What clause is used to order data when creating a view?

    a. The GROUP BY clause functions in a view much as the ORDER BY clause (or GROUP BY clause) does in a regular query.

4. What option can be used, when creating a view from a view, to check integrity constraints?

    a. The WITH CHECK OPTION.

5. You try to drop a view and receive an error, because there are one or more underlying views. What must you do to drop the view?

    a. Reexecute your DROP statement with the CASCADE option. This allows the DROP statement to succeed by also dropping all underlying views.

C

## Exercise Answers

1. Write a statement to create a view based on the total contents of the EMPLOYEE_TBL table.

   a.

   ```
   CREATE VIEW EMP_VIEW AS
   SELECT * FROM EMPLOYEE_TBL
   ```

2. Write a statement that creates a summarized view containing the average pay rate and average salary for each city in the EMPLOYEE_TBL table.

   a.

   ```
   CREATE VIEW AVG_PAY_VIEW AS
   SELECT E.CITY, AVG(P.PAY_RATE), AVG(P.SALARY)
   FROM EMPLOYEE_PAY_TBL P,
   EMPLOYEE_TBL E
   WHERE P.EMP_ID = E.EMP_ID
   GROUP BY E.CITY
   ```

3. Write statements that drop the two views that you created in Exercises 1 and 2.

   a.

   ```
   DROP VIEW EMP_VIEW
   DROP VIEW AVG_PAY_VIEW
   ```

# Hour 21, "Working with the System Catalog"

## Quiz Answers

1. The system catalog is also known as what?

   a. The system catalog is also known as the data dictionary.

2. Can a regular user update the system catalog?

   a. Not directly; however, when a user creates an object such as a table, the System Catalog is automatically updated.

3. What Sybase system table would be used to retrieve information about views that exist in the database?

   a. SYSVIEWS

4. Who owns the system catalog?

   a. The owner of the system catalog is often a privileged database user account called SYS or SYSTEM. The system catalog may also be owned by the owner of the database, but is not ordinarily owned by a particular schema in the database.

C

5. What is the difference between the Oracle system objects ALL_TABLES and DBA_TABLES?

    a. ALL_TABLES shows all tables that are accessible by a particular user where DBA_TABLES shows all tables that exist in the database.

6. Who makes modifications to the system tables?

    a. The database server itself.

# Hour 22, "Advanced SQL Topics"

## Quiz Answers

1. Can a trigger be altered?

    a. No, the trigger must be replaced or recreated.

2. When a cursor is closed, can you reuse the name?

    a. This is implementation specific. In some implementations, the closing of the cursor will allow you to reuse the name and even free the memory, while for other implementations you must use the deallocate statement before the name can be reused.

3. What command is used to retrieve the results after a Cursor has been opened?

    a. The FETCH command.

4. Are triggers executed before or after an INSERT, DELETE, or UPDATE?

    a. Triggers can be executed before or after an INSERT, DELETE, or UPDATE. There are many different types of triggers that can be created.

## Exercise Answers

1. Using your implementation's system catalog tables, write the SQL that creates the following SQL statements. Substitute the name of an actual object for the object names.

    a.

```
GRANT SELECT ON TABLE_NAME TO USERNAME;
```

    a.

```
SELECT 'GRANT SELECT ON '||TABLE_NAME|| ' TO '||
USERNAME||';'
FROM SYSTEM CATALOG TABLE_NAME
```

    b.

```
GRANT, CONNECT, RESOURCE TO USERNAME;
```

    b.

```
SELECT 'GRANT, CONNECT, RESOURCE TO '
||USERNAME||';'
FROM SYSTEM CATALOG TABLE_NAME
```

c.

```
SELECT COUNT(*) FROM TABLE_NAME;
```

c.

```
SELECT 'SELECT COUNT(*) FROM '||TABLE_NAME||';'
FROM SYSTEM CATALOG TABLE_NAME
```

2. Write a statement to create a stored procedure that deletes an entry from the PRODUCTS_TBL table; it should be similar to the example used in this hour to insert a new product.

   a.

   ```
   CREATE PROCEDURE DELETE_PRODUCT
   (OLD_PROD_ID IN VARCHAR2)
   AS
   BEGIN
       DELETE FROM PRODUCTS_TBL
       WHERE PROD_ID = OLD_PROD_ID;
       COMMIT;
   END;
   /
   ```

3. Write the statement that executes the stored procedure that you created in Exercise 2 to delete the row for PROD_ID '9999'.

   a.

   ```
   EXECUTE DELETE_PRODUCT ('9999');
   ```

# Hour 23, "Extending SQL to the Enterprise, the Internet, and the Intranet"

## Quiz Answers

1. Can a database on a server be accessed from another server?
   a. Yes; by using a middleware product. This is called accessing a remote database.

2. What can a company use to disseminate information to its own employees?
   a. An intranet.

3. Products that allow connections to databases are called what?
   a. Middleware.

4. Can SQL be embedded into Internet programming languages?
   a. Yes. SQL can be embedded in Internet programming languages such as Java.

5. How is a remote database accessed through a Web application?
   a. Via a Web server.

# Hour 24, "Extensions to Standard SQL"

## Quiz Answers

1. Is SQL a procedural or non-procedural language?

    a. SQL is a non-procedural, meaning that the database decides how to execute the SQL statement. The extensions discussed during this hour are procedural.

2. What are some of the reasons differences in SQL exist?

    a. Differences exist in SQL among the vendors because of storage requirements, advantages over competitors, ease of use, and performance considerations.

3. What are the three basic operations of a cursor outside of declaring the cursor?

    a. OPEN, FETCH, and CLOSE.

4. Procedural or non-procedural: With which does the database engine decide how to evaluate and execute SQL statements?

    a. Non-procedural.

## Exercise Answers

1. No specific answer.

2. Using the EMPLOYEE_TBL (see Appendix D), write the interactive SQL statement that returns the name of all employees who have a zip code of 46234. (Hint: Refer to the Oracle example in this hour for parameter passing.)

| Name | Null | Type |
|------|------|------|
| EMP_ID | NOT NULL | VARCHAR2(9) |
| LAST_NAME | NOT NULL | VARCHAR2(8) |
| FIRST_NAME | NOT NULL | VARCHAR2(8) |
| MID_INIT | | CHAR(1) |
| ADDRESS | NOT NULL | VARCHAR2(15) |
| CITY | NOT NULL | VARCHAR2(12) |
| STATE | NOT NULL | CHAR(2) |
| ZIP | NOT NULL | CHAR(5) |
| PHONE | | CHAR(10) |
| PAGER | | CHAR(10) |

a.

```
SELECT LAST_NAME, FIRST_NAME
FROM EMPLOYEE_TBL
WHERE ZIP = '&ZIP';

Enter value for zip: 46234
old   3: WHERE ZIP = '&ZIP'
new   3: WHERE ZIP = '46234'

Results of Query


LAST_NAM FIRST_NA
-------- --------
SPURGEON TIFFANY

1 row selected.
```

# Appendix **D**

# CREATE TABLE Statements for Book Examples

This appendix is very useful. The CREATE TABLE statements used in the examples are listed. You can use these statements to create your own tables to query.

## EMPLOYEE_TBL

```
create table EMPLOYEE_TBL
(
emp_id              varchar2(9)       not null,
last_name           varchar2(15)      not null,
first_name          varchar2(15)      not null,
middle_name         varchar2(15),
address             varchar2(30)      not null,
city                varchar2(15)      not null,
state               char(2)           not null,
```

```
zip                     number(5)               not null,
phone                   char(10),
pager                   char(10),
constraint emp_pk primary key (emp_id)
)
/
```

## EMPLOYEE_PAY_TBL

```
create table EMPLOYEE_PAY_TBL
(
emp_id                  varchar2(9)             not null        primary key,
position                varchar2(15)            not null,
date_hire               date,
pay_rate                number(4,2),
date_last_raise         date,
salary                  number(8,2),
bonus                   number(6,2),
constraint emp_fk foreign key  (emp_id) references employee_tbl (emp_id)
)
/
```

## CUSTOMER_TBL

```
create table CUSTOMER_TBL
(
cust_id                 varchar2(10)            not null        primary key,
cust_name               varchar2(30)            not null,
cust_address            varchar2(20)            not null,
cust_city               varchar2(15)            not null,
cust_state              char(2)                 not null,
cust_zip                number(5)               not null,
cust_phone              number(10),
cust_fax                number(10)
)
/
```

## ORDERS_TBL

```
create table ORDERS_TBL
(
ord_num                 varchar2(10)            not null        primary key,
cust_id                 varchar2(10)            not null,
prod_id                 varchar2(10)            not null,
qty                     number(6)               not null,
ord_date                date
)
/
```

# PRODUCTS_TBL

```
create table PRODUCTS_TBL
(
prod_id       varchar2(10)   not null       primary key,
prod_desc     varchar2(40)   not null,
cost          number(6,2)    not null
)
/
```

# Appendix **E**

# INSERT Statements for Data in Book Examples

This appendix contains the INSERT statements that were used to populate the tables that are listed in Appendix D, "CREATE TABLE Statements for Book Examples." These INSERT statements may be used to populate the tables after you create them.

## INSERT Statements

### EMPLOYEE_TBL

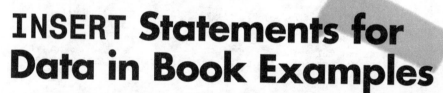

```
insert into employee_tbl values
('311549902', 'STEPHENS', 'TINA', 'DAWN',   'RR 3 BOX 17A', 'GREEN-
WOOD',
'IN',  '47890', '3178784465',  NULL)
/

insert into employee_tbl values
('442346889', 'PLEW', 'LINDA', 'CAROL', '3301 BEACON', 'INDIANAPO-
LIS',
'IN',  '46224', '3172978990', NULL)
/

insert into employee_tbl values
('213764555', 'GLASS', 'BRANDON', 'SCOTT', '1710 MAIN ST',
'WHITELAND',
'IN',  '47885', '3178984321', '3175709980')
/
```

```
insert into employee_tbl values
('313782439', 'GLASS', 'JACOB', NULL, '3789 WHITE RIVER BLVD',
'INDIANAPOLIS', 'IN', '45734', '3175457676',  '8887345678')
/

insert into employee_tbl values
('220984332', 'WALLACE', 'MARIAH', NULL, '7889 KEYSTONE AVE',
'INDIANAPOLIS', 'IN', '46741', '3173325986', NULL)
/

insert into employee_tbl values
('443679012', 'SPURGEON', 'TIFFANY',  NULL, '5 GEORGE COURT',
'INDIANAPOLIS', 'IN', '46234', '3175679007', NULL)
/
```

## EMPLOYEE_PAY_TBL

```
insert into employee_pay_tbl values
('311549902', 'MARKETING', '23-MAY-89',  NULL,  '01-MAY-97',  '40000', NULL)
/

insert into employee_pay_tbl values
('442346889', 'TEAM LEADER', '17-JUN-90', '14.75', '01-JUN-97', NULL, NULL)
/

insert into employee_pay_tbl values
('213764555', 'SALES MANAGER', '14-AUG-94',  NULL, '01-AUG-97', '30000', '2000')
/

insert into employee_pay_tbl values
('313782439', 'SALESMAN', '28-JUN-97',  NULL, NULL, '20000', '1000')
/

insert into employee_pay_tbl values
('220984332', 'SHIPPER', '22-JUL-96', '11.00', '01-JUL-97', NULL, NULL)
/

insert into employee_pay_tbl values
('443679012', 'SHIPPER', '14-JAN-91', '15.00', '01-JAN-97', NULL, NULL)
/
```

## CUSTOMER_TBL

```
insert into customer_tbl values
('232', 'LESLIE GLEASON', '798 HARDAWAY DR', 'INDIANAPOLIS',
'IN', '47856', '3175457690', NULL)
/

insert into customer_tbl values
('109', 'NANCY BUNKER', 'APT A 4556 WATERWAY', 'BROAD RIPPLE',
'IN', '47950', '3174262323', NULL)
/
```

**E**

```
insert into customer_tbl values
('345', 'ANGELA DOBKO', 'RR3 BOX 76', 'LEBANON', 'IN', '49967',
'7658970090', NULL)
/
insert into customer_tbl values
('090', 'WENDY WOLF', '3345 GATEWAY DR', 'INDIANAPOLIS', 'IN',
'46224', '3172913421', NULL)
/
insert into customer_tbl values
('12', 'MARYS GIFT SHOP', '435 MAIN ST', 'DANVILLE', 'IL', '47978',
'3178567221', 3178523434')
/

insert into customer_tbl values
('432', 'SCOTTYS MARKET', 'RR2 BOX 173', 'BROWNSBURG', 'IN',
'45687', '3178529835', '3178529836')
/

insert into customer_tbl values
('333', 'JASONS AND DALLAS GOODIES', 'LAFAYETTE SQ MALL',
'INDIANAPOLIS', 'IN', '46222', '3172978886', '3172978887')
/

insert into customer_tbl values
('21', 'MORGANS CANDIES AND TREATS', '5657 W TENTH ST',
'INDIANAPOLIS', 'IN', '46234', 3172714398, NULL)
/

insert into customer_tbl values
('43', 'SCHYLERS NOVELTIES', '17 MAPLE ST', 'LEBANON', 'IN',
'48990', '3174346758', NULL)
/

insert into customer_tbl values
('287', 'GAVINS PLACE', '9880 ROCKVILLE RD', 'INDIANAPOLIS',
'IN', '46244', '3172719991', 3172719992')
/

insert into customer_tbl values
('288', 'HOLLYS GAMEARAMA', '567 US 31 SOUTH', 'WHITELAND',
'IN', '49980', '3178879023', NULL)
/

insert into customer_tbl values
('590', 'HEATHERS FEATHERS AND THINGS', '4090 N SHADELAND AVE',
'INDIANAPOLIS', 'IN', '43278', '3175456768', NULL)
/

insert into customer_tbl values
('610', 'RAGANS HOBBIES INC', '451 GREEN ST', 'PLAINFIELD', 'IN',
'46818', '3178393441', 3178399090')
/

insert into customer_tbl values
('560', 'ANDYS CANDIES', 'RR 1 BOX 34', 'NASHVILLE', 'IN',
'48756', '8123239871', NULL)
/
```

```
insert into customer_tbl values
('221', 'RYANS STUFF', '2337 S SHELBY ST', 'INDIANAPOLIS', 'IN',
'47834', '3175634402', NULL)
/
```

## ORDERS_TBL

```
insert into orders_tbl values
('56A901', '232', '11235', '1', '22-OCT-97')
/
```

```
insert into orders_tbl values
('56A917', '12', '907', '100', '30-SEP-97')
/
```

```
insert into orders_tbl values
('32A132', '43', '222', '25', '10-OCT-97')
/
```

```
insert into orders_tbl values
('16C17', '090', '222', '2', '17-OCT-97')
/
```

```
insert into orders_tbl values
('18D778', '287', '90', '10', '17-OCT-97')
/
```

```
insert into orders_tbl values
('23E934', '432', '13', '20', '15-OCT-97')
/
```

## PRODUCTS_TBL

```
insert into products_tbl values
('11235', 'WITCHES COSTUME', '29.99')
/
```

```
insert into products_tbl values
('222', 'PLASTIC PUMPKIN 18 INCH', '7.75')
/
```

```
insert into products_tbl values
('13', 'FALSE PARAFFIN TEETH', '1.10')
/
```

```
insert into products_tbl values
('90', 'LIGHTED LANTERNS', '14.50')
/
```

```
insert into products_tbl values
('15', 'ASSORTED COSTUMES', '10.00')
/
```

E

```
insert into products_tbl values
('9', 'CANDY CORN', '1.35')
/

insert into products_tbl  values
('6', 'PUMPKIN CANDY', '1.45')
/

insert into products_tbl values
('87', 'PLASTIC SPIDERS', '1.05')
/

insert into products_tbl values
('119', 'ASSORTED MASKS', '4.95')
/
```

# Appendix F

# Glossary

**alias**   Another name or term for a table or column.

**ANSI**   American National Standards Institute.

**application**   A set of menus, forms, reports, and code that performs a business function using a database.

**buffer**   An area in memory for editing or execution of SQL.

**Cartesian product**   The result of not joining tables in the WHERE clause of a SQL statement. When tables in a query are not joined, every row in one table is paired with every row in all other tables.

**client**   The client is typically a PC, but can be another server that is dependent upon another computer for data, services, or processing.

**column**   A part of a table that has a name and a specific datatype.

**COMMIT**   Makes changes to data permanent.

**composite index**   An index that is composed of two or more columns.

**condition**   Search criteria in a query's WHERE clause that evaluates to true or false.

**constant**   A value that does not change.

**constraint**   Restrictions on data that are enforced at the data level.

**cursor**   A work area in memory where the current SQL statement is stored.

**data dictionary**   Another name for the System Catalog. See *system catalog*.

**database**   A collection of data.

**datatype**   Defines data as type, such as number, date, or character.

**DBA**   Database Administrator. An individual who manages a database.

**DDL**   Data Definition Language.

**default**   A value used when no specification has been made.

**distinct**   Unique; used in the SELECT clause to return unique values.

**DML**   Data Manipulation Language.

**DQL**   Data Query Language.

**end user**   Users whose job requires them to query or manipulate data in the database. The end user is the individual for which the database exists.

**field**   Another name for a column in a table. See *column*.

**foreign key**   One or more columns whose values are based on the primary key column values in another table.

**full table scan**   The search of a table from a query without the use of an index.

**function**   An operation that is predefined and may be used in a SQL statement to manipulate data.

**GUI**   Graphical User Interface.

**host**   The computer on which a database is located.

**index**   Pointers to table data that make access to a table more efficient.

**join**   Combines data from different tables by linking columns. Used in the WHERE clause of a SQL statement.

**key**   A column or columns that identify rows of a table.

**normalization**   Designing a database to reduce redundancy by breaking large tables down into smaller, more manageable tables.

**NULL value**   A value that is unknown.

**object**   Elements in a database, such as triggers, tables, views, procedures.

**F**

**operator**  A reserved word or symbol used to perform an operation, such as addition or subtraction.

**optimizer**  Part of the database that decides how to execute a SQL statement and return an answer.

**parameter**  A value or range of values that is used to resolve a part of a SQL statement or program.

**primary key**  A specified table column that uniquely identifies rows of the table.

**privilege**  Specific permissions that are granted to users to perform a specific action in the database.

**procedure**  A set of instructions that are saved for repeated calling and execution.

**public**  A database user account that represents all database users.

**query**  A SQL statement that is used to retrieve data from a database.

**record**  See *row*.

**referential integrity**  Assures that values from one column depend on the values from another column.

**relational database**  A database that is organized into tables that consist of rows, which contain the same sets of data items, where tables in the database are related to one another through common keys.

**ROLLBACK**  A command that undoes all transactions since the last COMMIT or SAVEPOINT commands issued.

**row**  Sets of records in a table.

**savepoint**  A specified point in a transaction to which you may roll back or undo changes.

**schema**  The owner of a set of objects in a database.

**security**  The process of ensuring that data in a database is fully protected at all times.

**SQL**  Structured Query Language.

**stored procedure**  SQL code that is stored in a database and ready to execute.

**subquery**  A SELECT statement embedded within another SQL statement.

**synonym**  Another name given to a table or view.

**syntax for SQL**  A set of rules that shows mandatory and optional parts of a SQL statement's construction.

**system catalog**  Collection of tables or views that contain information about the database.

**table**   The basic logical storage unit for data in a relational database.

**transaction**   One or more SQL statements that are executed as a single unit.

**trigger**   A stored procedure that executes upon specified events in a database, such as before or after an update of a table.

**variable**   A value that does not remain constant.

**view**   A database object that is created from one or more tables and can be used the same as a table. A view is a virtual table that has no storage requirements of its own.

# INDEX

# Sams' Teach Yourself SQL in 21 Days, Second Edition

*—Morgan, Perkins, Stephens, & Plew*

Fully updated and revised to include coverage of PL/SQL and Transact SQL, this easy-to-understand guide teaches users everything they need to know from database concepts and processes to implementing security and constructing and optimizing queries.

Q&A sections, step-by-step instructions, and review sections make learning easy and fun.

Shows how to create tables, modify data, incorporate security features, and tune the database for optimum performance. Emphasizes common database concepts, including SQL functions and queries.

Price: $39.99 USA/$56.95 CAN  New–Casual
ISBN: 0-672-31110-0  624 pages

# SQL Unleashed

*—Hans Ladanyi*

*SQL Unleashed* is broken into four distinct parts to help readers find the information they need:

Retrieving Information  The largest section focuses on the accurate, reliable, and efficient retrieval of information. Readers will become proficient at creating, testing, and improving select (simple, nested, or correlated).

Manipulating Information and Database Objects  This section deals with manipulating information and database objects. Readers will understand the best ways to manipulate single table data while controlling transactions. They will also learn the most efficient way to create tables and relationships, and to customize the appearance of tables through views.

Optimizing Issues  This section identifies the key optimization and performance issues that are vital to SQL programming. The reader will learn ways to improve performance, optimize statements, and avoid unnecessary database accesses.

Advanced Issues  A catch-all section for many difficult to classify topics, this final part keys on some specific issues that have not been addressed in other books. Ensuring the accuracy of complex queries, modularized reporting, data warehousing, integrating and scrubbing data, and security issues all are described in detail.

*SQL Unleashed* serves as the one comprehensive resource for SQL programming. The market lacks a large, encompassing SQL book. This book fills that void! SQL is the standard command set used to communicate with the most important relational database systems on the market today (Oracle, Informix, Sybase, DB2, MS SQL Server, and Access) and a working knowledge of SQL is needed by all database programmers and administrators.

Price:$49.99 USA/$70.95 CAN  New–Expert
ISBN: 0-672-31133-x  1,000 pages

# Sams' Teach Yourself PL/SQL in 21 Days

*—Jonathan Gennick and Tom Luers*

Leads the reader step-by-step to a solid understanding of PL/SQL (Oracle's powerful and flexible procedural language that is used to develop applications). PL/SQL is essential in order to program and develop with Oracle and to be able to take advantage of the Oracle tools capabilities. By using real-world examples in an easy-to-comprehend style, readers will learn how to use PL/SQL to build robust applications.

Covers PL/SQL

*Price:$39.99 USA/$56.95 CAN*　　　*Beginning–Casual*
*ISBN: 0-672-31123-2*　　　　　　　*700 pages*

# Sams' Teach Yourself Transact SQL in 21 Days

*—Bennett Wm. McEwan and David Solomon*

Based on the best-selling Sams' Teach Yourself series, this comprehensive book provides readers with the techniques they need to not only write flexible and effective applications that produce efficient results, but also decrease the performance demands on the server. In no time users will master methods that will improve productivity and maximize performance. Explores topics such as coding standards, the CASE function, bitmaps, and more. Q&A sections, exercises, and week-at-a-glance previews make learning a breeze.

Covers Transact-SQL for Microsoft SQL Server and Sybase SQL Server

*Price:$35.00 USA/$49.95 CAN*　　*New–Casual*
*ISBN: 0-672-31045-7*　　　　　　*500 pages*　　　*7 3/8 × 9 1/8*

# Sams' Teach Yourself Oracle8 in 21 Days

*—Ed Whalen*

*Sams' Teach Yourself Oracle8 in 21 Days* is a tutorial that will teach the reader the basics of using and administrating an Oracle database. This book focuses on using concrete examples to explain why things should be done in a certain way. The key topics are broken into three weeks:

Week One　Overview of the Oracle8 Architecture, Network Computing Architecture (NCA), Installing Oracle, Planning the Database, How to Administer Users' and How to Manage Processes.

Week Two　Administering Logs, Control Files, Datafiles, and Tablespaces; Controlling Rollback Segments; Building Tables and Views; Using Indexes and Clusters; and Security.

Week Three　Effective Backup Techniques, Recovering the Database, Administering Oracle Replication, Tuning and Optimizing the Database, Administering the Oracle Web Server, and Advanced Oracle Options.

This hands-on tutorial teaches the basics of Oracle8 in a short period of time. The book provides a step-by-step walk-through of the Oracle8 architecture, managing database storage, and database schema, including security, backup, recovery, tuning, and optimization.

Oracle8 is Oracle's new object-oriented RDBMS.

*Price:$39.99 USA/$56.95 CAN*　　*New–Advanced*
*ISBN: 0-672-31159-3*　　　　　　*600 pages*

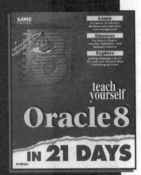

# Sams' Teach Yourself Oracle8 Database Development in 21 Days

*—David Lockman*

*Sams' Teach Yourself Oracle8 Database Development in 21 Days* is a tutorial that will teach the reader the basics of developing Oracle database applications. This book focuses on teaching the concepts behind logical and physical database design, a working knowledge of SQL and PL/SQL, and the basics of Developer/2000 and Oracle Power Objects. This is the first and only beginning-level book devoted entirely to Oracle development. This hands-on tutorial teaches the basics of Oracle development in a short period of time.

Covers logical and physical database design, a working knowledge of SQL and PL/SQL, and the basics of Developer/2000 and Oracle Power Objects.

*Price:$49.99 USA/$70.95 CAN*  *Beginning–Intermediate*
*ISBN: 0-672-31078-3*  *600 pages*

# Sams' Teach Yourself Microsoft SQL Server 6.5 in 21 Days

*—Rick Sawtell, Lance Mortensen, Richard Waymire, and Kalen Delaney*

*Sams' Teach Yourself Microsoft SQL Server 6.5 in 21 Days* covers issues such as installing SQL Server, backup and restore, creating user accounts, creating tables, importing and exporting data, data integrity, stored procedures and triggers, distributed data and performance, and tuning and optimization. Learn how to install, design, and create a SQL Server database. Configure SQL Server and build effective queries. Discover programming features of Transact-SQL.

*Price:$39.99 USA/$56.95 CAN*  *Beginning–Intermediate*
*ISBN: 0-672-31138-0*  *700 pages*

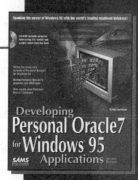

# Developing Personal Oracle7 for Windows 95 Applications, Second Edition

*—David Lockman*

An update to the successful first edition, this comprehensive reference takes users through the process of developing powerful applications while teaching them how to effectively use Personal Oracle7.

CD-ROM includes current versions of Personal Oracle7 for Windows 3.1 and Windows 95.

Covers Personal Oracle7 for Windows 3.1 and Windows 95

*Price:$49.99 USA/$70.95 CAN*  *New–Casual*
*ISBN: 0-672-31025-2*  *800 pages*  *7 3/8 × 9 1/8*

# Add to Your Sams Library Today with the Best Books for Programming, Operating Systems, and New Technologies

## The easiest way to order is to pick up the phone and call

# 1-800-428-5331

## between 9:00 a.m. and 5:00 p.m. EST.

## For faster service please have your credit card available.

| ISBN | Quantity | Description of Item | Unit Cost | Total Cost |
|---|---|---|---|---|
| 0-672-31110-0 | | Sams' Teach Yourself SQL in 21 Days, 2E | $39.99 | |
| 0-672-31133-x | | SQL Unleashed | $49.99 | |
| 0-672-31123-2 | | Sams' Teach Yourself PL/SQL in 21 Days | $39.99 | |
| 0-672-31045-7 | | Sams' Teach Yourself Transact SQL in 21 Days | $35.00 | |
| 0-672-31159-3 | | Sams' Teach Yourself Oracle8 in 21 Days | $39.99 | |
| 0-672-31078-3 | | Sams' Teach Yourself Oracle8 Database Development in 21 Days | $49.99 | |
| 0-672-31138-0 | | Sams' Teach Yourself Microsoft SQL Server 6.5 in 21 Days | $39.99 | |
| 0-672-31025-2 | | Developing Personal Oracle7 for Windows 95 Applications, 2E | $49.99 | |
| | | Shipping and Handling: See information below. | | |
| | | TOTAL | | |

Shipping and Handling: $4.00 for the first book, and $1.75 for each additional book. Floppy disk: add $1.75 for shipping and handling. If you need to have it NOW, we can ship product to you in 24 hours for an additional charge of approximately $18.00, and you will receive your item overnight or in two days. Overseas shipping and handling adds $2.00 per book and $8.00 for up to three disks. Prices subject to change. Call for availability and pricing information on latest editions.

**201 W. 103rd Street, Indianapolis, Indiana 46290**

**1-800-428-5331 — Orders    1-800-835-3202 — FAX    1-800-858-7674 — Customer Service**

Book ISBN 0-672-31245-x